GPU Programming
in MATLAB

GPU Programming
in MATLAB

Nikolaos Ploskas

Nikolaos Samaras

AMSTERDAM • BOSTON • HEIDELBERG • LONDON
NEW YORK • OXFORD • PARIS • SAN DIEGO
SAN FRANCISCO • SINGAPORE • SYDNEY • TOKYO

Morgan Kaufmann is an imprint of Elsevier

Morgan Kaufmann is an imprint of Elsevier
50 Hampshire Street, 5th Floor, Cambridge, MA 02139, United States

Library of Congress Cataloging-in-Publication Data
A catalog record for this book is available from the Library of Congress

British Library Cataloguing-in-Publication Data
A catalogue record for this book is available from the British Library

ISBN: 978-0-12-805132-0

For information on all Morgan Kaufmann publications
visit our website at https://www.elsevier.com/

Working together
to grow libraries in
developing countries

www.elsevier.com • www.bookaid.org

Publisher: Todd Green
Acquisition Editor: Todd Green
Editorial Project Manager: Lindsay Lawrence
Production Project Manager: Priya Kumaraguruparan
Cover Designer: Mark Rogers

Typeset by SPi Global, India

To my family
– Nikolaos Ploskas

To my son, Stathis
– Nikolaos Samaras

Contents

About the Authors

Nikolaos Ploskas is a Postdoctoral Researcher at the Department of Chemical Engineering, Carnegie Mellon University, USA. He received his Bachelor of Science degree, Master's degree, and Ph.D. in Computer Systems from the Department of Applied Informatics of the University of Macedonia, Greece. His primary research interests are in

Operations research,
Mathematical programming,
Linear programming,
Parallel programming,
GPU programming,
Decision support systems.

Dr. Ploskas has participated in several international and national research projects. He is the author or co-author of writings in more than 40 publications, including high-impact journals and book chapters, and conference publications. He has also served as a reviewer for many scientific journals. He received an honorary award from HELORS (Hellenic Operations Research Society) for the best doctoral dissertation in operations research (2014).

Nikolaos Samaras is a Professor at the Department of Applied Informatics, School of Information Sciences, University of Macedonia, Greece. Professor Samaras's current research interests are at the interface between computer science and operations research, which apply to a variety of engineering and scientific systems:

Linear/Non Linear optimization: theory, algorithms, and software
Network optimization: theory, algorithms, and software
Scientific computing: HPC, and GPU-programming

He has served on the editorial board of the *Operations Research: An International Journal*, and as a reviewer in many scientific journals. He has also held numerous positions within HELORS (Hellenic Operations Research Society). He was awarded with the Thomson ISI/ASIS&T Citation Analysis Research Grant (2005).

Dr. Samaras has published more than 35 journal papers in high-impact journals, including *Computational Optimization and Applications, Computers and Operations Research, European Journal of Operational Research, Annals of Operations Research, Journal of Artificial Intelligence Research, Discrete Optimization, Applied Mathematics and Computation, International Journal of Computer Mathematics, Electronics Letters, Computer Applications in Engineering Education, Journal of Computational Science, and Applied Thermal Engineering*. He has also published more than 85 conference papers.

Foreword

This book represents an important addition to the library of professional MATLAB reference texts. Whereas most other MATLAB-related texts typically focus on a specific engineering domain, this book targets general MATLAB users, who are already familiar with MATLAB and wish to improve their program's speed using multicore and GPU parallelization. Until recently, parallelization was employed by supercomputers and were outside the reach of the regular MATLAB user. But with multiple CPU cores and powerful GPU cards ubiquitous in modern computers, parallelization is now available to anyone, and it would seem a waste not to use all this available power for our compute-intensive MATLAB programs. Unfortunately, MATLAB users have few resources explaining the fine details about how *exactly* to make their MATLAB programs run on the GPU. MATLAB's internal documentation, good as it may be, may not be enough for professional development. I believe that this book successfully fills this gap. A detailed discussion of GPU programming in MATLAB is presented, starting with a general overview, continuing with a discussion about how to employ easy-to-use gpuArrays, all the way to the detailed intricacies of compiling CUDA kernels and integrating GPU code into MEX-files. The reader therefore benefits from a discussion at various levels of increasing complexity. Multiple usage examples are presented to enable users in different engineering disciplines to understand the material, including a discussion about real-world limitations such as memory or bandwidth. MATLAB error messages, which are sometimes difficult to understand and overcome, are explained alongside suggested solutions/workarounds. Multiple tips and best practices are suggested throughout the book. While this book does not cover other aspects of MATLAB performance tuning in any great detail, its discussion of GPU programming for MATLAB is very detailed and quite up-to-date. With GPU programming becoming commonplace, such a dedicated, detailed and highly readable book about this subject is a welcome addition. This textbook should be on the bookself of any MATLAB programmer who plans to employ GPU parallelization.

Yair Altman
"Accelerating MATLAB Performance," http://UndocumentedMatlab.com

Preface

MATLAB is a high-level language for technical computing. It is widely used as a rapid prototyping tool in many scientific areas. Many researchers and companies use MATLAB to solve computationally intensive problems and run their codes faster. MATLAB provides the Parallel Computing Toolbox that allows users to solve their computationally intensive problems using multicore processors, computer clusters, and GPUs.

With the advances made in hardware, GPUs have gained a lot of popularity in the past decade and have been widely applied to computationally intensive applications. There are currently two major models for programming on GPUs: CUDA and OpenCL. CUDA is more mature and stable. In order to access the CUDA architecture, a programmer can write codes in C/C++ using CUDA C or Fortran using the PGI's CUDA Fortran, among others.

This book, however, takes another approach. This book is intended for students, scientists, and engineers who develop or maintain applications in MATLAB and would like to accelerate their codes using GPU programming without losing the many benefits that MATLAB offers. The readers of this book likely have some or a lot of experience with MATLAB coding, but they are not familiar with parallel architectures.

The main aim of this book is to help readers implement their MATLAB applications on GPUs in order to take advantage of their hardware and accelerate their codes. This book includes examples for every concept that is introduced in order to help its readers apply the knowledge to their applications. We preferred to follow a tutorial rather than a case study approach when writing this book because MATLAB's users have different backgrounds. Hence, the examples presented in this book aim to focus the interest of the readers on the techniques used to implement an application on a GPU and not on a specific application domain. The examples provided are common problems in many scientific areas such as image processing, signal processing, optimization, communications systems, statistics, etc.

MATLAB's documentation for GPU computing is very helpful, but the information is not available in one location and important implementation issues on GPU programming are not discussed thoroughly. Various functions and toolboxes have been created since MATLAB introduced GPU support in 2010, so information is scattered. The aim of this book is to fill this gap. In addition, we provide many real-world examples in various scientific areas in order to demonstrate MATLAB's GPU capabilities. Readers with some experience of CUDA C/C++ programming will also be able to obtain more advanced knowledge by utilizing CUDA C/C++ code in MATLAB or by profiling and optimizing their GPU applications.

The main emphasis of this book is addressed on two fronts:

- The features that MATLAB inherently provides for GPU programming. This part is divided into three parts:

  1. GPU-enabled MATLAB built-in functions that require the existence of the Parallel Computing Toolbox.

  2. Element-wise operations for GPUs that do not require the existence of the Parallel Computing Toolbox.

  3. GPU-enabled MATLAB functions found in several toolboxes other than Parallel Computing Toolbox, including Communications System Toolbox, Image Processing Toolbox, Neural Network Toolbox, Phased Array System Toolbox, Signal Processing Toolbox, and Statistics and Machine Learning Toolbox.

- Linking MATLAB with CUDA C/C++ codes either when MATLAB cannot execute an existing piece of code on GPUs or when the user wants to use highly optimized CUDA-accelerated libraries.

The main target groups of this book are:

- Undergraduate and postgraduate students who take a course on GPU programming and want to use MATLAB to exploit the parallelism in their applications.
- Scientists who develop or maintain applications in MATLAB and would like to accelerate their codes using GPUs without losing the many benefits that MATLAB offers.
- Engineers who want to accelerate their computationally intensive applications in MATLAB without the need to rewrite them in another language, such as CUDA C/C++ or CUDA Fortran.

We are thankful to MathWorks for providing us an academic license for MATLAB through their MathWorks Book Program. We also thank NVIDIA for hardware donations in the context of the NVIDIA Academic Partnership program. Special thanks to Ioannis Athanasiadis for providing ideas and implementing examples for GPU-enabled functions of MATLAB toolboxes. Finally, we thank our families for their love and support over many years.

Nikolaos Ploskas
Nikolaos Samaras

Introduction

CHAPTER OBJECTIVES

This Chapter introduces some key features of parallel programming and GPU programming on CUDA-capable GPUs. Furthermore, some real-world examples that can be accelerated through GPUs are presented. After reading this Chapter, you should be able to:

- understand the key concepts of parallel programming.
- understand the key concepts of GPU programming.
- describe the architecture of a CUDA-capable GPU.
- list those applications where parallel and GPU programming can be used.

1.1 PARALLEL PROGRAMMING

1.1.1 INTRODUCTION TO PARALLEL COMPUTING

A software that has been written for serial computation is executed on a single processor. Hence, the problem is broken into a discrete series of instructions, and those instructions are executed sequentially one after another (Fig. 1.1).

For example, consider that we want to calculate the dot product of two column vectors:

$$a = \begin{bmatrix} a_1 \\ a_2 \\ \vdots \\ a_n \end{bmatrix}, \quad b = \begin{bmatrix} b_1 \\ b_2 \\ \vdots \\ b_n \end{bmatrix}$$

The following serial program in MATLAB will calculate the dot product (inner product) of these vectors:

GPU Programming in MATLAB. http://dx.doi.org/10.1016/B978-0-12-805132-0.00001-1

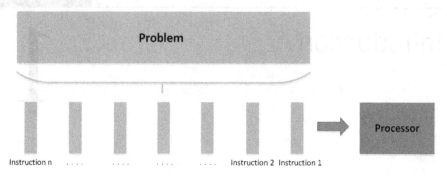

FIG. 1.1

Serial computing overview.

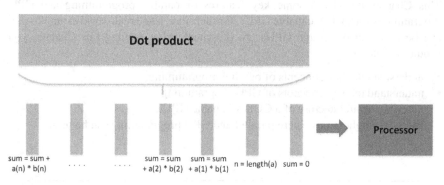

FIG. 1.2

Serial computing example.

```
1.    sum = 0;
2.    n = length(a);
2.    for i = 1:n
3.        sum = sum + a(i) * b(i);
4.    end
```

The instructions will be executed sequentially on a single processor (Fig. 1.2).

On the other hand, a software that has been written for parallel computation is executed on multiple compute resources. Hence, the problem is broken into discrete parts that can be solved concurrently, and parts are further broken into a series of instructions. The instructions from each part are executed simultaneously on different compute resources. Of course, the instructions of a single part are executed sequentially one after another on a specific compute resource (Fig. 1.3).

Considering that we want to calculate the dot product over a large number of vectors, we can calculate the dot product of two vectors on each compute resource (Fig. 1.4).

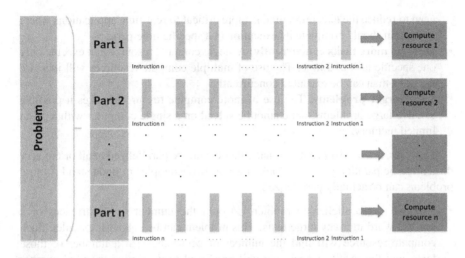

FIG. 1.3

Parallel computing overview.

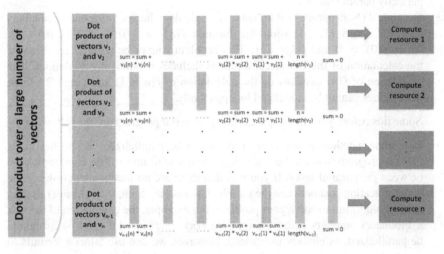

FIG. 1.4

Parallel computing example.

The compute resources can be typically either cores (on a single computer with one processor) or processors (either on a single computer or on different computers connected by a network).

Parallel computing is mainly used for the following reasons:

- **Reduce the execution time of a program:** The use of more compute resources to execute a program will possibly reduce the execution time of this program, and sometimes this reduction to the execution time also offers cost savings. The need to reduce the execution time is more critical to real-time applications where a program should complete its execution in a specific time period.

- **Perform more tasks concurrently:** A single compute resource can execute only one specific task at a time. The use of multiple compute resources will increase the tasks than can be executed concurrently.
- **Solve larger problems:** The use of more compute resources makes it possible to solve large problems that cannot be solved on a single computer with a given limited memory.

However, there exist problems that either cannot be parallelized at all or are very difficult to be parallelized. Let's look closer at two examples to understand if those problems can be actually parallelized:

- Example 1 (Parallelizable problem): Count the number of occurrences of a specific word in many large texts. This problem can be solved in parallel. Each compute resource will find the number of occurrences in a number of those texts, and the result of each one will be shared to determine the final number of occurrences in all texts. These type of problems, where there exists little or no dependency between the parallel tasks, are called embarrassingly parallel tasks or perfectly parallel tasks.
- Example 2 (Non-parallelizable problem): Calculate the first n Fibonacci numbers $(0, 1, 1, 2, 3, 5, 8, 13, \ldots)$ using the formula $f(n) = f(n-1) + f(n-2)$, where $f(0) = 0$ and $f(1) = 1$. This problem cannot be parallelized because the calculation of the Fibonacci numbers includes dependent calculations. The calculation of $f(n)$ depends on the calculation of $f(n-1)$ and $f(n-2)$; these three values cannot be calculated independently.

Some tips before you start to parallelize your serial program are the following:

- Determine whether or not your problem can be parallelized. Try to find parts of your program that can be run independently with no or little communication between the parallel tasks. If you find that there are no independent tasks or the communication cost between the parallel tasks is very high, then consider finding another algorithm to solve your problem. For example, the calculation of the first n Fibonacci numbers using the formula $f(n) = f(n-1) + f(n-2)$ cannot be parallelized, as already mentioned. However, we can use Binet's formula to calculate the nth Fibonacci number as $f(n) = \dfrac{\left(1+\sqrt{5}\right)^n - \left(1-\sqrt{5}\right)^n}{2^n \sqrt{5}}$. Using this formula, we can easily parallelize the calculation of the first n Fibonacci numbers.
- Find the hotspots on your program. Try to use profilers or performance analysis tools to identify the parts of your program that perform the most time-consuming tasks. Then, focus to parallelize those tasks.
- Identify possible bottlenecks that cause parallelizable tasks to halt.
- Use third-party highly optimized parallel libraries when possible.

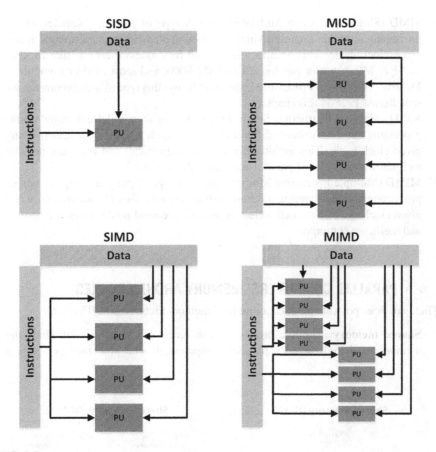

FIG. 1.5

Classification of parallel computers.

1.1.2 CLASSIFICATION OF PARALLEL COMPUTERS

According to Flynn's taxonomy [1], multiprocessor computer architectures can be classified into two independent dimensions: (i) instruction stream (I) and (ii) data stream (D). Each of these dimensions has one of two possible states: (i) single (S) and (ii) multiple (M). Hence, there are four possible types of computers (Fig. 1.5):

• SISD (Single Instruction Single Data): A sequential computer whose processing unit executes a single instruction on a single data stream at any given clock cycle. This architecture is very old and was used by the oldest type of computers with a single processor/core.

- SIMD (Single Instruction Multiple Data): A type of parallel computer whose processing units can execute a single instruction on different data streams at any given clock cycle. This architecture is used by processor arrays, like MasPas MP-1 & MP-2; vector pipelines, like IBM 9000; and most modern computers. Moreover, Graphical Processing Units (GPUs) use this type of architecture, as we will discuss later on this chapter.
- MISD (Multiple Instruction Single Data): A type of parallel computer whose processing units can execute different instructions on a single data stream at any given clock cycle. This architecture is more theoretical, and there are not any well-known examples of parallel computers that use it.
- MIMD (Multiple Instruction Multiple Data): A type of parallel computer whose processing units can execute different instructions on different data streams at any given clock cycle. This architecture is used by the most modern supercomputers and multicore computers.

1.1.3 PARALLEL COMPUTERS' MEMORY ARCHITECTURES

There are three possible parallel computers' memory architectures (Fig. 1.6):

- **Shared memory:** Multiple processors can access independently but share the memory in shared memory parallel computers. If one processor performs a

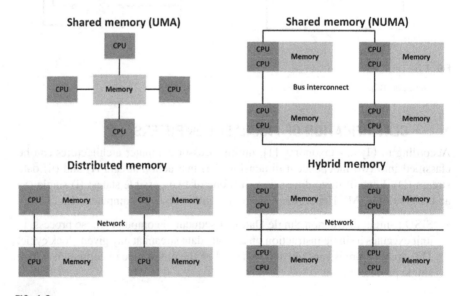

FIG. 1.6

Types of parallel computers' memory architectures.

change in a memory location, then this change is visible to all other processors. Shared memory parallel computers can be further classified into:

(1) **Uniform Memory Access** (UMA): identical processors have equal access times to memory. This architecture is used by symmetric multiprocessor (SMP) computers.

(2) **Non-Uniform Memory Access** (NUMA): many SMPs are linked, and one SMP can directly access the memory of another SMP. Hence, not all processors have equal access times to the memories of all SMPs. Moreover, the access to a memory across the link is slower.

- **Distributed memory:** All processors have their own local memory and can access it independently. All computers are connected through a network, for example, Ethernet, and can request data from other computers (a computer does not have access to the memory of another computer, but data can be transmitted from one computer to another programmatically). The type of network used to connect the computers affects the speed of transmission.

- **Hybrid memory:** Most modern supercomputers use a hybrid type of memory architecture combining both shared and distributed memory architectures. All processors in a machine can share the memory and can request data from other computers (a computer does not have access to the memory of another computer, but data can be transmitted from one computer to another programmatically).

1.2 GPU PROGRAMMING

A Graphical Processing Unit (GPU) enables you to run high-definition graphics on your computer. Like the CPU, GPU is a single-chip multicore processor. However, GPU has hundreds of cores aligned in a particular way forming a single hardware unit. A GPU can have thousands of concurrent hardware threads. GPU is utilized for data-parallel and computationally intensive portions of an algorithm. Data-parallel algorithms are well suited for such devices because the hardware can be classified as SIMT (Single Instruction Multiple Threads). GPUs outperform CPUs in terms of GFLOPS (Giga FLoating point OPerations per Second). For example, concerning the equipment utilized to measure the execution time of the CPU- and GPU-based applications presented in this book, a high-end Core i7 processor with 3.46 GHz delivers up to a peak of 55.36 GFLOPs, whereas a high-end NVIDIA Tesla K40 delivers up to a peak of 5 TFLOPs.

GPUs offer good computational performance and efficient memory bandwidth. The impressive computational power and memory bandwidth of a GPU make it an attractive architecture to run computationally intensive algorithms. There are currently two major programming models available for programming on GPUs, CUDA (Compute Unified Device Architecture) [2], and OpenCL (Open Computing Language) [3]. NVIDIA introduced CUDA in late 2006, and it is only available with

NVIDIA GPUs, while Apple introduced OpenCL in 2008, and it is available on GPUs of different vendors and even on CPUs. General programming languages, like CUDA and OpenCL, are based on the stream processing model. This model makes GPU programming hard due to its low level nature.

The primary job of a GPU is to calculate 3D functions because these types of calculations are very time-consuming if executed on the CPU. However, GPUs have now evolved into general computing and can be used to handle other tasks. Algorithms that are massively parallel will run efficiently on the GPU. The sequential part of an application runs on the CPU and the time-consuming parts can be accelerated by using a GPU. If we execute the complex tasks of an application to the GPU, then we can free the CPU, which can be utilized for other tasks. On the other hand, GPUs are not always better than CPUs on all types of tasks. For example, CPUs are more efficient for performing different tasks of the operating system, like job scheduling and memory management. In addition, CPUs are very efficient on task-parallel programs, whereas GPUs are very efficient on data-parallel programs. To sum up, the design of CPUs is optimized for sequential code performance, whereas the GPUs are designed for handling numerically intensive computations. Therefore, most applications should use both the CPU and the GPU; the sequential part of an application should be executed on the CPU, and the time-consuming parts can be accelerated by a GPU.

1.3 CUDA ARCHITECTURE

NVIDIA introduced CUDA, a technology that enables users to solve many complex problems on their GPU cards. NVIDIA CUDA is an architecture that manages data-parallel computations on a GPU. CUDA C/C++ is an extension, introduced by NVIDIA, of the C/C++ programming languages for general-purpose computations on NVIDIA GPUs. CUDA enables users to execute programs on their GPUs, and it is based on the SIMT programming model. The CUDA programming model allows a programmer to assign a hard computing problem to a highly processing architecture. A CUDA program includes two portions, one that is executed on the CPU and another that is executed on the GPU. The CPU should be viewed as the host device, whereas the GPU should be viewed as the coprocessor. The part of the program that can be parallelized is executed on the GPU as kernels, whereas the rest is executed on the CPU. A kernel is a Single Program Multiple Data (SPMD) computation that is executed using a large number of parallel threads. CPU starts the execution of each portion of program and invokes a kernel function, so, the execution is moved to the GPU. The connection between the CPU memory and the GPU memory is through a fast PCIe 16x point to point link.

Fig. 1.7 shows the architecture of a CUDA-capable GPU. The GPU is organized into an array of highly threaded Streaming Multiprocessors (SMs). A number of SMs (two in Fig. 1.7) forms a building block, and each SM has a number of Streaming Processors (SPs; eight in Fig. 1.7) that share control logic and instruction cache. Finally, GPUs have also a Graphics Double Data Rate (GDDR) memory; modern

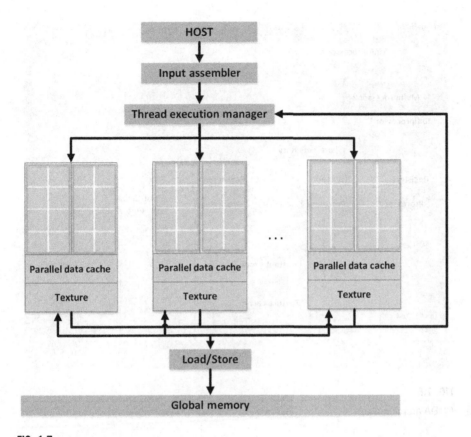

FIG. 1.7

Architecture of a CUDA-capable GPU.

GPUs come with a memory of some gigabytes. This off-chip memory has a very high bandwidth and more latency compared to the system memory.

NVIDIA Tesla K40, which is used to measure the execution time in the applications presented in this book, consists of 15 SMs with 192 cores each, resulting in 2880 total cores. Moreover, it has 12 GB of memory and 288 GB/s of memory bandwidth.

On a CUDA-capable GPU, many processors can be executed at once. This feature enables software developers to take advantage of a data-parallel programming methodology. Each SM also has a small amount of on-chip shared memory and specialized hardware for caching data formatted as textures or cast as constants (Fig. 1.8). A CUDA-capable GPU has the following types of memory:

- **Register memory:** This is the fastest type of memory. In most cases, accessing a register consumes zero clock cycles per instruction. A set of register memory is given to each thread for fast storage and retrieval of a small amount of data, for

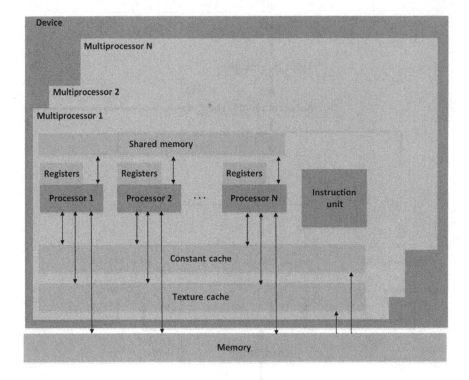

FIG. 1.8

CUDA architecture.

example, counters, and it lasts only for the lifetime of that thread. Data stored in register memory is visible only to that thread.

- **Local memory:** This type of memory is generally used for data that cannot be fit into registers. It is not a physical type of memory, but an abstraction of the global memory. Hence, local memory is slow and uncached.
- **Shared memory:** This type of memory is visible to all threads in a block and lasts only for the lifetime of that block. Shared memory allows threads in a block to communicate and share data between them. Shared memory performance is comparable to register memory. However, consecutive access to data by many threads may cause bottlenecks.
- **Constant memory:** This type of memory stores constants and kernel arguments that will not change over the course of a kernel execution. It is slow and read only.
- **Texture memory:** It is also a cached on-chip read only memory. Texture caches are specially designed for graphics applications where memory access patterns exhibit a great deal of spatial locality.
- **Global memory:** This type of memory is visible to all threads within the application, including the host, and lasts only for the lifetime of the host allocation. It is slow and uncached memory.

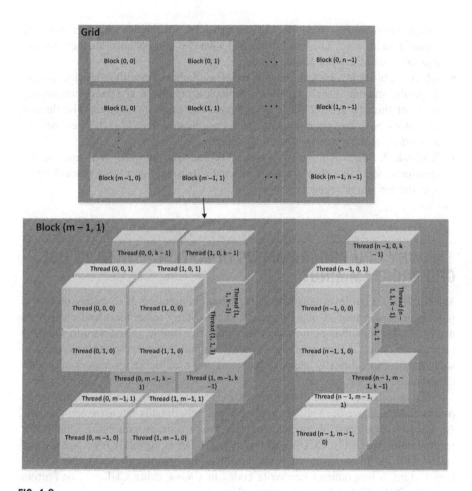

FIG. 1.9

CUDA structure.

Each program that is executed on the GPU is divided into many threads. Each thread executes the same program independently on different data. A thread block is a group of threads that cooperate via shared memory and synchronize their execution to coordinate their memory accesses. A grid consists of a group of thread blocks and a kernel is executed on a group of grids. A kernel is the resulting program after the compilation. The hierarchical structure of the CUDA architecture in Fig. 1.9 consists of the following basic units:

- **Grid:** A grid is a group of threads that run the same kernel. A grid is organized as a two-dimensional array of blocks. Every call from the CPU is made through one grid. The threads in a grid are organized into a two-level hierarchy using unique coordinates, called blockId and threadId. All threads in a grid share the same blockId value. The blocks in a grid have two components: the x coordinate *blockId.x*, and the y coordinate *blockId.y*.

- **Block:** A block is a logical unit containing a number of coordinating threads and a specific amount of shared memory. A block is organized as a three-dimensional array of threads. All blocks in a grid have the same dimensions. The threads in a block have three components: the x coordinate *threadId.x*, the y coordinate *threadId.y*, and the z coordinate *threadId.z*.
- **Thread:** A thread is a part of a block. Threads run on individual cores of the multiprocessors, but they are not restricted to a single core. Each thread has a specific amount of register memory.

1.4 WHY GPU PROGRAMMING IN MATLAB? WHEN TO USE GPU PROGRAMMING?

MATLAB is a high-level language for technical computing. It is widely used as a rapid prototyping tool in many scientific areas. Many researchers and companies use MATLAB for solving computationally intensive problems and need to run their codes faster. MATLAB provides the Parallel Computing Toolbox that allows users to solve their computationally intensive problems using multicore processors, computer clusters, and GPUs.

With the advances made in hardware, GPUs have gained a lot of popularity in the past decade and have been widely applied to computationally intensive applications. As already mentioned, there are currently two major programming models for programming on GPUs, CUDA and OpenCL. CUDA is currently more mature and stable with the most advanced development tools. In order to access the CUDA architecture, a programmer can write codes in C/C++ using CUDA C or Fortran using the PGI's CUDA Fortran, among others.

This book pertains to another approach. This book is intended for students, scientists, and engineers who develop or maintain applications in MATLAB and would like to accelerate their codes using GPUs. These students, scientists, and engineers want to exploit GPU programming without losing the many benefits that MATLAB offers. The readers of this book have some or a lot of experience on MATLAB coding, but they are not familiar with parallel architectures. The main aim of this book is to help students, scientists, and engineers implement their MATLAB applications on GPUs to take advantage of their hardware and accelerate their codes. This book includes examples for every concept that is introduced to help its readers apply the provided knowledge to their applications. We preferred to follow a tutorial rather than a case study approach when writing this book because MATLAB's users have different backgrounds. Hence, the examples presented in this book aim to focus the interest of the readers on the techniques used to implement an application on a GPU and not on a specific application domain.

Engineers and scientists are successfully employing GPU technology to accelerate their discipline-specific programs. MATLAB offers them the opportunity to accelerate their software with minimal effort and without extensive knowledge of GPUs and low-level CUDA programming. However, MATLAB also allows experienced with CUDA programming users to integrate their CUDA kernels into MATLAB programs without any additional C/C++ programming.

Not all MATLAB programs can be accelerated with the GPUs. A program must satisfy some certain criteria:

- **Massively parallel:** the computations can be broken down into hundreds or thousands of independent units of work. The best performance will be obtained when all cores of the GPU are kept busy.
- **Computationally intensive:** the time spent on computation is significantly larger than the time spend on communication, that is, transferring data from and to the GPU memory.

If a program satisfies these criteria, then it is a good candidate to accelerate it using MATLAB's GPU capabilities. Common GPU programming goals are: (i) maximize parallel execution, (ii) minimize global memory access, (iii) improve thread occupancy, and (iv) keep high arithmetic intensity of computations. On the other hand, a program that does not satisfy these criteria might actually run slower on a GPU than on a CPU.

The first thing that you should find out to determine whether your program is a good candidate for GPU computing is which function is consuming the majority of the execution time. If you find out that some custom functions or lines of code consume the majority of the execution time, then this is probably a good indicator that your program is a good candidate for GPU computing. On the other hand, if you find out that built-in functions that are not GPU-enabled MATLAB functions consume the majority of the execution time, then this is a bad indicator. The next step is to identify the type and size of data that is processed in the custom functions and lines of code that consume the most execution time. If those parts handle simple data types, for example, arrays, and large data, then this is a good indicator that your program is a good candidate for GPU computing. On the other hand, if you find out that those parts handle complicated data types, for example, multilevel structures, or small data, then this is a bad indicator.

Two real-world examples are presented next to demonstrate the use of GPU programming in MATLAB. The first example uses filtering to highlight the watery areas in a large aerial photograph [4]. Function *findWateryAreas* (filename: findWateryAreas.m) takes as input an array that represents the initial image (Fig. 1.10A) and outputs an array that represents the final image (Fig. 1.10B).

```
1.    function outputImage = findWateryAreas(inputImage)
2.    % Filename: findWateryAreas.m
3.    % Description: This function uses filtering to highlight
4.    % the watery areas of an image
5.    % Authors: Ploskas, N., & Samaras, N.
```

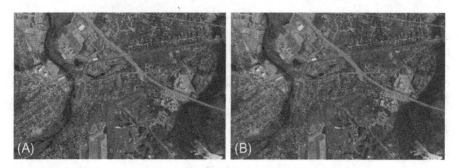

FIG. 1.10

Highlight watery areas in a large aerial photograph. (A) Initial image. (B) Final image.

```
6.    % Syntax: outputImage = findWateryAreas(inputImage)
7.    % Input:
8.    %    -- inputImage: the image for which we want to highlight
9.    %       the watery areas
10.   % Output:
11.   %    -- outputImage: the image with highlighted watery
12.   %       areas
13.
14.   % convert the RGB image to a grayscale image
15.   imGray = rgb2gray(inputImage);
16.   % keep only the pixels with values of 70 or less
17.   imWater = imGray < 70;
18.   % remove points that do not represent water
19.   imWaterMask = imopen(imWater, strel('disk', 4));
20.   imWaterMask = bwmorph(imWaterMask, 'erode', 3);
21.   % blur the mask image
22.   blurH = fspecial('gaussian', 20, 5);
23.   imWaterMask = imfilter(single(imWaterMask) * 10, blurH);
24.   % boost the blue channel to identify the watery areas
25.   blueChannel = inputImage(:, :, 3);
26.   blueChannel = imlincomb(1, blueChannel, 6, uint8(imWaterMask));
27.   % create the output image
28.   outputImage = inputImage;
29.   outputImage(:, :, 3) = blueChannel;
30.   end
```

This function uses some built-in functions (*rgb2gray*, *imopen*, *bwmorph*, *fspecial*, *imfilter*, and *imlincomb*) of MATLAB's Image Processing Toolbox that are GPU-enabled. Hence, we can execute this code on a GPU (details about how to transfer matrix *inputImage* to the GPU will be discussed in Chapter 4). If we measure the execution time both on the CPU (Intel Core i7) and on the GPU (Tesla K40) using an 2,036 × 3,060 pixels image, we find out that the GPU is about 4 times faster than the CPU.

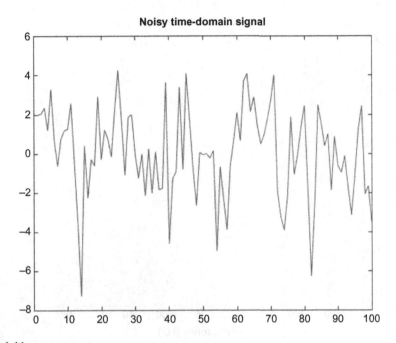

FIG. 1.11

Noisy time-domain signal.

The second example identifies the frequency components of a signal buried in a noisy time-domain signal [5]. Function *findPowerSpectrum* (filename: findPowerSpectrum.m) takes as input the data that simulates the signal (*sampleFrequency* and *numSamples*), adds some random noise to the signal (Fig. 1.11), and outputs a frequency vector and an array of the power spectral density that measures the energy at various frequencies (Fig. 1.12).

```
1.    function powerSpectrum = findPowerSpectrum(sampleFrequency, ...
2.        numSamples)
3.    % Filename: findPowerSpectrum.m
4.    % Description: This function identifies the frequency
5.    % components of a signal buried in a noisy time-domain signal
6.    % Authors: Ploskas, N., & Samaras, N.
7.    % Syntax: powerSpectrum = findPowerSpectrum(sampleFrequency, ...
8.    %     numSamples)
9.    % Input:
10.   %     -- sampleFrequency: the sampling frequency
11.   %     -- numSamples: the number of samples
12.   % Output:
13.   %     -- powerSpectrum: the power spectral density
14.
15.   % set up the time vector
```

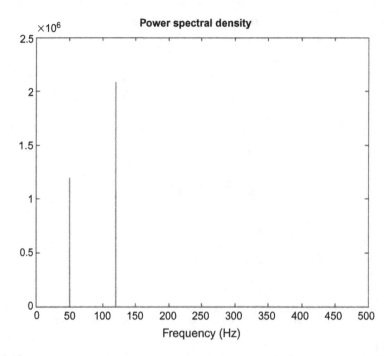

FIG. 1.12

Power spectral density.

```
16.    sampleTime = 1 / sampleFrequency;
17.    timeVec = (0:numSamples - 1) * sampleTime;
18.    % calculate signal as a combination of two sinusoids at
19.    % frequencies freq1 and freq2
20.    freq1 = 2 * pi * 50;
21.    freq2 = 2 * pi * 120;
22.    signal = sin(freq1 .* timeVec) + sin(freq2 .* timeVec);
23.    % add some random noise to the signal
24.    signal = signal + 2 * randn(size(timeVec));
25.    % transform the signal using fft
26.    transformedSignal = fft(signal);
27.    % calculate the power spectral density
28.    powerSpectrum = transformedSignal .* ...
29.        conj(transformedSignal) ./ numSamples;
30.    end
```

This function uses some built-in functions (*sin*, *randn*, *fft*, and *conj*) and operators that are GPU-enabled. Hence, we can execute this code on a GPU (details about how to transfer input data to the GPU and modify the syntax of some built-in functions, for example, *randn*, when using the GPU will be discussed in Chapter 4). If we measure the execution time both on the CPU (Intel Core i7) and on the GPU (Tesla K40) using a signal of 1,000 Hz sampling frequency and 2^{23} samples, we find out that the GPU is about 16 times faster than the CPU.

1.5 OUR APPROACH: ORGANIZATION OF THE BOOK

The scope of this book is twofold. First, the reader will learn all features that are provided through the Parallel Computing Toolbox and other MATLAB toolboxes for GPU computing. This will allow the reader to implement straightforwardly his/her applications on GPUs without special knowledge about GPU programming. This part of this book will cover concepts about GPU-enabled built-in MATLAB functions, element-wise operations on GPUs, and taking advantage of multiple GPUs on a multicore machine or on different machines, among others. Finally, the reader will obtain more advanced knowledge by utilizing CUDA C/C++ code in MATLAB or by profiling and optimizing his/her GPU applications.

The main emphasis of this book is given on two aspects:

- The features that MATLAB inherently provides for GPU programming. This part is divided on three parts:

    (1) GPU-enabled MATLAB built-in functions that require the existence of the Parallel Computing Toolbox.
    (2) Element-wise operations for GPUs that do not require the existence of the Parallel Computing Toolbox.
    (3) GPU-enabled MATLAB functions on several toolboxes other than Parallel Computing Toolbox, like Communications System Toolbox, Image Processing Toolbox, Neural Network Toolbox, Phased Array System Toolbox, Signal Processing Toolbox, and Statistics and Machine Learning Toolbox.

- Linking MATLAB with CUDA C/C++ codes either when MATLAB cannot execute an existing piece of code on GPUs or when you want to use highly-optimized CUDA-accelerated libraries.

    The main target group of this book is

- Undergraduate and postgraduate students that take a course on GPU programming and want to use MATLAB to exploit the parallelism in their applications.
- Scientists who develop or maintain applications in MATLAB and would like to accelerate their codes using GPUs without losing the many benefits that MATLAB offers.
- Engineers that want to accelerate their computationally intensive applications in MATLAB without the need to rewrite them in another language, like CUDA C/C++ or CUDA Fortran.

The readers of this book have some or a lot of experience on MATLAB coding, but they are not familiar with parallel architectures. Some advanced features, like CUDA kernels and MEX files, covered at the end of this book are only for those that are familiar with CUDA C/C++.

Note that this book is dealing only with GPU programming in MATLAB. We also make a brief introduction on MATLAB's parallel capabilities through its Parallel Computing Toolbox and present some tips to tune MATLAB's performance, but we do not intend to cover these topics in depth. There are several good books that cover parallel programming and performance tuning features in MATLAB [6–8].

The rest of this book is organized as follows. Chapter 2 presents the software and hardware needed for GPU programming in MATLAB. Installation steps are presented for Windows, Linux, and MAC users.

In Chapter 3, the Parallel Computing Toolbox is presented. More specifically, the reader can get the whole picture of MATLAB's parallel capabilities through its Parallel Computing Toolbox. Representative didactical examples are given on each section of this chapter.

Chapter 4 covers one of the most important topics of this book, the inherent GPU programming features that MATLAB provides. More specifically, Chapter 4 introduces the GPU arrays, arrays that are stored on GPUs. These arrays can be used in computations by built-in MATLAB functions for GPUs and element-wise MATLAB operations. Chapter 4 includes a variety of examples, both didactical and real-world examples.

Chapter 5 aims to explore GPU-enabled MATLAB functions on several toolboxes other than the Parallel Computing Toolbox, like the Communications System Toolbox, Image Processing Toolbox, Neural Network Toolbox, Phased Array System Toolbox, Signal Processing Toolbox, and Statistics and Machine Learning Toolbox. Chapter 5 presents the GPU-enabled functions on these toolboxes with a variety of real-world examples.

Chapter 6 covers a hot topic about utilizing multiple GPUs. Chapter 6 presents the use of multiple GPUs both on a multicore machine and on different machines. Multiple GPUs are used to improve the performance on task- or data-parallel codes and when working with data that cannot fit in the memory of a single GPU. Chapter 6 includes a variety of examples, both didactical and real-world examples.

Chapter 7 explains how to create an executable kernel for a CUDA C/C++ code or PTX code and run that kernel on a GPU by calling it through MATLAB. The steps to create and run an executable kernel for a CUDA C code or PTX code are covered. Moreover, a brief introduction of CUDA C is presented. Furthermore, two classic examples, vector addition and matrix multiplication, are presented.

Chapter 8 explains how to create a MATLAB MEX file that contains CUDA code and run it on a GPU by calling it through MATLAB. The steps to create and run a MATLAB MEX file that contains CUDA code are covered. Furthermore, two classic examples, vector addition and matrix multiplication, are presented.

Chapter 9 presents the CUDA-accelerated libraries *cuBLAS*, *cuFFT*, *cuRAND*, *cuSOLVER*, *cuSPARSE*, *NPP*, and *Thrust*, that are incorporated into CUDA Toolkit.

These libraries provide highly optimized algorithms that can be incorporated into MATLAB applications through MEX files. Examples are presented for each library.

Chapter 10 presents two advanced topics for better utilization of GPUs on computationally heavy applications: (i) profiling a code running on GPUs, and (ii) improving GPU performance. Didactical examples are given in this chapter for the reader to understand these topics. Moreover, best practices that you should follow to improve GPU performance are discussed in detail.

1.6 CHAPTER REVIEW

This chapter introduced some key features of parallel programming and GPU programming on CUDA-capable GPUs. The architecture of CUDA-capable GPUs has been presented in brief, and the terminology used on GPU computing has been described. In addition, the steps to identify whether a program is a good candidate to accelerate it using MATLAB's GPU capabilities have been introduced. Moreover, two real-world applications that can be accelerated on GPUs have been presented. Finally, the approach and the organization of this book have been described.

To sum up, GPU computing can help you accelerate your computationally intensive applications in MATLAB. However, not all problems can be accelerated using GPU computing in MATLAB. In general, if a program is massively parallel and computationally intensive, then it is a good candidate to accelerate it using MATLAB's GPU capabilities.

Getting started

2

CHAPTER OBJECTIVES

This Chapter presents the software and hardware needed for GPU programming in MATLAB. Installation steps are presented for Windows, Linux and MAC users. After reading this Chapter, you should be able to:

- identify if your NVIDIA GPU is CUDA-capable.
- install NVIDIA CUDA toolkit.
- install MATLAB.
- verify that the installation was successful and that you can use MATLAB's GPU capabilities.

2.1 HARDWARE REQUIREMENTS

There are a couple of issues to take into account before installing the required software to use MATLAB's GPU capabilities. Initially, your computer should be running a 64-bit version of a selected operating system; MathWorks has already ended 32-bit support for Linux and will also end 32-bit support for Windows in R2016a version. MathWorks publishes a platform road map for IT planning purposes for releases of Microsoft Windows, Apple Mac OS, and selected Linux distributions. Table 2.1 presents operating systems supported by MathWorks and the system requirements for MATLAB (as of MATLAB R2015b) [9].

Moreover, you should have a CUDA-capable NVIDIA GPU with compute capability 2.0 or higher. A CUDA-capable GPU is a GPU that can take advantage of CUDA-accelerated applications. NVIDIA maintains a list of all CUDA-capable GPUs [10]. Most recent GPUs have a compute capability 2.0 or higher and can be used for CUDA programming. A list of some widely used CUDA-capable GPUs can be found in Table 2.2. The most well-known NVIDIA GPU families are the following:

Table 2.1 MathWorks' platform road map

Operating system		Support (at least) until	Processor	RAM	Disk space	GPU
Windows	Windows 10	R2017a	Any Intel or AMD x86 processor supporting SSE2 instruction set	2 GB at least; 4 GB is recommended	3–4 GB for a typical installation	Hardware accelerated graphics card supporting OpenGL 3.3 with 1 GB GPU memory recommended.
	Windows 8.1	R2017a				
	Windows 8	R2017a				
	Windows 7	R2017a				
Mac OS	Mac OS X 10.11 (El Capitan)	R2017a	All Intel-based Mac with an Intel Core 2 or later	2 GB at least; 4 GB is recommended	3–4 GB for a typical installation	Hardware accelerated graphics card supporting OpenGL 3.3 with 1 GB GPU memory recommended.
	Mac OS X 10.10 (Yosemite)	R2017a				
	Mac OS X 10.9.5 (Mavericks)	R2015b				
Linux	Ubuntu 14.04 LTS & 14.10	R2017a	Any Intel or AMD x86 processor supporting SSE2 instruction set	2 GB at least; 4 GB is recommended	3–4 GB for a typical installation	Hardware accelerated graphics card supporting OpenGL 3.3 with 1 GB GPU memory recommended.
	Red Hat Enterprise Linux 6 & 7	R2017a				
	SUSE Linux Enterprise Desktop 11.3+	R2017a				
	Debian 7.x	R2017a				

Table 2.2 CUDA-capable GPUs

Processor families	GPU	Compute capability
Tesla Products	Tesla K80	3.7
	Tesla K40	3.5
	Tesla K20	3.5
	Tesla C2075	2.0
	Tesla C2050/C2070	2.0
Quadro Products	Quadro M6000	5.2
	Quadro K6000	3.5
	Quadro M5000	5.2
	Quadro K5000	3.0
	Quadro M4000	5.2
	Quadro K4000	3.0
	Quadro K2000	3.0
GeForce Products	GeForce GTX TITAN X	5.2
	GeForce GTX TITAN Z	3.5
	GeForce GTX TITAN	3.5
	GeForce GTX 980M	5.2
	GeForce GTX 880M	3.0
	GeForce GTX 780M	3.0
	GeForce GTX 680M	3.0
	GeForce GTX 580M	2.1

(1) Tesla: GPUs designed for general-purpose scientific and high-performance computing (appropriate for servers and workstations)

(2) Quadro: GPUs designed for professional 2D and 3D applications (appropriate for desktops)

(3) GeForce: GPUs designed for mainstream and gaming use (appropriate for desktops and laptops)

2.2 SOFTWARE REQUIREMENTS

In order to use MATLAB's GPU capabilities, the NVIDIA CUDA toolkit and MATLAB with Parallel Computing Toolbox should be installed. The following subsections present the installation steps to install the appropriate software for Windows, Linux, and MAC users.

2.2.1 NVIDIA CUDA TOOLKIT
WINDOWS

Before installing the NVIDIA CUDA toolkit, you should verify that your computer has a CUDA-capable GPU and a supported version of Microsoft Windows, as explained in Section 2.1. Moreover, a supported version of Microsoft Visual Studio should be installed. For example, NVIDIA CUDA toolkit 7.5 supports Visual Studio 2012 and Visual Studio 2013. You can download for free and install Visual Studio 2012/2013 Express (https://www.microsoft.com/en-us/download/details.aspx?id=34673).

Initially, download the latest version of NVIDIA CUDA toolkit from NVIDIA's website (https://developer.nvidia.com/cuda-downloads). Select your operating system and the installer type (the network installer allows you to download only the files you need, while the local installer is a stand-alone installer with a large initial download) and download the installation file (Fig. 2.1).

Run the installer and follow the instructions in the installation wizard to complete the installation (Fig. 2.2).

In order to verify the installation of the NVIDIA CUDA toolkit, navigate to the CUDA Samples' *deviceQuery* directory (Fig. 2.3).

Open the *deviceQuery* Visual Studio solution file for the version of Visual Studio that you have installed and build and run the solution. If CUDA is installed and configured correctly, the output should look similar to Fig. 2.4. The output might be different on your system. The important outcomes are that a device was found and that the device matches what is installed in your system.

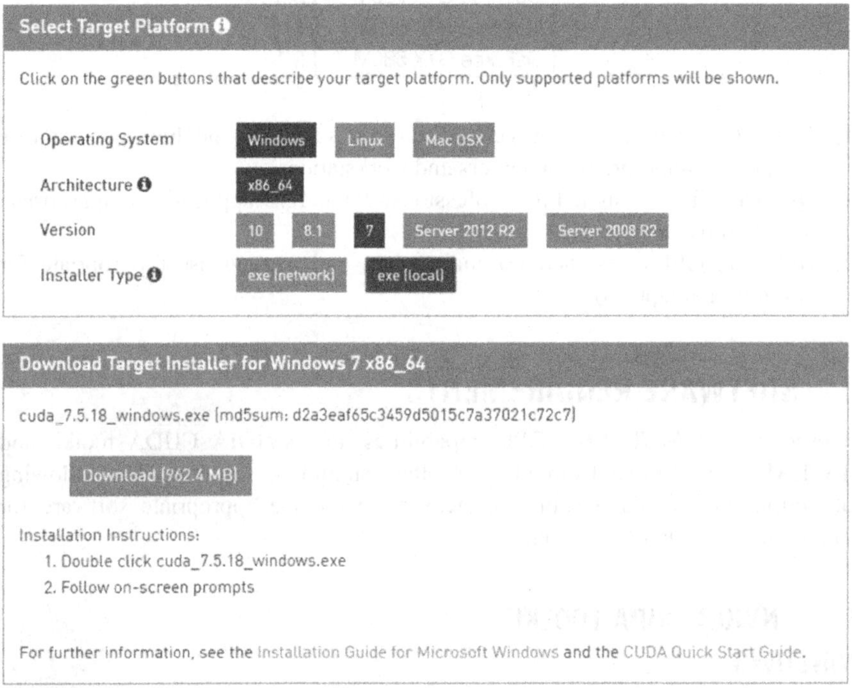

FIG. 2.1

Download NVIDIA CUDA toolkit for Windows.

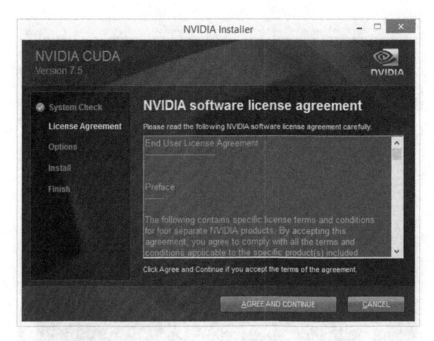

FIG. 2.2

Install NVIDIA CUDA toolkit in Windows.

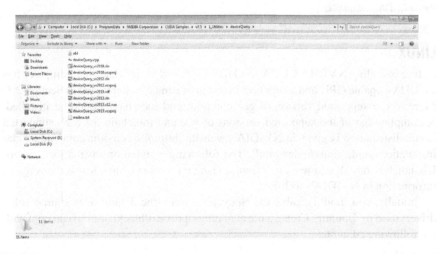

FIG. 2.3

Navigate to CUDA Samples' deviceQuery directory.

FIG. 2.4

Verify CUDA installation.

LINUX

Before installing NVIDIA CUDA toolkit, you should verify that your computer has a CUDA-capable GPU and a supported version of Linux, as explained in Section 2.1. Moreover, a supported version of gcc compiler and toolchain should be installed. A complete list of the supported versions of gcc and toolchain for each supported Linux distribution is given in NVIDIA's website (http://docs.nvidia.com/cuda/cuda-installation-guide-linux/index.html). The following installation instructions are for Ubuntu, but they should work in a similar fashion for other Linux distributions (more information in NVIDIA's website).

Initially, you should disable the Nouveau drivers (the default open source video drivers used by Ubuntu). Create a file at /etc/modprobe.d/blacklist-nouveau.conf with the following contents:

```
blacklist nouveau
options nouveau modeset=0
```

Then, regenerate the kernel initramfs:

```
$ sudo update-initramfs -u
```

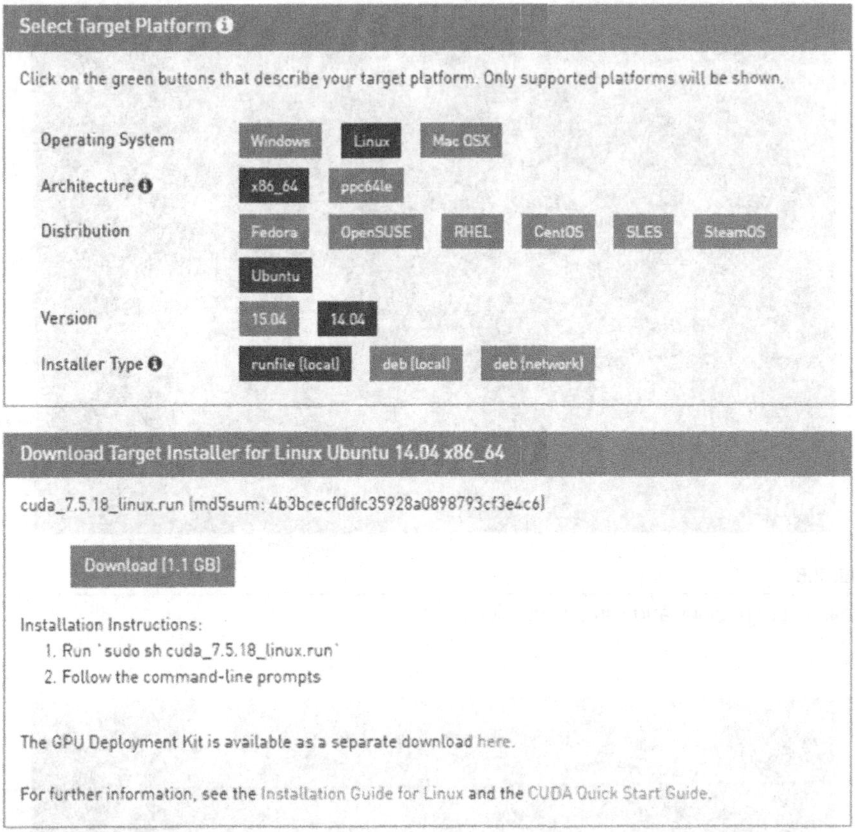

FIG. 2.5

Download NVIDIA CUDA toolkit for Ubuntu.

Next, reboot into runlevel 3 by temporarily adding the number "3" and the word "nomodeset" to the end of the system's kernel boot parameters. Then, download the latest version of NVIDIA CUDA toolkit from NVIDIA's website (https://developer.nvidia.com/cuda-downloads). Select your operating system and the installer type (the network installer allows you to download only the files you need, while the local installer is a stand-alone installer with a large initial download), and download the installation file (Fig. 2.5).

Change the permissions of the downloaded file and run the installer (Fig. 2.6).

Follow the instructions in the installation wizard to complete the installation (Fig. 2.7).

Next, create an xorg.conf file to use the NVIDIA GPU for display:

```
$ sudo nvidia-xconfig
```

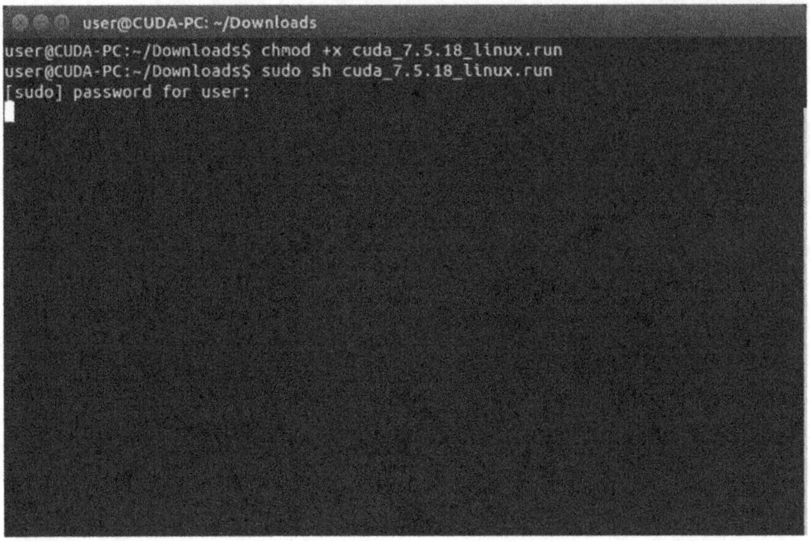

FIG. 2.6

Change permissions and run the installer in Linux.

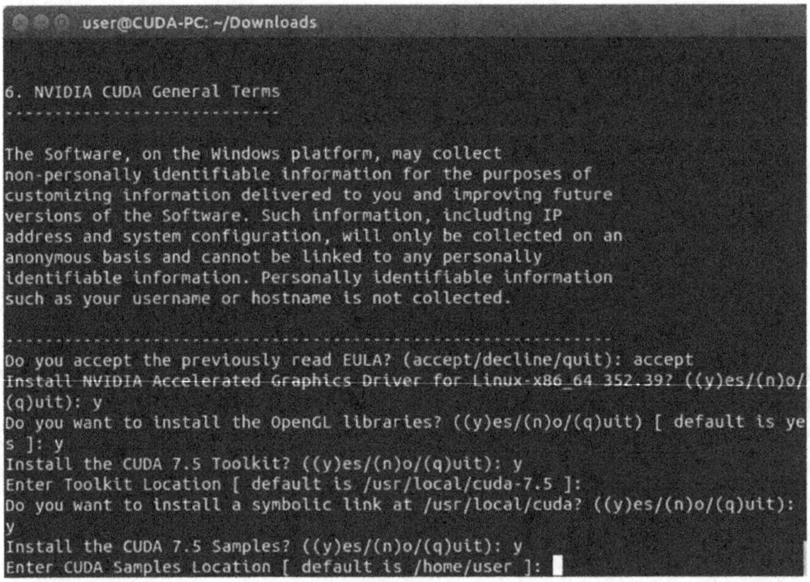

FIG. 2.7

Install the NVIDIA CUDA toolkit in Linux.

Then, reboot the system to load the graphical interface. Next, set up the development environment by modifying the PATH and LD_LIBRARY_PATH variables:

```
$ export PATH=/usr/local/cuda-7.5/bin:$PATH
$ export LD_LIBRARY_PATH=/usr/local/cuda-7.5/lib64:$LD_LIBRARY_PATH
```

Finally, install a writable copy of the samples and build and run the *deviceQuery* sample to verify the installation of the NVIDIA CUDA toolkit. If CUDA is installed and configured correctly, the output should look similar to Fig. 2.4. The output might be different on your system. The important outcomes are that a device was found and that the device matches what is installed in your system.

```
$ cuda-install-samples-7.5.sh ~
$ cd ~/NVIDIA_CUDA-Samples_7.5/1_Utilities/deviceQuery/
$ make
$ ./deviceQuery
```

MAC OS

Before installing the NVIDIA CUDA toolkit, you should verify that your computer has a CUDA-capable GPU and a supported version of MAC OS, as explained in Section 2.1. Moreover, a supported version of Clang compiler and toolchain should be installed using Xcode. A complete list of the supported versions of Clang and toolchain for each supported MAC OS version is given in NVIDIA's website (http://docs.nvidia.com/cuda/cuda-installation-guide-mac-os-x/index.html).

Initially, download the latest version of the NVIDIA CUDA toolkit from NVIDIA's website (https://developer.nvidia.com/cuda-downloads). Select your operating system and the installer type (the network installer allows you to download only the files you need, while the local installer is a stand-alone installer with a large initial download), and download the installation file (Fig. 2.8).

Run the installer, and follow the instructions in the installation wizard to complete the installation (Fig. 2.9). Select to install the CUDA driver, the CUDA toolkit, and the samples (Fig. 2.10).

Next, set up the development environment by modifying the PATH and DYLD_LIBRARY_PATH variables:

```
$ export PATH=/Developer/NVIDIA/CUDA-7.5/bin:$PATH
$ export DYLD_LIBRARY_PATH=/Developer/NVIDIA/CUDA-7.5/lib:$DYLD_LIBRARY_PATH
```

Then, install Xcode via the App Store. Moreover, install Xcode command-line tools:

```
$ xcode-select --install
```

Finally, install a writable copy of the samples and build and run the *deviceQuery* sample to verify the installation of the NVIDIA CUDA toolkit. If CUDA is installed and configured correctly, the output should look similar to Fig. 2.4. The output might be different on your system. The important outcomes are that a device was found and that the device matches what is installed in your system.

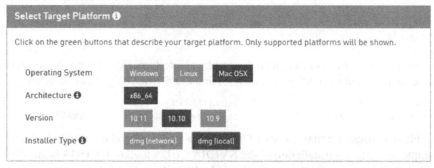

FIG. 2.8

Download the NVIDIA CUDA toolkit for MAC OS.

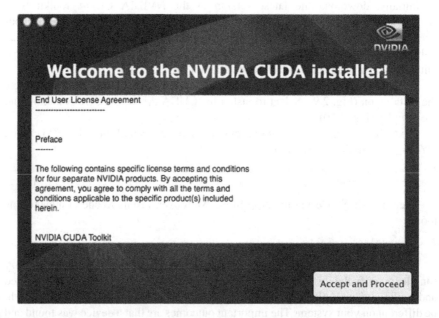

FIG. 2.9

Run the NVIDIA CUDA toolkit installer in MAC OS.

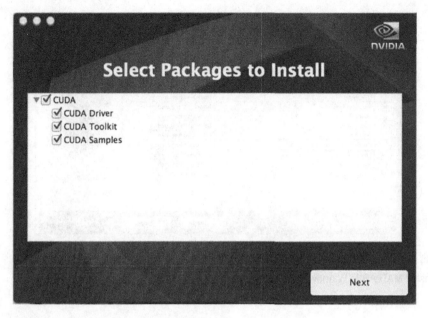

FIG. 2.10

Install the NVIDIA CUDA toolkit in MAC OS.

```
$ cuda-install-samples-7.5.sh ~
$ cd ~/NVIDIA_CUDA-Samples_7.5/1_Utilities/deviceQuery/
$ make
$ ./deviceQuery
```

2.2.2 MATLAB
WINDOWS

Run the installer, and follow the instructions in the installation wizard to complete the installation. Note that in order to use MATLAB's GPU capabilities, you should purchase and install at least the Parallel Computing Toolbox. If you also want to run your code in a computer cluster, grid, or cloud, then you should also install the Distributed Computing Server [11]. You should also install other toolboxes if you want to use their enhanced GPU support (Fig. 2.11).

Open MATLAB, and type the command *gpuDevice* to verify that you have installed correctly MATLAB and the NVIDIA CUDA toolkit. If MATLAB and CUDA are installed and configured correctly, the output should look similar to Fig. 2.12. The output might be different on your system depending on the installed GPU.

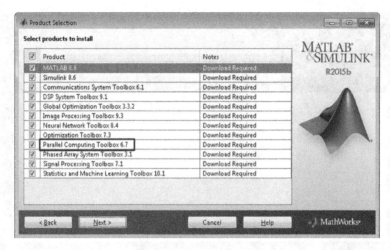

FIG. 2.11

Install MATLAB in Windows.

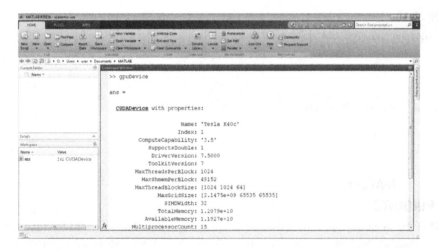

FIG. 2.12

Verify CUDA installation using MATLAB.

LINUX

Run the installer, and follow the instructions in the installation wizard to complete the installation (Fig. 2.13). Note that in order to use MATLAB's GPU capabilities, you should purchase and install at least the Parallel Computing Toolbox. If you also want to run your code in a computer cluster, grid, or cloud, then you should also install the

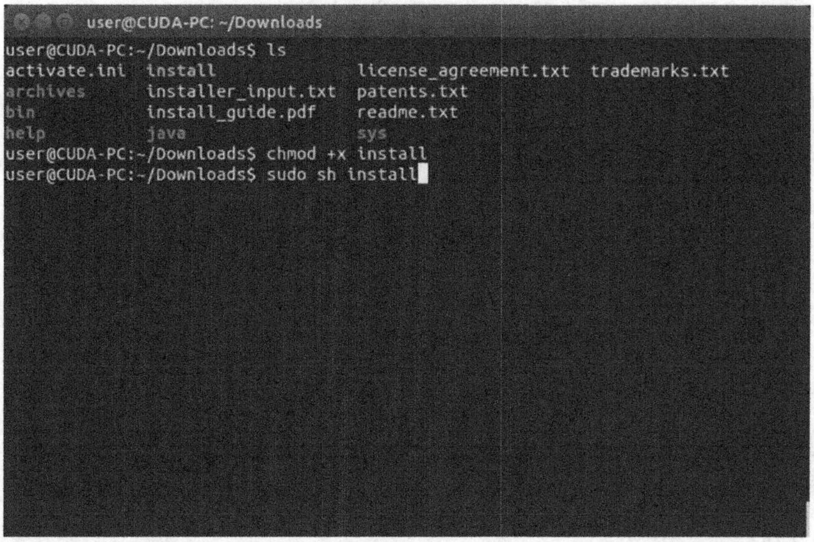

FIG. 2.13

Run MATLAB installer in Linux.

Distributed Computing Server [11]. You should also install other toolboxes if you want to use their enhanced GPU support (Fig. 2.14).

Open MATLAB, and type the command *gpuDevice* to verify that you have installed correctly MATLAB and the NVIDIA CUDA toolkit. If MATLAB and CUDA are installed and configured correctly, the output should look similar to Fig. 2.12. The output might be different on your system depending on the installed GPU.

MAC OS

Run the installer, and follow the instructions in the installation wizard to complete the installation (Fig. 2.15). Note that in order to use MATLAB's GPU capabilities, you should purchase and install at least the Parallel Computing Toolbox. If you also want to run your code in a computer cluster, grid, or cloud, then you should also install the Distributed Computing Server [11]. You should also install other toolboxes if you want to use their enhanced GPU support (Fig. 2.16).

Open MATLAB and type the command *gpuDevice* to verify that you have installed correctly MATLAB and NVIDIA CUDA toolkit. If MATLAB and CUDA are installed and configured correctly, the output should look similar to Fig. 2.12. The output might be different on your system depending on the installed GPU.

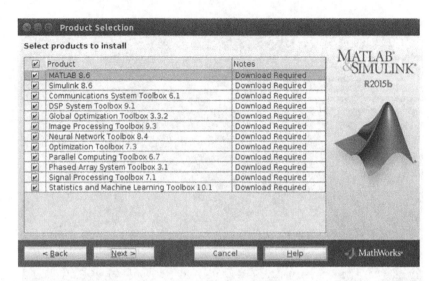

FIG. 2.14

Install MATLAB in Linux.

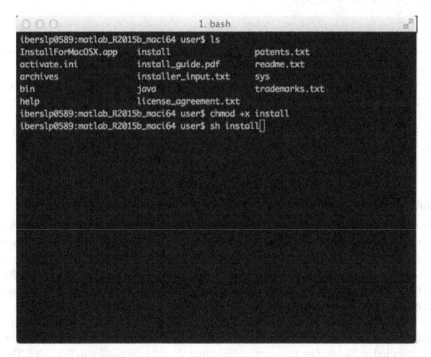

FIG. 2.15

Run MATLAB installer in MAC OS.

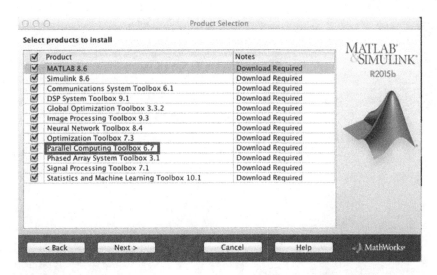

FIG. 2.16

Install MATLAB in MAC OS.

2.3 CHAPTER REVIEW

This chapter presented the software and hardware needed for GPU programming in MATLAB. Installation steps were presented for Windows, Linux, and MAC users. In order to be able to utilize MATLAB's GPU capabilities, some hardware and software issues should be considered. Initially, your computer should have a CUDA-capable GPU and a supported version of Microsoft Windows, Linux, or MAC OS. Finally, you should install the NVIDIA CUDA toolkit and MATLAB with Parallel Computing Toolbox.

Parallel Computing Toolbox

3

CHAPTER OBJECTIVES

This Chapter introduces the key features of MATLAB's Parallel Computing Toolbox. Task- and data-parallel applications can be parallelized using the features provided by Parallel Computing Toolbox. After reading this Chapter, you should be able to:

- understand the key features of Parallel Computing Toolbox.
- execute loop iterations in parallel using a *parfor-loop*.
- execute code in parallel on MATLAB workers using an *spmd* statement.
- use *distributed* and *codistributed* arrays across many MATLAB workers.
- work interactively with a communicating job using the *pmode* functionality.
- create and submit jobs on a computer cluster.

3.1 PRODUCT DESCRIPTION AND OBJECTIVES

MATLAB's Parallel Computing Toolbox allows users to solve computationally and data-intensive problems using multicore and multiprocessor computers, computer clusters, and GPUs. Users can use high-level MATLAB functions to parallelize applications without OpenMP, MPI, and CUDA programming. One of the important features of MATLAB's Parallel Computing Toolbox is that the same application can be executed on a simple core, a multicore processor, or a computer cluster without changing the code. Combining Parallel Computing Toolbox with Distributed Computing Server, users can run their MATLAB programs on computer clusters, grids, and clouds.

Other MATLAB products can take advantage of parallel computing resources and speedup users' codes. As of MATLAB R2015b, the toolboxes that have parallel capabilities are presented in Table 3.1 [12].

The toolboxes that provide GPU support will be presented in Chapter 5. Readers who are interested in utilizing Parallel Computing Toolbox in other toolboxes presented in Table 3.1 are directed to toolboxes user's guides provided by MathWorks. The rest of this chapter will present the most important programming features of the Parallel Computing Toolbox.

GPU Programming in MATLAB. http://dx.doi.org/10.1016/B978-0-12-805132-0.00003-5

Table 3.1 Parallel computing support in MATLAB and Simulink products

Product name	Parallel capabilities
Simulink	Run multiple Simulink simulations using simcommand with parfor. Run multiple simulations in rapid accelerator mode using parfor with prebuilt Simulink models.
Embedded Coder	Generate and build code in parallel using model blocks.
Simulink Coder	Generate and build code in parallel using model blocks.
Bioinformatics Toolbox	Distribute pairwise alignments to a computer cluster using functions for progressive alignment of multiple sequences and pairwise distance between sequences.
Robust Control Toolbox	Tune fixed-structure control systems with the looptune, systune, and hinfstruct commands.
Simulink Control Design	Perform frequency response estimation of Simulink models.
Simulink Design Optimization	Estimate model parameters and optimize system response.
Image Processing Toolbox	Improve performance in Batch Image Processor. Improve performance of block processing tasks in blockproc function. **Improve performance of many functions using a GPU.**
Computer Vision System Toolbox	Improve performance of functions in bag-of-words workflow.
Global Optimization Toolbox	Explore simultaneously local solution space in genetic algorithm, particle swarm, and pattern search solvers.
Model-Based Calibration Toolbox	Fit multiple models to experimental data. Run of multiple optimizations in parallel.
Neural Network Toolbox	Improve performance of training and simulation. **Improve performance of training and simulation using a GPU.**
Optimization Toolbox	Accelerate gradient estimation in selected constrained nonlinear solvers. Launch parallel computations from optimtool GUI.
Statistics and Machine Learning Toolbox	Improve performance of many resampling functions. Fit multiclass support vector machines and other classifiers. Generate reproducible random streams in parallel. Improve performance of many D-optimal design generation functions. Improve performance of many functions with multiple starting points. **Improve performance of many functions using a GPU.**
Communications System Toolbox	**Improve performance of many System objects using a GPU.** **MATLAB Compiler support for GPU System objects.**
Phased Array System Toolbox	Accelerate clutter model simulation using parfor. **Accelerate clutter model simulation using a GPU.**
Signal Processing Toolbox	**Improve performance of many functions using a GPU.**
SystemTest	Run test iterations on multiple processors or machines.

The Parallel Computing Toolbox can be used to improve the performance of various types of applications:

- Applications that involve repetitive segments of code. Different iterations can be evaluated in parallel using parallel *for-loops* (Section 3.2). Applications can include many iterations that might not take long to execute or few iterations that take long to execute. The only restriction on parallel *for-loops* is that each iteration is not allowed to depend on any other iteration.
- Applications that run a series of independent tasks. Different tasks can be evaluated in parallel using parallel *for-loops* (Section 3.2).
- Applications evaluating the same code on multiple data sets. Multiple workers can be used to run the same code on multiple data sets (Section 3.3).
- Applications involving data that is too large for your computer's memory. Arrays can be distributed among multiple MATLAB workers, and each MATLAB worker can operate only on its part of the array (Sections 3.3 and 3.4).
- Applications that their execution in parallel can improve their performance (Sections 3.2 and 3.3).
- Applications that their execution on GPUs can improve their performance (Section 3.6).

3.2 PARALLEL FOR-LOOPS (*parfor*)

It is well-known that a *for-loops* is a series of statements that are executed over a range of values. Similarly, a *parfor-loop* in MATLAB is the same as the standard *for-loops* with the difference that the loop iterations can be executed in parallel. To understand better the concept of the *parfor-loop*, let's introduce some terminology. The MATLAB client is the MATLAB instance that initiated the execution of the *parfor-loop*, while the MATLAB worker is a MATLAB process that runs in parallel without a graphical user interface. Several MATLAB workers can be used to evaluate a *parfor-loop*. As of MATLAB R2015b, a maximum number of 512 MATLAB workers can be used in parallel. To set the number of the MATLAB workers on your machine, select the Parallel Preferences option from MATLAB's workspace (Fig. 3.1). Then, select the Cluster Profile Manager option (Fig. 3.2). Finally, select a cluster profile (the default is named 'local'), click on Edit, and enter a value for the number of workers that you want to use (Fig. 3.3). The default option is the number of cores. If multithreading is enabled, you can set the number of workers equal to the number of threads.

Before running a code that includes a *parfor-loop* or an *spmd* statement, you should open a parallel pool. To open a parallel pool using a specific cluster, e.g., 'local', and a specific size, e.g., 4, type the following command:

```
>> parpool('local', 4)
```

After running your code, you can shut down the parallel pool by typing the following commands (*gcp* returns the current parallel pool):

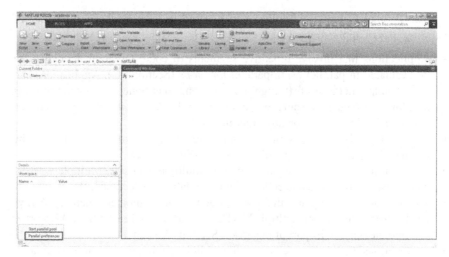

FIG. 3.1

Select the parallel preferences option.

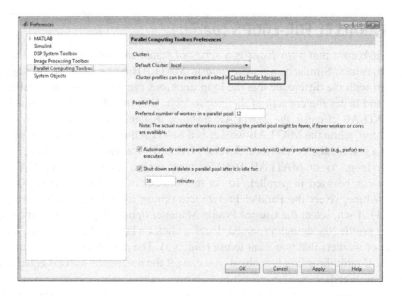

FIG. 3.2

Select the cluster profile manager option.

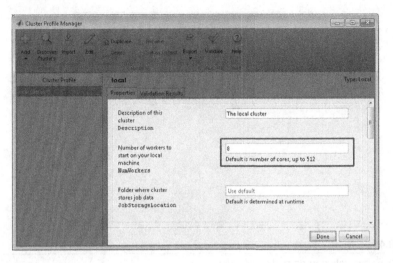

FIG. 3.3

Set the number of workers.

```
>> p = gcp;
>> delete(p)
```

A *parfor-loop* is initiated on the MATLAB client, and the MATLAB client sends the necessary data to the MATLAB workers. Each MATLAB worker performs the computations that were assigned to it and sends the results back to the MATLAB client. Finally, the MATLAB client pieces the results together. There is no guarantee that all MATLAB workers will be assigned the same number of iterations. If the number of MATLAB workers is equal to the number of the iterations, then each MATLAB worker performs one iteration. If there are more iterations, then some MATLAB workers may perform more iterations than others. Moreover, the iterations are evaluated in no particular order and independent of each other. For example, let's consider the following example:

```
parfor i = 1:8
    disp(i)
end
```

Using a parallel pool with 4 MATLAB workers, let's execute the preceding code twice (Fig. 3.4). The results show that the iterations are evaluated in no particular order.

Moreover, each iteration must be independent of all other iterations. For instance, the MATLAB worker evaluating the third iteration might not be the same MATLAB worker evaluating the fifth iteration. Thus, each iteration cannot use data used in other iterations. Let's take, for example, the following code in which the first n Fibonacci numbers are calculated.

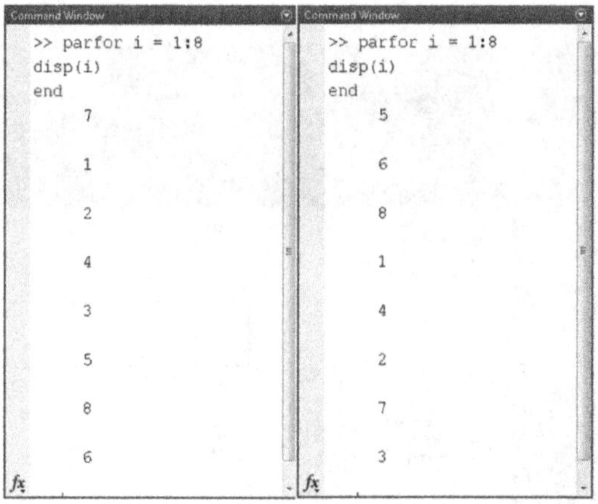

FIG. 3.4

Iterations evaluation in no particular order.

```
n = 10;
fib = zeros(1, n);
fib(1) = 0;
fib(2) = 1;
for i = 3:n
    fib(i) = fib(i - 1) + fib(i - 2);
end
```

As you may already know, the sequence F_n of Fibonacci numbers is defined by the recurrence relation $F_n = F_{n-1} + F_{n-2}$. The statement in each iteration depends on results that are calculated in previous iterations. For instance, to compute the fifth Fibonacci number ($i = 5$), the fourth Fibonacci number ($i = 4$) and the third Fibonacci number ($i = 3$) are needed. However, as mentioned earlier, each iteration must be independent of all other iterations, and the iterations are evaluated in no particular order. Thus, we cannot use *parfor* in this example. Even if we used the *parfor* to parallelize the *for-loop*, MATLAB outputs an error that cannot classify the variable *fib* in the *parfor-loop* (Fig. 3.5). Note that the calculation of the first n Fibonacci numbers can be calculated in parallel if we use Binet's formula,

$$f(n) = \frac{\left(1+\sqrt{5}\right)^n - \left(1-\sqrt{5}\right)^n}{2^n \sqrt{5}}, \text{ as already mentioned in Chapter 1.}$$

MATLAB classifies the variables found in a *parfor-loop* in one of the following categories:

(1) Loop Variables: Loop variables define the loop index value for each iteration. A loop variable is set at the beginning line of a *parfor-loop*:

```
parfor i = 1:100
    ...
end
```

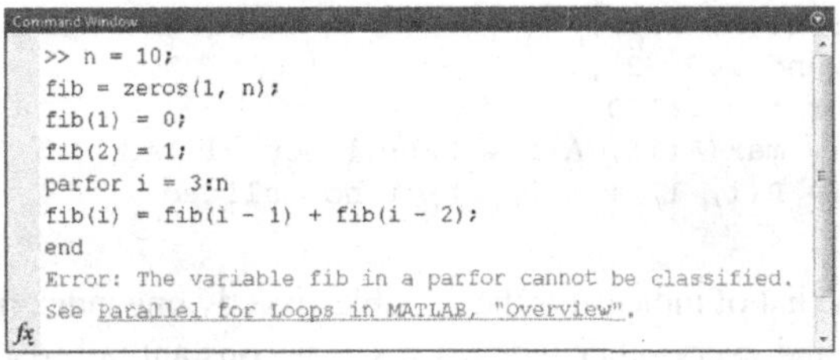

```
Command Window
>> n = 10;
fib = zeros(1, n);
fib(1) = 0;
fib(2) = 1;
parfor i = 3:n
fib(i) = fib(i - 1) + fib(i - 2);
end
Error: The variable fib in a parfor cannot be classified.
See Parallel for Loops in MATLAB, "Overview".
```

FIG. 3.5

Wrong use of parfor in non-independent iterations.

There are some restrictions while using a loop variable:

- A loop variable must evaluate to ascending consecutive integers. Hence, the *parfor* statements *parfor i = 1:100* and *parfor i = -10:10* are valid, while the *parfor* statements *parfor i = -100:-1:1*, *parfor i = 1:2:100*, and *parfor i = 1:0.5:10* are not valid.
- Assignments to the loop variable are not allowed. Hence, the following *parfor-loop* is not valid:

```
parfor i = 1:100
    i = i + 2; % not valid
    ...
end
```

- A loop variable cannot be indexed or subscripted. Hence, the following *parfor-loop* is not valid:

```
parfor i = 1:100
    x = i(1); % not valid
    y = i.a; % not valid
end
```

(2) **Sliced Variables**: Sliced variables are arrays whose segments are manipulated by different workers on different loop iterations. Sliced variables are used to reduce the communication time between the MATLAB client and MATLAB workers because only those slices needed by a worker are sent to it when it starts working on a particular range of indices. Let i be a loop variable. A variable is sliced if it has all the following characteristics [5]:

- The first level of indexing is enclosed in either parentheses '()' or braces '{}'. After the first level, any valid MATLAB indexing can be used. Hence, the variable *A.p{i}* is not sliced, while the variables *A{i}*, *A(i)*, *A(i, 5)*, and *A(i).p* are sliced.
- Within the first-level parenthesis or braces, the list of indices is the same for all occurrences of a given variable. In the following code, variables *A* and *B* are not sliced because *A* is indexed by i and $i + 1$ in different places and *B* is indexed by $(i, 1)$ and $(i, 2)$ in different places.

```
>> A = rand(1, 101);
>> B = rand(100, 2);
>> parfor i = 1:100
      x = max(A(i), A(i + 1)); % not sliced
      y = B(i, 1) + B(i, 2); % not sliced
   end
```

- Within the list of indices for the variable, exactly one index involves the loop variable, and every other index is a scalar constant, a broadcast variable, a nested *for-loop* index, *colon*, or *end*. Hence, *A(i, i + 1)* and *B(i, 20:30, end)* are not sliced, while *A(i, :, end)* and *B(i + 2, j, :, 3)* are sliced.
- The sliced variable maintains a constant shape (no deletion or insertion operators are allowed). In the following code, variables *A* and *B* are not sliced because they change their shape by adding or deleting elements.

```
>> A = rand(100, 2);
>> B = rand(100);
>> parfor i = 1:100
      A(i, :) = []; % not sliced
      B(end + 1) = i; % not sliced
   end
```

All sliced variables have the characteristics of being input or output. Some sliced variables have both characteristics. Sliced input variables are transmitted from the MATLAB client to the MATLAB workers, sliced output variables are transmitted from the MATLAB workers to the MATLAB client, and sliced input and output variables are transmitted in both directions. In the following code, variable *A* is a sliced input variable, variable *B* is a sliced output variable, and variable *C* is a sliced input and output variable.

```
>> A = rand(100);
>> C = rand(100);
>> parfor i = 1:100
      B(i) = A(i);
      if rand < 0.5
         C(i) = 0;
      end
   end
```

(3) Broadcast Variables: Broadcast variables are variables other than loop and sliced variables that are defined before a *parfor-loop* and are used inside the loop but never modified. The MATLAB client sends the broadcast variables to all MATLAB workers at the start of a *parfor-loop*. In the following code, variables a and *B* are broadcast variables.

```
>> a = 0.4;
>> B = rand(101, 1);
>> C = zeros(100, 1);
>> parfor i = 1:100
      if B(i) + B(i + 1) < a
         C(i) = 0;
```

```
      else
          C(i) = 1;
      end
  end
```

Note that variable B is not a sliced variable because it is indexed by i and $i + 1$ in different places. Large broadcast variables can cause a lot of communication between the MATLAB client and the MATLAB workers, and degrade performance. In some cases it is more efficient to use temporary instead of broadcast variables, if possible.

(4) Reduction Variables: Reduction variables accumulate a value that depends on all the iterations together. This is the only exception to the rule that loop iterations must be independent. However, the value of the reduction variable is independent of the iteration order. Reductions variables appear on both sides of an assignment statement. Table 3.2 presents all the possible assignments in which a reduction variable can appear (*expr* is a MATLAB expression).

In the following code, the usage of a reduction variable X is illustrated:

```
>> A = rand(100, 1);
>> X = 0;
>> parfor i = 1:100
       X = X + A(i);
   end
```

The value of variable X is not transmitted from the MATLAB client to MATLAB workers or from a MATLAB worker to another. Rather, each MATLAB worker performs a number of additions of $A(i)$ and transmits back to the MATLAB client the result. The MATLAB client receives the results from each MATLAB worker and adds these into X. Some other rules for the reduction variables are the following:

Table 3.2 Possible assignments involving a reduction variable X

Assignment	Assignment
X = X + expr	X = expr + X
X = X - expr	
X = X .* expr	X = expr .* X
X = X * expr	X = expr * X
X = X & expr	X = expr & X
X = X | expr	X = expr | X
X = [X, expr]	X = [expr, X]
X = [X; expr]	X = [expr; X]
X = min(X, expr)	X = min(expr, X)
X = max(X, expr)	X = max(expr, X)
X = union(X, expr)	X = union(expr, X)
X = intersect(X, expr)	X = intersect(expr, X)

- For any reduction variable, the same reduction function or operation must be used in all reduction assignments for that variable. For example, the following *parfor-loop* is not valid because the reduction assignment uses '+' in one instance and '*' in another.

```
>> X = 0;
>> parfor i = 1:100
      if rand < 0.5
          X = X + 5;
      else
          X = X * 2;
      end
   end
```

On the other hand, the following *parfor-loop* is valid.

```
>> X = 0;
>> parfor i = 1:100
      if rand < 0.5
          X = X + 5;
      else
          X = X + i + 2;
      end
   end
```

- If the reduction assignment uses '*' or '[,]' or '[;]', then in every reduction assignment for *X*, *X* must be consistently specified as the first argument or consistently specified as the second. For example, the following code is not valid because variable *X* does not occur in the same argument position in all reduction assignments.

```
>> X = 0;
>> parfor i = 1:100
      if rand < 0.5
          X = X * 5;
      else
          X = 2 * X;
      end
   end
```

On the other hand, the following *parfor-loop* is valid.

```
>> X = 0;
>> parfor i = 1:100
      if rand < 0.5
          X = [X, 5];
      else
          X = [X, i + 2];
      end
   end
```

- The logical operators && and || are not allowed in reduction assignments.

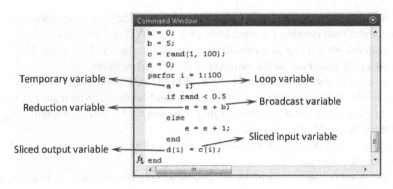

FIG. 3.6

Types of *parfor* variables.

(5) Temporary Variables: Temporary variables are variables that are the target of direct non-indexed assignments, but they are not reduction variables. Temporary variables exist only in a MATLAB worker's workspace and are not transferred back to the MATLAB client. In the following code, variables a and *b* are temporary variables.

```
>> a = 0;
>> parfor i = 1:100
       a = i;
       if rand < 0.5
           b = 0;
       else
           b = 1;
       end
   end
```

To sum up, Fig. 3.6 presents an example where all different types of *parfor* variables are used.

If a *parfor-loop* contains a variable that cannot be uniquely classified into one of the preceding categories or a variable violates its category restrictions, MATLAB generates an error, as shown in Fig. 3.5. Understanding the different types of *parfor* variables will help you find performance degrades.

You should also consider the following limitations/concerns before parallelizing your application using a *parfor-loop*:

- A code including a *parfor-loop* may result in better execution times in a multicore machine but not in a computer cluster due to the communication cost.
- You cannot use a *parfor-loop* if an iteration depends on the results of other iterations.
- There might be no benefit to using a *parfor-loop* if there is a small number of simple calculations due to the communication cost.

- When running a *parfor-loop* in a computer cluster, the communication cost will be greater than running the same code on local MATLAB workers.
- Be careful when using *cd*, *addpath*, and *rmpath* on a *parfor-loop* as the MATLAB search path might not be the same on all MATLAB workers.
- If an error occurs in one iteration, then all MATLAB workers terminate.
- Be careful when using commands like *input* and *keyboard*, which are not strictly computational in nature, as they might not have a visible effect or might hang the corresponding MATLAB worker.
- Any graphical output, for example, a figure, will not be displayed at all if it is used inside a *parfor-loop*.
- If you want to use objects inside a loop, then explicitly assign them to a variable, as they are not automatically propagated to the client.
- If you want to call a function handle with the loop variable as an argument, use *feval*.
- The body of a *parfor-loop* cannot make reference to a nested function, but it can call a nested function by means of a function handle.
- The body of a *parfor-loop* cannot contain another *parfor-loop*. Hence, if you have a code with two nested *for-loops*, you can parallelize either of the nested loops. Usually, the best strategy is to convert the outer *for-loop* to a *parfor-loop*.
- The range of a *for-loop* nested in a *parfor-loop* must be defined by constant numbers or variables and not by using function calls, like *length(A)*.
- When using a nested *for-loop* variable for indexing a sliced variable, you must use the variable in plain form and not as part of an expression (e.g., you can use *A(j)* but not *A(j + 1)*, where *j* is the nested *for-loop* variable and *A* a sliced variable).
- If you index into a sliced variable inside a nested *for-loop*, you cannot use that variable elsewhere in the *parfor-loop*.
- If you index into a sliced variable inside multiple *for-loops* (not nested) in a *parfor-loop*, they must loop over the same range of values.
- A sliced output variable can be used in only one nested *for-loop*.
- The body of a *parfor-loop* cannot contain *break* or *return* statements.
- You cannot clear variables from a MATLAB worker's workspace (e.g., clear x;), but instead you can set its value to empty (e.g., x = [];).
- You cannot use functions *eval*, *evalc*, *evalin* if the variables involved in these functions are not visible in the *parfor-loop* (e.g., they are declared prior to the *parfor-loop*).
- You cannot use *save* and *load* inside a *parfor-loop* unless the output of *load* is assigned to a variable.

There are mainly two types of applications that the use of a *parfor-loop* will improve their computation time:

- Applications that involve repetitive segments of code and include many iterations that do not take long to execute
- Applications that involve repetitive segments of code and include few iterations that take long to execute

Example: Monte Carlo simulation to approximate the area of a figure

A Monte Carlo simulation is a useful method to approximate the area of a figure. In some cases, it is difficult to find the exact area of a figure; so, this approximation method is very useful. A Monte Carlo method performs the following steps to find the area of a figure:

- Generates uniformly n random points on the square that encloses the figure and counts the number of points (*counter*) that lie inside the figure.
- Calculates the ratio *counter*/n, which approximates the ratio between the area of the figure and the square that encloses the figure.
- Computes the area of the given figure by multiplying the calculated ratio with the known area of the square that encloses the figure.

For instance, the previously mentioned Monte Carlo simulation will be applied to compute the area of the following definite integral:

$$\int_0^2 x(x-2)^6 dx$$

The area of this definite integral is the area under the curve $y = x(x-2)^6$ from $x = 0$ to $x = 2$ (Fig. 3.7).

A single-threaded MATLAB code to compute the area of the above definite integral is the following:

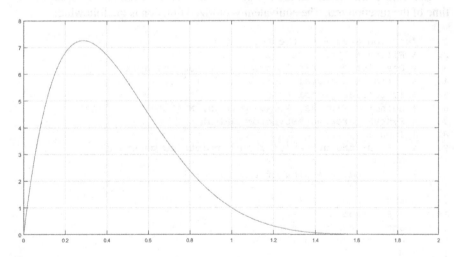

FIG. 3.7

Plot of the curve $y = x(x-2)^6$ from $x = 0$ to $x = 2$.

```
1.    function area = test(n)
2.    % Filename: test.m
3.    % Description: This function computes the area of the
4.    % definite integral int(x * (x - 2) ^ 6, x = 0..2)
5.    % (single-threaded version)
6.    % Authors: Ploskas, N., & Samaras, N.
7.    % Syntax: area = test(n)
8.    % Input:
9.    %    -- n: the number of random points to generate
10.   % Output:
11.   %    -- area: the area of the integral
12.
13.   counter = 0;
14.   for i = 1:n
15.       x = 2 * rand;
16.       y = 8 * rand;
17.       if(y <= x * (x - 2) ^ 6)
18.             counter = counter + 1;
19.       end
20.   end
21.   area = counter / n * 2 * 8;
22.   end
```

The number of the uniformly n random points that will be generated is an important part of each Monte Carlo method. The higher the number, the more accurate will be the calculation of the area. So, let's use 1,000,000,000 random points to calculate the area. The *test* function runs in 188.89 seconds.

Someone could argue that the use of vectorized code will improve the execution time of the function *test*. The equivalent vectorized function is the following:

```
1.    function area = testVectorized(n)
2.    % Filename: testVectorized.m
3.    % Description: This function computes the area of the
4.    % definite integral int(x * (x - 2) ^ 6, x = 0..2)
5.    % (vectorized version)
6.    % Authors: Ploskas, N., & Samaras, N.
7.    % Syntax: area = testVectorized(n)
8.    % Input:
9.    %    -- n: the number of random points to generate
10.   % Output:
11.   %    -- area: the area of the integral
12.
13.   x = 2 * rand(n, 1);
14.   y = 8 * rand(n, 1);
15.   counter = sum(y < (x .* (x - 2) .^ 6));
16.   area = counter / n * 2 * 8;
17.   end
```

The *testVectorized* function runs in 56.45 seconds, a ~3.35× speedup compared to the *test* function. This is a very good speedup and it was expected because the vectorized function is executed in multiple threads. However, the *testVectorized* function requires 16 Gb of RAM to create and store variables *x* and *y*. This is a huge amount of memory that is not available in many computers.

Assuming that our computer has a smaller amount of memory, we can modify the *test* function to take advantage of the vectorized code. Instead of generating vectors *x* and *y* with 1,000,000,000 values, we will generate them with 10,000,000 values and perform the *for-loop* 100 times. So, the following code only uses 160 MB for variables *x* and *y*.

```
1.   function area = test2(n)
2.   % Filename: test2.m
3.   % Description: This function computes the area of the
4.   % definite integral int(x * (x - 2) ^ 6, x = 0..2)
5.   % (single-threaded semi-vectorized version)
6.   % Authors: Ploskas, N., & Samaras, N.
7.   % Syntax: area = test2(n)
8.   % Input:
9.   %    -- n: the number of random points to generate
10.  % Output:
11.  %    -- area: the area of the integral
12.
13.  n = n / 100;
14.  counter = 0;
15.  for i = 1:100
16.      x = 2 * rand(n, 1);
17.      y = 8 * rand(n, 1);
18.      counter = counter + sum(y < (x .* (x - 2) .^ 6));
19.  end
20.  area = counter / (n * 100) * 2 * 8;
21.  end
```

The *test2* function runs in 56.83 seconds, a ~3.32× speedup compared to the *test* function.

Initially, let's use a *parfor-loop* to parallelize the *test* function.

```
1.   function area = testparfor(n)
2.   % Filename: testparfor.m
3.   % Description: This function computes the area of the
4.   % definite integral int(x * (x - 2) ^ 6, x = 0..2)
5.   % (multi-threaded version using parfor)
6.   % Authors: Ploskas, N., & Samaras, N.
7.   % Syntax: area = testparfor(n)
8.   % Input:
9.   %    -- n: the number of random points to generate
10.  % Output:
11.  %    -- area: the area of the integral
12.
13.  counter = 0;
14.  parfor i = 1:n
15.      x = 2 * rand;
16.      y = 8 * rand;
17.      if(y <= x * (x - 2) ^ 6)
```

```
18.              counter = counter + 1;
19.        end
20.    end
21.    area = counter / n * 2 * 8;
22.    end
```

The *testparfor* function runs in 36.12 seconds using 8 MATLAB workers, a ~5.23× speedup compared to the *test* function. We cannot achieve a linear speedup of 8× due to the communication cost.

Next, let's use a *parfor-loop* to parallelize the *test2* function.

```
1.     function area = testparfor2(n)
2.     % Filename: testparfor2.m
3.     % Description: This function computes the area of the
4.     % definite integral int(x * (x - 2) ^ 6, x = 0..2)
5.     % (multi-threaded semi-vectorized version using parfor)
6.     % Authors: Ploskas, N., & Samaras, N.
7.     % Syntax: area = testparfor2(n)
8.     % Input:
9.     %    -- n: the number of random points to generate
10.    % Output:
11.    %    -- area: the area of the integral
12.
13.    n = n / 100;
14.    counter = 0;
15.    parfor i = 1:100
16.        x = 2 * rand(n, 1);
17.        y = 8 * rand(n, 1);
18.        counter = counter + sum(y < (x .* (x - 2) .^ 6));
19.    end
20.    area = counter / (n * 100) * 2 * 8;
21.    end
```

The *testparfor2* function runs in 25.95 seconds using 8 MATLAB workers, a ~7.28× speedup compared to the *test* function and a ~2.19× speedup compared to the *test2* function.

3.3 SINGLE PROGRAM MULTIPLE DATA (*spmd*)

The single programming multiple data (*spmd*) statement allows seamless interleaving of serial and parallel programming. A block of code to run simultaneously on multiple MATLAB workers can be defined in an *spmd* statement. An *spmd* statement is used when we want to execute an identical code on multiple data. Each MATLAB worker will execute the same code on different data. Before and after an *spmd* statement, the code is executed on the MATLAB client, and the code inside an *spmd* statement is executed on the MATLAB workers. Hence, the general form of an *spmd* statement is the following:

```
... % statements executed on the MATLAB client
spmd
    ... % statements executed on multiple MATLAB workers
end
... % statements executed on the MATLAB client
```

You can also define the number of MATLAB workers to be used in an *spmd* statement:

```
spmd(n)
    ...
end
```

or

```
spmd(m, n)
    ...
end
```

In the first case (*spmd(n)*), the *spmd* statement requires that *n* MATLAB workers will run the *spmd* block of code. If the pool is large enough, but *n* MATLAB workers are not available, the statement waits until enough MATLAB workers are available. In the second case (*spmd(m, n)*), the *spmd* statement requires a minimum of *m* MATLAB workers, and it uses a maximum of *n* MATLAB workers, if available in the pool.

Each MATLAB worker used in an *spmd* statement has a unique value of *labindex* that can be used to run codes on specific MATLAB workers or access unique data. The total number of MATLAB workers used in an *spmd* statement can be obtained using the *numlabs* value. For example, we can create different sized arrays depending on *labindex*, as shown in the following code:

```
spmd
    if labindex == 1
        A = rand(3, 3);
    elseif labindex == numlabs
        A = rand(4, 4);
    else
        A = rand(2, 2);
    end
    maximum = max(max(A));
end
```

In the preceding example *A* and *maximum* are *composite* objects (Fig. 3.8). *Composite* objects contain references to the values stored on the MATLAB workers and can be retrieved on the MATLAB client using cell-array indexing (Fig. 3.9).

There are two ways to create *composite* objects:

•   Define variables on MATLAB workers inside an *spmd* statement. These variables are accessible by the MATLAB client after the *spmd* statement, as shown in the previous example (Figs. 3.8 and 3.9).

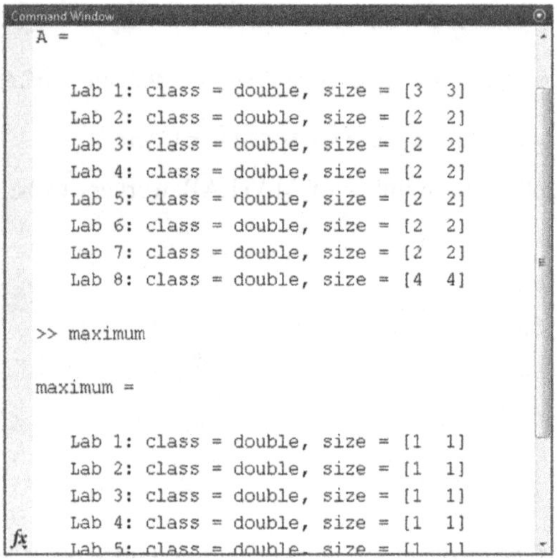

FIG. 3.8

Composite objects.

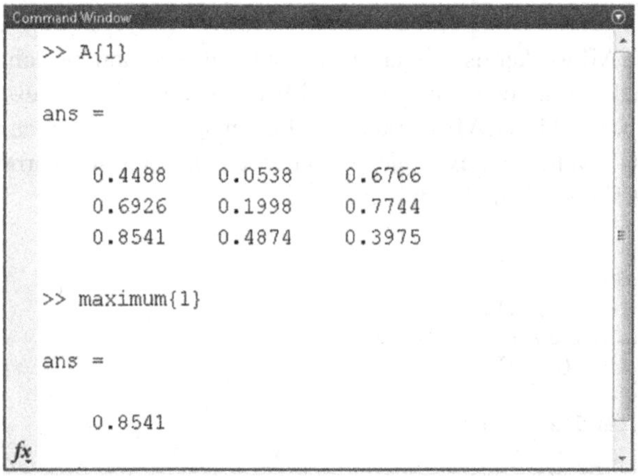

FIG. 3.9

Retrieving *composite* objects on the MATLAB client.

- Use the *Composite* function on the MATLAB client. The MATLAB client may create a *composite* object prior to an *spmd* statement, and the MATLAB workers can access the *composite* object inside an *spmd* statement.

```
>> A = Composite();
>> for i = 1:numel(A)
       A{i} = rand(3, 3);
   end
```

Table 3.3 Functions used by MATLAB workers to communicate with each other

Function	Description
gcat	Global concatenation of an array performed across all MATLAB workers.
gop	Global reduction using binary associative operation performed across all MATLAB workers.
gplus	Global addition performed across all MATLAB workers.
labBarrier	Block execution until all MATLAB workers reach this call.
labBroadcast	Send data to all MATLAB workers or receive data sent to all MATLAB workers.
labProbe	Test to see if messages are ready to be received from other MATLAB worker.
labReceive	Receive data from another MATLAB worker.
labSend	Send data to another MATLAB worker.
labSendReceive	Simultaneously send data to and receive data from another MATLAB worker.

```
>> spmd
      maximum = max(max(A));
   end
```

The *composite* objects are retained on the MATLAB workers until they are cleared on the MATLAB client or until the pool is closed. Moreover, multiple *spmd* statements can use *composite* objects defined in previous *spmd* statements.

The MATLAB workers can communicate with each other using a number of functions. First of all, *distributed* and *codistributed* arrays can be used to partition large data sets. *Distributed* and *codistributed* arrays will be thoroughly presented in Section 3.4. Moreover, a number of functions can be used from the MATLAB workers to communicate with each other (Table 3.3).

You should also consider the following limitations/concerns before parallelizing your application using an *spmd* statement:

- When running an *spmd* statement in a computer cluster, the communication cost will be greater than running the same code on local MATLAB workers.
- Any graphical output, for example, *plot*, will not be displayed at all because the MATLAB workers are sessions without graphical output.
- Be careful when using *cd*, *addpath*, and *rmpath* on an *spmd* statement as the MATLAB search path might not be the same on all MATLAB workers.
- If an error occurs on a worker, then all MATLAB workers terminate.
- The body of an *spmd* statement cannot make any direct reference to a nested function, but it can call a nested function by means of a variable defined as a function handle to the nested function.

- The body of an *spmd* statement cannot define an anonymous function, but it can reference an anonymous function by means of a function handle.
- The body of an *spmd* statement cannot directly contain another *spmd* statement, but it can call a function that contains another *spmd* statement. However, the inner *spmd* statement runs serially in a single thread on the worker running its containing function.
- The body of a *parfor-loop* cannot contain an *spmd* statement and an *spmd* statement cannot contain a *parfor-loop*.
- The body of an *spmd* statement cannot contain *break* and *return* statements.
- The body of an *spmd* statement cannot contain global or persistent variable declarations.

There are mainly two types of applications in which the use of an *spmd* statement will improve their computation time:

- Applications that take a long time to execute: several MATLAB workers compute solutions simultaneously.
- Applications that use large data sets: data is distributed to multiple MATLAB workers.

Example: Monte Carlo simulation to approximate the area of a figure

Let's consider again the example presented in Section 3.2. Initially, let's use an *spmd* statement to parallelize the *test* function.

```
1.   function area = testspmd(n)
2.   % Filename: testspmd.m
3.   % Description: This function computes the area of the
4.   % definite integral int(x * (x - 2) ^ 6, x = 0..2)
5.   % (multi-threaded version using spmd)
6.   % Authors: Ploskas, N., & Samaras, N.
7.   % Syntax: area = testspmd(n)
8.   % Input:
9.   %    -- n: the number of random points to generate
10.  % Output:
11.  %    -- area: the area of the integral
12.
13.  spmd(8)
14.      iterations = floor(n / 8);
15.      if labindex <= mod(n, 8)
16.          iterations = iterations + 1;
17.      end
18.      counter = 0;
19.      for i = 1:iterations
20.          x = 2 * rand;
21.          y = 8 * rand;
22.          counter = counter + sum(y < (x * (x - 2) ^ 6));
23.      end
24.  end
25.  counterStruct = gplus(counter);
```

```
26.    counter = 0;
27.    for i = 1:8
28.        counter = counter + counterStruct{i};
29.    end
30.    area = counter / n * 2 * 8;
31.    end
```

The *testspmd* function runs in 35.20 seconds using 8 MATLAB workers, a ~5.37× speedup compared to the *test* function and almost the same execution time with the *testparfor* function.

Next, let's use an *spmd* statement to parallelize the *test2* function.

```
1.    function area = testspmd2(n)
2.    % Filename: testspmd2.m
3.    % Description: This function computes the area of the
4.    % definite integral int(x * (x - 2) ^ 6, x = 0..2)
5.    % (multi-threaded semi-vectorized version using spmd)
6.    % Authors: Ploskas, N., & Samaras, N.
7.    % Syntax: area = testspmd2(n)
8.    % Input:
9.    %     -- n: the number of random points to generate
10.   % Output:
11.   %     -- area: the area of the integral
12.
13.   n = n / 100;
14.   spmd(8)
15.       iterations = floor(100 / 8);
16.       if labindex <= mod(100, 8)
17.           iterations = iterations + 1;
18.       end
19.       counter = 0;
20.       for i = 1:iterations
21.           x = 2 * rand(n, 1);
22.           y = 8 * rand(n, 1);
23.           counter = counter + sum(y < (x .* (x - 2) .^6 ));
24.       end
25.   end
26.   counterStruct = gplus(counter);
27.   counter = 0;
28.   for i = 1:8
29.       counter = counter + counterStruct{i};
30.   end
31.   area = counter / (n * 100) * 2 * 8;
32.   end
```

The *testparfor2* function runs in 25.79 seconds using 8 MATLAB workers, a ~7.32× speedup compared to the *test* function, a ~2.20× speedup compared to the *test2* function and almost the same execution time with the *testparfor2* function.

3.4 DISTRIBUTED AND CODISTRIBUTED ARRAYS

The MATLAB client can create a *distributed* array and distribute it across all MATLAB workers. A *codistributed* array can be created inside an *spmd* statement and partitioned among the MATLAB workers. The difference between *distributed* and *codistributed* arrays is one of perspective. *Codistributed* arrays are partitioned among the MATLAB workers from which you execute code to create or manipulate them. *Distributed* arrays are partitioned among workers in the parallel pool. When a *codistributed* array is created in an *spmd* statement, it can be accessed as a *distributed* array on the MATLAB client. When a *distributed* array is created on the MATLAB client, it can be accessed as a *codistributed* array inside an *spmd* statement. The details of distribution cannot be controlled when creating a *distributed* array; a *distributed* array is distributed in one dimension, along the last non-singleton dimension, and as evenly as possible along that dimension among the MATLAB workers. On the other hand, the details of distribution can be controlled when creating a *codistributed* array.

A *distributed* array can be created using one of the following ways:

- Use the *distributed* function to distribute an existing array from the MATLAB client's workspace to the MATLAB workers of a parallel pool. In the following example, A and B are *distributed* arrays. Each MATLAB worker stores only a part of A and B (Fig. 3.10).

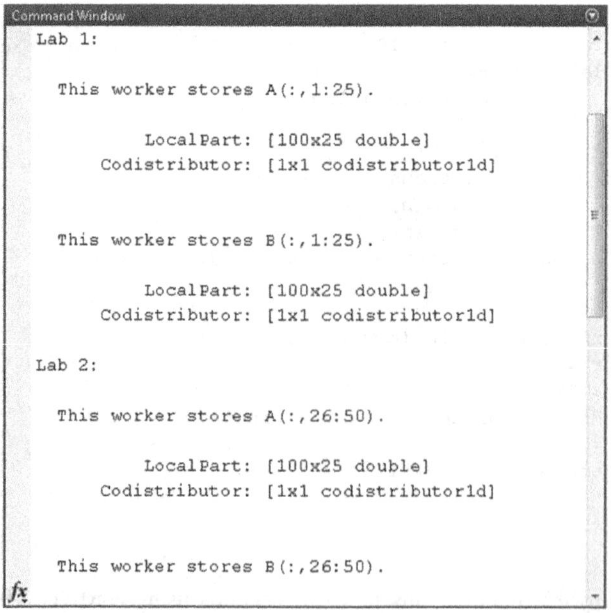

```
Command Window
  Lab 1:

    This worker stores A(:,1:25).

            LocalPart: [100x25 double]
        Codistributor: [1x1 codistributor1d]


    This worker stores B(:,1:25).

            LocalPart: [100x25 double]
        Codistributor: [1x1 codistributor1d]

  Lab 2:

    This worker stores A(:,26:50).

            LocalPart: [100x25 double]
        Codistributor: [1x1 codistributor1d]


    This worker stores B(:,26:50).
```

FIG. 3.10

Part of *distributed* arrays stored on each MATLAB worker.

```
>> parpool('local', 4);
>> A = rand(100, 100);
>> A = distributed(A);
>> spmd
      B = A * 2;
   end
>> delete(gcp);
```

- Use any of the overloaded *distributed* object methods to directly construct a *distributed* array on the MATLAB workers (Table 3.4). In the following example, *A* and *B* are *distributed* arrays. Each MATLAB worker stores only a part of *A* and *B* (Fig. 3.10).

```
>> parpool('local', 4);
>> A = rand(100, 100, 'distributed');
>> spmd
      B = A * 2;
>> end
>> delete(gcp);
```

- Create a *codistributed* array inside an *spmd* statement and access it as a *distributed* array outside the *spmd* statement (see examples for *codistributed* arrays later in this section).

A *codistributed* array can be created using one of the following ways:

- Use the *codistributed* function inside an *spmd* statement, a communicating job or *pmode* to codistribute data already existing on the MATLAB workers running that job. In the following example, *A* and *B* are *codistributed* arrays. Each MATLAB worker stores only a part of *A* and *B* (Fig. 3.10).

```
>> parpool('local', 4);
>> spmd
      A = rand(100, 100);
      A = codistributed(A);
      B = A * 2;
   end
>> delete(gcp);
```

In the preceding code, *codistributed(A)*, which is the same as *codistributed(A, codistributor('1d', 2))*, tells MATLAB to distribute array *A* along its second dimension, that is, columns. If you want to distribute array *A* along its first dimension, that is, rows, use *codistributed(A, codistributor('1d', 1))* (Fig. 3.11).

As an alternative to distributing by a single dimension of rows or columns, you can distribute an array by blocks using '2dbc' or two-dimensional block-cyclic distribution. In the following example, *A* and *B* are distributed with a 50 × 50 block in 2-by-2 arrangement (Figs. 3.12 and 3.13).

```
>> parpool('local', 4);
>> spmd
      A = rand(100, 100);
```

Table 3.4 Overloaded MATLAB functions for *distributed* arrays

Function	Description
distributed.cell	Create a distributed cell array.
distributed.colon(a, d, b)	Create a distributed array from the vector a:d:b.
distributed.eye	Create a distributed identity matrix.
distributed.false	Create a distributed array of logical zeros.
distributed.Inf	Create a distributed array with Inf values in all elements.
distributed.linspace	Create a distributed linearly spaced vector.
distributed.logspace	Create a distributed logarithmically spaced vector.
distributed.NaN	Create a distributed array with Nan values in all elements.
distributed.ones	Create a distributed array of ones.
distributed.rand	Create a distributed array of uniformly distributed pseudo-random numbers.
distributed.randi	Create a distributed array of uniformly distributed pseudo-random integer numbers.
distributed.randn	Create a distributed array of normally distributed pseudo-random numbers.
distributed.spalloc	Allocate space for a sparse distributed array.
distributed.speye	Create a distributed sparse identity array.
distributed.sprand	Create a distributed sparse array of uniformly distributed pseudo-random values.
distributed.sprandn	Create a distributed sparse array of normally distributed pseudo-random values.
distributed.true	Create a distributed array of logical ones.
distributed.zeros	Create a distributed array of zeros.
eye(..., 'distributed')	Create a distributed identity matrix.
false(..., 'distributed')	Create a distributed array of logical zeros.
Inf(..., 'distributed')	Create a distributed array with Inf values in all elements.
NaN(..., 'distributed')	Create a distributed array with Nan values in all elements.
ones(..., 'distributed')	Create a distributed array of ones.
rand(..., 'distributed')	Create a distributed array of uniformly distributed pseudo-random numbers.
randi(..., 'distributed')	Create a distributed array of uniformly distributed pseudo-random integer numbers.
randn(..., 'distributed')	Create a distributed array of normally distributed pseudo-random numbers.
true(..., 'distributed')	Create a distributed array of logical ones.
zeros(..., 'distributed')	Create a distributed array of zeros.

```
Command Window                                          ⊙
  Lab 1:

    This worker stores A(1:25,:).

            LocalPart: [25x100 double]
         Codistributor: [1x1 codistributor1d]


    This worker stores B(1:25,:).

            LocalPart: [25x100 double]
         Codistributor: [1x1 codistributor1d]

  Lab 2:

    This worker stores A(26:50,:).

            LocalPart: [25x100 double]
         Codistributor: [1x1 codistributor1d]


    This worker stores B(26:50,:).
fx
```

FIG. 3.11

Codistributed arrays along their first dimension.

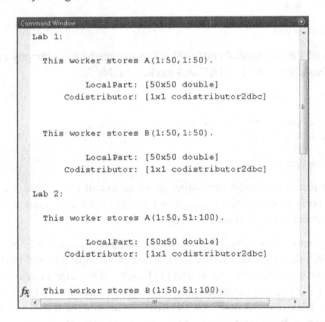

```
Command Window                                          ⊙
  Lab 1:

    This worker stores A(1:50,1:50).

            LocalPart: [50x50 double]
         Codistributor: [1x1 codistributor2dbc]


    This worker stores B(1:50,1:50).

            LocalPart: [50x50 double]
         Codistributor: [1x1 codistributor2dbc]

  Lab 2:

    This worker stores A(1:50,51:100).

            LocalPart: [50x50 double]
         Codistributor: [1x1 codistributor2dbc]

fx  This worker stores B(1:50,51:100).
```

FIG. 3.12

Codistributed arrays using '2dbc' distribution.

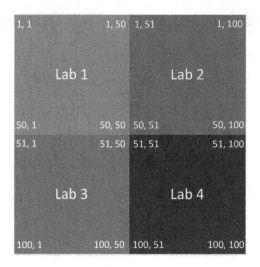

FIG. 3.13

Codistributed arrays using '2dbc' distribution.

```
        A = codistributed(A, codistributor('2dbc', [2 2], 50));
        B = A * 2;
>> end
>> delete(gcp);
```

• Use any of the overloaded *codistributed* object methods to directly construct a *codistributed* array on the MATLAB workers (Table 3.5).

```
>> parpool('local', 4);
>> spmd
        A = rand(100, 100, codistributor1d());
        B = A * 2;
>> end
>> delete(gcp);
```

• Create a *distributed* array outside an *spmd* statement and access it as a *codistributed* array inside the *spmd* statement running on the same pool (see examples for *distributed* arrays earlier in this section).

Indexing into a non-distributed array is straightforward; each dimension is indexed within the range of 1 to the final subscript given by the *end* keyword. The length of any dimension can be determined using either *size* or *length* function. On the other hand, these values are not so easily obtained for *codistributed* arrays because the index range depends on the distribution scheme that was used to distribute the *codistributed* array. MATLAB provides the *globalIndices* function, which provides a correlation between the local and global indexing of the *codistributed* array.

Table 3.5 Overloaded MATLAB functions for *codistributed* arrays

Function	Description
codistributed.build	Build a codistributed array from local parts.
codistributed.cell	Create a codistributed cell array.
codistributed.colon(a, d, b)	Create a codistributed array from the vector a:d:b.
codistributed.eye	Create a codistributed identity matrix.
codistributed.false	Create a codistributed array of logical zeros.
codistributed.linspace	Create a codistributed linearly spaced vector.
codistributed.logspace	Create a codistributed logarithmically spaced vector.
codistributed.Inf	Create a codistributed array with Inf values in all elements.
codistributed.NaN	Create a codistributed array with Nan values in all elements.
codistributed.ones	Create a codistributed array of ones.
codistributed.rand	Create a codistributed array of uniformly distributed pseudo-random numbers.
codistributed.randi	Create a codistributed array of distributed pseudo-random integer numbers.
codistributed.randn	Create a codistributed array of normally distributed pseudo-random numbers.
codistributed.spalloc	Allocate space for a sparse codistributed array.
codistributed.speye	Create a codistributed sparse identity array.
codistributed.sprand	Create a codistributed sparse array of uniformly distributed pseudo-random values.
codistributed.sprandn	Create a codistributed sparse array of normally distributed pseudo-random values.
codistributed.true	Create a codistributed array of logical ones.
codistributed.zeros	Create a codistributed array of zeros.
eye(..., 'codistributed')	Create a codistributed identity matrix.
false(..., 'codistributed')	Create a codistributed array of logical zeros.
Inf(..., 'codistributed')	Create a codistributed array with Inf values in all elements.
NaN(..., 'codistributed')	Create a codistributed array with Nan values in all elements.
ones(..., 'codistributed')	Create a codistributed array of ones.
rand(..., 'codistributed')	Create a codistributed array of uniformly distributed pseudo-random numbers.
randi(..., 'codistributed')	Create a codistributed array of distributed pseudo-random integer numbers.
randn(..., 'codistributed')	Create a codistributed array of normally distributed pseudo-random numbers.
sparse(..., codist)	Create a sparse codistributed matrix.
true(..., 'codistributed')	Create a codistributed array of logical ones.
zeros(..., 'codistributed')	Create a codistributed array of zeros.

Moreover, MATLAB offers *for drange* loop to iterate through a *codistributed* array, as shown below:

```
>> n = 100;
>> A = 1:n;
>> spmd
      B = zeros(1, n, codistributor());
      for i = drange(1:n)
         B(i) = A(i) * 2;
      end
   end
```

Finally, many functions in MATLAB are overloaded so that they operate on *codistributed* arrays in the same way they operate on non-distributed arrays. For a full list, see [5].

3.5 INTERACTIVE PARALLEL DEVELOPMENT (*pmode*)

MATLAB provides the *pmode* functionality where you can work interactively with a communicating job running simultaneously on multiple MATLAB workers. *pmode* and *spmd* are very similar; the main difference to *spmd* is that *pmode* does not allow you to freely interleave serial and parallel work as *spmd* does. When a *pmode* session is terminated, its job is destroyed and all data stored on the MATLAB workers lost. Commands that are typed at the *pmode* prompt are executed on all MATLAB workers at the same time. Each worker has its own workspace. All communication functions supported in *spmd* statements can also be used in *pmode* and the variables can be transferred between the MATLAB client and the MATLAB workers. As with *spmd*, MATLAB workers are sessions without display. Moreover, the MATLAB workers running *pmode* can be on a computer cluster.

We can start *pmode* using the local profile with 4 local workers (Fig. 3.14):

```
>> pmode start local 4
```

Codistributed arrays can be distributed among the MATLAB workers (Fig. 3.15):

```
>> A = rand(100, 100, codistributor());
```

The *gather* function can be used to gather an entire array into the workspace of all MATLAB workers. Moreover, the *client2lab* function can be used to copy a variable from the MATLAB client to all/specified MATLAB workers, while *lab2client* function can be used to copy a variable from a MATLAB worker to the MATLAB client. Note that a *codistributed* array cannot be transferred from a MATLAB worker to the MATLAB client because the MATLAB worker stores only a local portion of the *codistributed* array. To overcome that limitation, the *gather* function must first be used to assemble the entire array into the workspace of all MATLAB workers and then use the *lab2client* function to transfer the *codistributed* array to the MATLAB client.

FIG. 3.14

pmode's parallel command window.

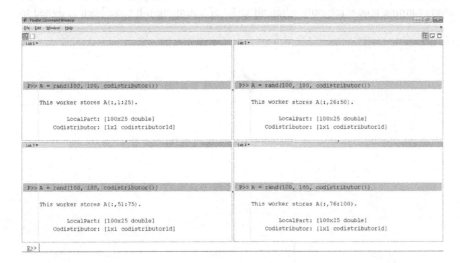

FIG. 3.15

Codistributed array in *pmode*'s parallel command window.

3.6 GPU COMPUTING

For the sake of completeness, we have also included this section about GPU computing because the Parallel Computing Toolbox enables you to program MAT-LAB to use GPUs. However, we will not present MATLAB's GPU capabilities in this section because GPU computing will be extensively discussed in the next chapters of this book.

3.7 CLUSTERS AND JOB SCHEDULING

The Parallel Computing Toolbox and MATLAB Distributed Computing Server let you solve task- and data-parallel algorithms on many multicore and multiprocessor computers. A job is a large operation that you need to perform in MATLAB. A job can be divided into segments called tasks. These tasks can be identical or not. The MATLAB session in which the job is defined is called the MATLAB client. The Parallel Computing Toolbox should be installed on the MATLAB client. If the job is executed on a local cluster, no other MATLAB toolbox is needed. On the other hand, if the job is executed on a computer cluster, the MATLAB Distributed Computing Server should be installed on the machines of the cluster (Fig. 3.16). A job scheduler is needed to coordinate the execution of jobs and the evaluation of their tasks. MATLAB provides the MATLAB Job Scheduler (MJS) for this reason. However, the use of the MJS is optional; third-party schedulers, such as Microsoft Windows HPC Server and IBM Platform LSF, can also be used [13].

The MJS can be run on any machine on the network. The MJS runs jobs in the order in which they are submitted, unless any job in its queue is promoted, demoted, canceled or deleted. The MJS distributes the tasks to MATLAB workers, and the MATLAB workers execute the tasks and return the results to the MJS. The MJS starts running a new job only when all tasks of a running job have been assigned to

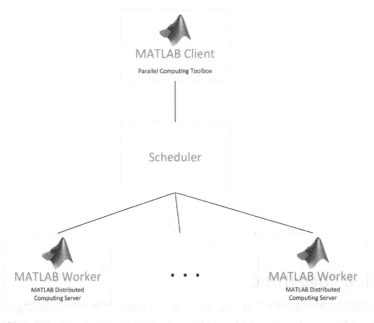

FIG. 3.16

Running a job on a computer cluster.

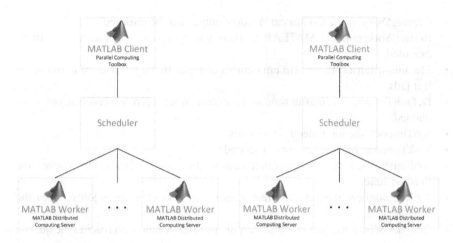

FIG. 3.17

Multiple MATLAB clients and MJSs.

MATLAB workers. In an independent job, the MATLAB workers evaluate tasks one at a time as available, perhaps simultaneously, perhaps not. In a communicating job, the MATLAB workers evaluate tasks simultaneously. Finally, the MJS returns all the results of all the tasks of a job to the MATLAB client.

In a large network, several MATLAB clients and MJSs may be used. Each client can create, run, and access jobs on any MJS, but a MATLAB worker is registered with and dedicated to only one MJS at a time (Fig. 3.17).

A cluster profile can be created either automatically (by discovering a MATLAB Distributed Computing Server cluster on the network) or manually. To create a cluster profile manually, on the *Home* tab in the *Environment* section, click *Parallel → Manage Cluster Profiles*. The following information should be given to create a cluster profile:

- Description: the description of the cluster profile.
- Host: the hostname of the machine where the MJS is running (required).
- MJSName: the name of the MJS (required if multiple MJSs exist on the host machine).
- Username: the username for MJS access (required if the MJS uses security level 1–3).
- LicenseNumber: the license number.
- AutoAttachFiles: if code files will automatically be sent to the cluster.
- AttachedFiles: the files and folders to copy from the MATLAB client to cluster nodes.
- AdditionalPaths: the folders to add to the MATLAB workers' search path.
- NumWorkersRange: the range of number of MATLAB workers to run a job.

- CaptureDiary: if the Command Window output will be returned.
- RestartWorker: if the MATLAB workers will be restarted before a job will be executed.
- MaximumRetries: the maximum number of times that a job will try to run again if it fails.
- DefaultTimeout: the master timeout in seconds when a job or a task timeout is not defined.
- JobTimeout: the job timeout in seconds.
- TaskTimeout: the task timeout in seconds.
- JobFinishedFcn: the function that runs on the client when a job reaches the finished state.
- JobRunningFcn: the function that runs on the client when a job reaches the running state.
- JobQueuedFcn: the function that runs on the client when a job reaches the queued state.
- TaskFinishedFcn: the function that runs on the client when a task reaches the finished state.
- TaskRunningFcn: the function that runs on the client when a task reaches the running state.

When a job is created and executed, it progresses through the following stages:

- Pending: the job's first state is pending. This is when a job is defined by adding tasks to it.
- Queued: when a job is submitted, the MJS places the job in a queue.
- Running: when a job reaches the top of the queue, the MJS distributes the job's tasks to MATLAB workers for evaluation.
- Finished: when all of a job's tasks have been evaluated, the job is moved to the finished state.
- Failed: if a third-party scheduler is used instead of the MJS, a job might fail if the scheduler encounters an error while attempting to execute its commands or access necessary files.
- Deleted: when a job's data has been removed from its data location or from the MJS, the state of the job on the MATLAB client is deleted.

As already mentioned, two type of jobs can be created:

- **Independent job**: an independent job is one whose tasks do not directly communicate with each other, that is, its tasks are independent of each other. The tasks do not need to run simultaneously and a MATLAB worker might run several tasks of the same job in succession. The following example creates (*createJob* function) and executes (*submit* function) an independent job with three simple tasks (the calculation of a vector's maximum and minimum element and the calculation of the sum of a vector's elements). Finally, the results from all tasks of the job are collected (*fetchOutputs* function) after the job is finished (*wait* function).

```
>> parallel.defaultClusterProfile('local');
>> c = parcluster();
>> j = createJob(c);
>> createTask(j, @max, 1, {rand(1, 10)});
>> createTask(j, @min, 1, {rand(1, 10)});
>> createTask(j, @sum, 1, {rand(1, 10)});
>> submit(j);
>> wait(j)
>> results = fetchOutputs(j)
```

- **Communicating job**: a communicating job is one in which the MATLAB workers can communicate with each other during the evaluation of their tasks. A communicating job consists of only a single task that runs simultaneously on several MATLAB workers, usually with different data. The task is duplicated on each MATLAB worker, so each MATLAB worker can perform the task on a different set of data or on a particular segment of a large data set. The following example creates (*createCommunicatingJob* function) and executes (*submit* function) a communicating job with a simple task (the calculation of the sum of a magic square). The task is defined in *totalSum* function which is attached to all MATLAB workers. The first MATLAB worker creates and sends to all other MATLAB workers a magic square (*labBroadcast* function), each of which calculates the sum of one column of the matrix. All of these column sums are combined to calculate the total sum of the elements of the original magic square (*gplus* function). Finally, the results from all tasks of the job are collected (*fetchOutputs* function) after the job is finished (*wait* function).

```
function total_sum = totalSum
    if labindex == 1
        A = labBroadcast(1, magic(numlabs));
    else
        A = labBroadcast(1);
    end
    colSum = sum(A(:, labindex));
    total_sum = gplus(colSum);
end

>> parallel.defaultClusterProfile('local');
>> c = parcluster();
>> j = createCommunicatingJob(c, 'Type', 'SPMD');
>> j.AttachedFiles = {'totalSum.m'};
>> j.NumWorkersRange = 8;
>> createTask(j, @totalSum, 1, {})
>> submit(j);
>> wait(j)
>> results = fetchOutputs(j)
```

FIG. 3.18

Job monitor.

The jobs can be monitored using the Job Monitor by clicking *Parallel → Monitor Jobs* on the *Home* tab in the *Environment* section (Fig. 3.18).

3.8 CHAPTER REVIEW

This chapter presented the key features of MATLAB's Parallel Computing Toolbox. The Parallel Computing Toolbox allows users to solve computationally- and data-intensive problems using multicore and multiprocessor computers, computer clusters, and GPUs. The *parfor-loop* and the *spmd* statement, which enable users to parallelize their code, have been presented in detail. Moreover, the *pmode* functionality, where you can work interactively with a communicating job running simultaneously on multiple MATLAB workers, was also introduced. Finally, the combination of the Parallel Computing Toolbox with the Distributed Computing Server has been described to show how codes can be executed on computer clusters, grids, and clouds.

To sum up, the Parallel Computing Toolbox offers many features to execute task- and data-parallel applications on a single core, a multicore processor, or a computer cluster. In general, Parallel Computing Toolbox can be used to improve the performance of the following types of applications: (i) applications that involve repetitive segments of code, (ii) applications that run a series of independent tasks, (iii) applications evaluating the same code on multiple data sets, and (iv) applications involving data that is too large for your computer's memory.

Introduction to GPU programming in MATLAB

4

CHAPTER OBJECTIVES

This Chapter covers one of the most important topics of this book, the inherent GPU programming features that MATLAB provides. More specifically, this Chapter introduces the GPU arrays, arrays that are stored on GPUs. These arrays can be used in computations by built-in MATLAB functions for GPUs and element-wise MATLAB operations. This Chapter includes a variety of examples, both didactical and real-world examples. After reading this Chapter, you should be able to:

- Understand MATLAB's GPU Programming features.
- Transfer arrays between the MATLAB workspace and the GPU.
- Execute code on GPU using GPU-enabled built-in MATLAB functions.
- Execute code on GPU using element-wise operations.
- Measure the execution time of a code running on GPU.

4.1 GPU PROGRAMMING FEATURES IN MATLAB

Besides multicore and multiprocessor computers and computer clusters, MATLAB's Parallel Computing Toolbox allows users to solve computationally- and data-intensive problems on CUDA-enabled GPUs. GPU computing was first introduced in MATLAB release R2010b. A special array type *gpuArray* was provided for various built-in functions. Subsequent releases further extended GPU support in various ways by:

- Adding more GPU-enabled built-in functions
- Improving the performance of GPU computing
- Supporting calls to CUDA kernels
- Supporting *gpuArray* indexing
- Providing *arrayfun*, *bsxfun*, and *pagefun* support
- Adding GPU support in various toolboxes

GPU Programming in MATLAB. http://dx.doi.org/10.1016/B978-0-12-805132-0.00004-7

MATLAB allows us to execute codes on GPUs with various ways:

- Using a special array type *gpuArray* and taking advantage of the various GPU-enabled built-in functions (see Section 4.3).
- Using a *gpuArray* on codes with element-wise operations (see Section 4.4).
- Using the GPU-enabled functions in toolboxes: Communications System Toolbox, Image Processing Toolbox, Neural Network Toolbox, Phased Array Systems Toolbox, Signal Processing Toolbox, and Statistics and Machine Learning Toolbox (see Chapter 5).
- Creating an executable kernel for a CUDA C/C++ code or PTX code and running that kernel on a GPU by calling it through MATLAB (see Chapter 7).
- Creating a MATLAB MEX file that contains CUDA code and running it on a GPU by calling it through MATLAB (see Chapters 8–9).

In this chapter, the inherent GPU programming features that MATLAB provides are thoroughly presented. More specifically, this chapter introduces the GPU arrays, arrays that are stored on GPUs. These arrays can be used in computations by built-in MATLAB functions for GPUs and element-wise MATLAB operations.

4.2 GPU ARRAYS

The easiest approach to use GPU computing is straightforward and does not require modification of the original code (running on a CPU), except converting the input data into the *gpuArray* special type. A *gpuArray* is an array that is stored on the GPU. The use of the *gpuArray* function will transfer an array from MATLAB workspace to the GPU, whereas the *gather* function will transfer an array from the GPU to the MATLAB workspace (Fig. 4.1):

```
>> A = magic(4);
>> gpuA = gpuArray(A);
>> B = gather(gpuA);
```

Note that the 108 bytes that *gpuArray gpuA* reserves in main memory are not for its actual data because it is stored on the GPU. For example, both a 2×2 random *gpuArray* and a $1,000 \times 1,000$ random *gpuArray* reserve the same amount in the main memory (108 bytes) that is used for indexing purposes (Fig. 4.2). We can use the *gpuDevice* command to display how much memory the GPU has and how much is being used (Fig. 4.3). The amount of memory used on the GPU may be not entirely used by MATLAB because other applications may also use the GPU.

gpuA is a MATLAB *gpuArray* object that represents the magic square stored on the GPU. The input provided to *gpuArray* must be numeric or logical. You can also specify the precision when transferring an array from MATLAB workspace to the GPU. For example, the following code creates an array of double-precision random values in MATLAB workspace and then transfers the array as single-precision from MATLAB workspace to the GPU:

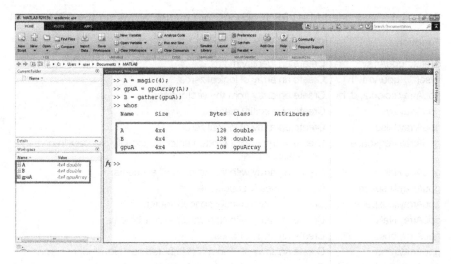

FIG. 4.1

Array stored on the GPU.

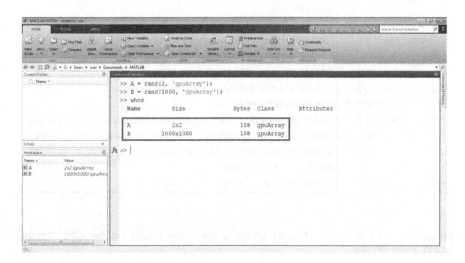

FIG. 4.2

Amount of main memory used by *gpuArray* objects.

```
>> A = rand(4);
>> gpuA = gpuArray(single(A));
```

Moreover, a number of methods on the *gpuArray* class allows you to directly create arrays on the GPU without having to transfer arrays from the MATLAB workspace. This is more efficient because it does not involve CPU memory allocation and transferring data between the CPU and the GPU. You can use any of the methods

Table 4.1 Overloaded MATLAB functions for creating arrays on the GPU

Function	Description
eye(..., 'gpuArray')	Create an identity matrix.
false(..., 'gpuArray')	Create an array of logical zeros.
gpuArray.colon(a, d, b)	Create an array from the vector a:d:b.
gpuArray.eye	Create an identity matrix.
gpuArray.false	Create an array of logical zeros.
gpuArray.freqspace	Create a frequency range vector for equally spaced frequency responses.
gpuArray.Inf	Create an array with Inf values in all elements.
gpuArray.linspace	Create a linearly spaced vector.
gpuArray.logspace	Create a logarithmically spaced vector.
gpuArray.NaN	Create an array with Nan values in all elements.
gpuArray.ones	Create an array of ones.
gpuArray.rand	Create an array of uniformly distributed pseudo-random numbers.
gpuArray.randi	Create an array of distributed pseudo-random integer numbers.
gpuArray.randn	Create an array of normally distributed pseudo-random numbers.
gpuArray.randperm	Create a vector containing a random permutation of a set of integers.
gpuArray.speye	Create a sparse identity array.
gpuArray.true	Create an array of logical ones.
gpuArray.zeros	Create an array of zeros.
Inf(..., 'gpuArray')	Create an array with Inf values in all elements.
NaN(..., 'gpuArray')	Create an array with Nan values in all elements.
ones(..., 'gpuArray')	Create an array of ones.
rand(..., 'gpuArray')	Create an array of uniformly distributed pseudo-random numbers.
randi(..., 'gpuArray')	Create an array of distributed pseudo-random integer numbers.
randn(..., 'gpuArray')	Create an array of normally distributed pseudo-random numbers.
true(..., 'gpuArray')	Create an array of logical ones.
zeros(..., 'gpuArray')	Create an array of zeros.

presented in Table 4.1 to directly create a *gpuArray* object on the GPU (as of MATLAB R2015b).

To get a complete list of available static methods in any release, type *methods('gpuArray')*. The constructors appear at the bottom of the output from this command. Moreover, you can display the documentation of these constructors by typing *help gpuArray/functionname*, for example, *help gpuArray/eye* (Fig. 4.4).

For example, the following code creates an identity array directly on the GPU with two different ways (Fig. 4.5):

```
>> A = eye(5, 'gpuArray');
>> B = gpuArray.eye(5);
```

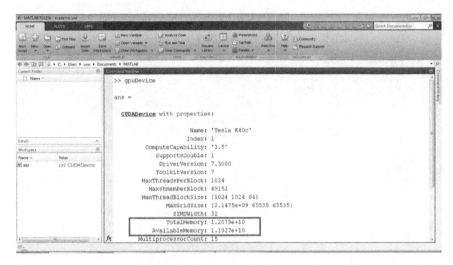

FIG. 4.3

Amount of memory used on the GPU.

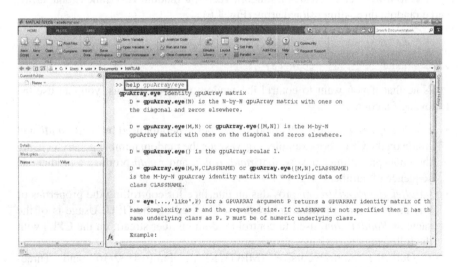

FIG. 4.4

Display documentation of *gpuArray* constructors.

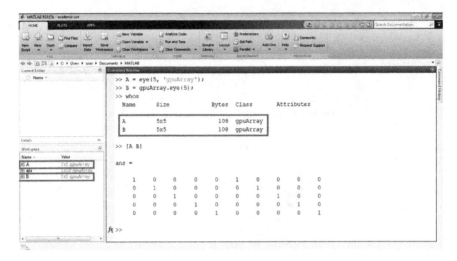

FIG. 4.5

Create arrays directly on the GPU.

The following code creates a random vector, a random two-dimensional array, and a random three-dimensional array (Fig. 4.6):

```
>> A = rand(1, 5, 'gpuArray');
>> B = rand(2, 'gpuArray');
>> C = rand(2, 2, 3, 'gpuArray');
```

Note that if you want to control the random number streams, you can use the following functions:

- *parallel.gpu.rng*: controls the random number generator used by *rand*, *randi*, and *randn* on the GPU. For example, *rng(s)* seeds the random number generator using the nonnegative integer *s*, so that *rand*, *randi*, and *randn* produce a predictable sequence of numbers (Fig. 4.7).
- *parallel.gpu.RandStream*: provides an interface for controlling the properties of one or more random number streams to be used on the GPU. Usage is of the same as *RandStream* (used to control random number stream on the CPU) with the following restrictions:
  - Only the "combRecursive" (MRG32K3A), "Philox4x32-10", and "Three-fry4x64-20" generators are supported.
  - The "Inversion" normal transform is supported for all generators.
  - The "BoxMuller" normal transform is supported only for the "Philox4x32-10" and "Threefry4x64-20" generators.
  - Setting the substream property is not allowed.

For example, you can use the following code to generate the same sequence of random numbers on CPU and GPU (Fig. 4.8):

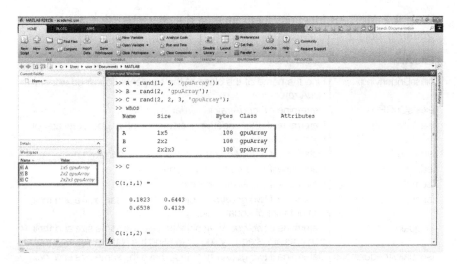

FIG. 4.6

Create multidimensional arrays directly on the GPU.

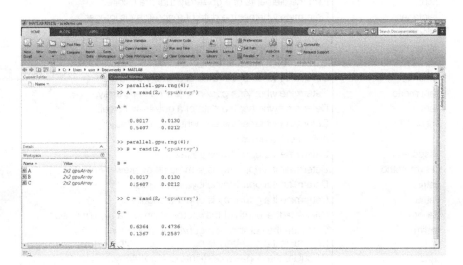

FIG. 4.7

Control random number streams using *parallel.gpu.rng*.

Table 4.2 MATLAB functions for examining the characteristics of a *gpuArray* object

Function	Description
classUnderlying	Find the name of the class of the elements contained within a *gpuArray*.
existsOnGPU	Determine if a *gpuArray* is available on GPU.
isaUnderlying	Determine if the underlying elements of a *gpuArray* are of specified class.
isbanded	Determine if a *gpuArray* is within a specific bandwidth.
isdiag	Determine if a *gpuArray* is diagonal.
isempty	Determine if a *gpuArray* is empty.
isequal	Determine if two *gpuArray* objects have the same size and their contents are of equal value.
isequaln	Determine if two *gpuArray* objects have the same size and their contents are of equal value by treating the NaN values as equal.
isequalwithequalnans	Determine if two *gpuArray* objects have the same size and their contents are of equal value by treating the NaN values as equal.
isfinite	Find the elements of a *gpuArray* that are finite.
isfloat	Determine whether the data of a *gpuArray* is float.
ishermitian	Determine if a *gpuArray* is Hermitian or skew-Hermitian.
isinf	Find the elements of a *gpuArray* that are infinite.
isinteger	Determine whether the data of a *gpuArray* is integer.
islogical	Determine whether the data of a *gpuArray* is logical.
ismember	Determine whether the elements of a *gpuArray* are members of set array.
isnan	Determine whether the data of a *gpuArray* is NaN.
isnumeric	Determine whether a *gpuArray* is a numeric array.
isreal	Determine whether the data of a *gpuArray* is real.
issorted	Determine whether the elements of a *gpuArray* are in sorted order.
issparse	Determine if a *gpuArray* is sparse.
issymmetric	Determine if a *gpuArray* is symmetric or skew-symmetric.
istril	Determine if a *gpuArray* is lower triangular.
istriu	Determine if a *gpuArray* is upper triangular.
length	Calculate the length of the vector or largest array dimension.
ndims	Calculate the number of a *gpuArray* dimensions.
ne	Determine if a *gpuArray* is not equal to another array.
nnz	Calculate the nonzero elements of a *gpuArray*.
nonzeros	Calculate the nonzero elements of a *gpuArray*.
norm	Calculate the norm of a *gpuArray*.
normest	Calculate an estimate of the 2-norm of a *gpuArray*.
numel	Calculate the number of elements of a *gpuArray*.
nzmax	Calculate the amount of storage allocated for the nonzero matrix elements of a *gpuArray*.
size	Calculate the size of a *gpuArray* object dimensions.

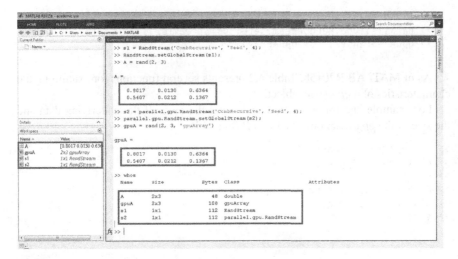

FIG. 4.8

Control random number streams using *RandStream* on CPU and GPU.

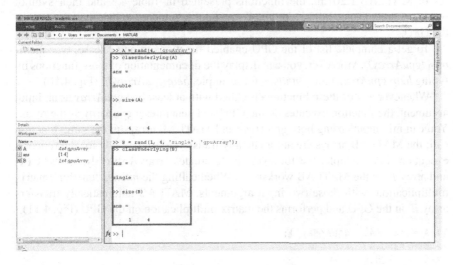

FIG. 4.9

Examine the characteristics of a *gpuArray*.

```
>> s1 = RandStream('CombRecursive', 'Seed', 4, ...
      'NormalTransform', 'Inversion');
>> RandStream.setGlobalStream(s1);
>> A = rand(2, 3)
>> s2 = parallel.gpu.RandStream('CombRecursive', 'Seed', 4, ...
```

```
          'NormalTransform', 'Inversion');
>> parallel.gpu.RandStream.setGlobalStream(s2);
>> gpuA = rand(2, 3, 'gpuArray')
```

As of MATLAB R2015b, Table 4.2 presents several functions for examining the characteristics of a *gpuArray* object:

For example, the following code examines the class of the underlying data and the size of the *gpuArray* objects *A* and *B* (Fig. 4.9):

```
>> A = rand(4, 'gpuArray');
>> classUnderlying(A)
>> size(A)
>> B = rand(1, 4, 'single', 'gpuArray');
>> classUnderlying(B)
>> size(B)
```

4.3 BUILT-IN MATLAB FUNCTIONS FOR GPUs

As of MATLAB R2015b, the functions presented in Table 4.3 and their symbol operators are enhanced to accept *gpuArray* input arguments so that they execute on the GPU.

To get a complete list of the GPU-enabled functions in any release, type *methods('gpuArray')*. Moreover, you can display the documentation of these functions by typing *help gpuArray/functionname*, for example, *help gpuArray/fft* (Fig. 4.10).

Whenever any of these functions is called with at least one *gpuArray* as an input argument, the function executes on the GPU and generates a *gpuArray* as the result. You can mix inputs using both *gpuArray* and MATLAB arrays in the same function call; the MATLAB arrays are automatically transferred to the GPU for the function execution. For example, the following code creates array *A* directly on the GPU and array *B* on the MATLAB workspace. When calling the *mtimes* function (matrix multiplication) with those two input arguments, MATLAB automatically transfers array *B* on the GPU and performs the matrix multiplication on the GPU (Fig. 4.11).

```
>> A = rand(4, 'gpuArray');
>> B = rand(4);
>> C = A * B;
```

The following code uses the *fft* function along with the arithmetic operator *. All calculations are performed on the GPU. Function *gather* retrieves the data from the GPU back to the MATLAB workspace (Fig. 4.12).

```
>> A = rand(1000);
>> gpuA = gpuArray(A);
>> gpuB = fft(gpuA) * 5;
>> B = gather(gpuB);
```

Table 4.3 Built-in MATLAB functions for GPUs

Function	Function	Function	Function
abs	edge	interp2	qmr
accumarray	eig	interp3	qr
acos	end	interpn	quiver
acosd	eps	interpstreamspeed	quiver3
acosh	eq	intersect	rad2deg
acot	erf	inv	radon
acotd	erfc	ipermute	rdivide
acoth	erfcinv	iradon	real
acsc	erfcx	isaUnderlying	reallog
acscd	erfinv	isbanded	realpow
acsch	errorbar	isdiag	realsqrt
all	existsOnGPU	isempty	reducepatch
and	exp	isequal	reducevolume
angle	expm	isequaln	regionprops
any	expm1	isequalwithequalnans	rem
applylut	ezcontour	isfinite	repmat
area	ezcontourf	isfloat	reshape
arrayfun	ezgraph3	ishermitian	rgb2gray
asec	ezmesh	isinf	rgb2hsv
asecd	ezmeshc	isinteger	rgb2ycbcr
asech	ezplot	islogical	ribbon
asin	ezplot3	ismember	roots
asind	ezpolar	isnan	rose
asinh	ezsurf	isnumeric	rot90
assert	ezsurfc	isocaps	round
atan	factorial	isocolors	scatter3
atan2	feather	isonormals	sec
atan2d	fft	isosurface	secd
atand	fft2	isreal	sech
atanh	fftfilt	issorted	semilogx
bandwidth	fftn	issparse	semilogy
bar	fill	issymmetric	setdiff
bar3	fill3	istril	setxor
bar3h	filter	istriu	shiftdim

Continued

Table 4.3 Built-in MATLAB functions for GPUs—cont'd

Function	Function	Function	Function
barh	filter2	ldivide	shrinkfaces
besselj	find	le	sign
bessely	fix	legendre	sin
beta	flip	length	sind
betainc	flipdim	line	single
betaincinv	fliplr	log	sinh
betaln	flipud	log10	size
bicg	floor	log1p	slice
bicgstab	fplot	log2	smooth3
bicgstabl	fprintf	logical	sort
bitand	full	loglog	sortrows
bitcmp	gamma	lsqr	sparse
bitget	gammainc	lt	spfun
bitor	gammaincinv	lu	spones
bitset	gammaln	mat2gray	sprintf
bitshift	gather	mat2str	spy
bitxor	ge	max	sqrt
bsxfun	gmres	mean	stairs
bwdist	gpuArray	medfilt2	std2
bwlabel	gradient	mesh	stdfilt
bwlookup	gt	meshc	stem
bwmorph	hist	meshgrid	stem3
cast	histc	meshz	stream2
cat	histcounts	min	stream3
cconv	histeq	minres	streamline
cdf2rdf	histogram	minus	streamparticles
ceil	horzcat	mldivide	streamribbon
cgs	hsv2rgb	mod	streamslice
chol	hypot	mode	streamtube
circshift	idivide	mpower	stretchlim
clabel	ifft	mrdivide	sub2ind
classUnderlying	ifft2	mtimes	subsasgn
comet	ifftn	ndgrid	subsindex
comet3	im2double	ndims	subspace
compass	im2int16	ne	subsref
complex	im2single	nextpow2	subvolume
cond	im2uint16	nnz	sum
coneplot	im2uint8	nonzeros	superiorfloat
conj	imabsdiff	norm	surf
contour	imadjust	normest	surfc
contour3	imag	normxcorr2	surfl

Table 4.3 Built-in MATLAB functions for GPUs—cont'd

Function	Function	Function	Function
contourc	image	not	svd
contourf	imagesc	nthroot	swapbytes
contourslice	imbothat	null	symmlq
conv	imclose	num2str	tan
conv2	imcomplement	numel	tand
convn	imdilate	nzmax	tanh
corr2	imerode	or	tfqmr
corrcoef	imfill	orth	times
cos	imfilter	padarray	transpose
cosd	imgaussfilt	pagefun	trapz
cosh	imgaussfilt3	pareto	tril
cot	imgradient	patch	trimesh
cotd	imgradientxy	pcg	trisurf
coth	imhist	pcolor	triu
cov	imlincomb	permute	typecast
csc	imnoise	pie	uint16
cscd	imopen	pie3	uint32
csch	imreconstruct	planerot	uint64
ctranspose	imregdemons	plot	uint8
cummax	imregionalmax	plot3	uminus
cummin	imregionalmin	plotmatrix	union
cumprod	imresize	plotyy	unique
cumsum	imrotate	plus	unwrap
curl	imrotate_old	polar	uplus
deg2rad	imshow	poly	var
del2	imtophat	polyder	vertcat
det	ind2sub	polyfit	vissuite
diag	inpolygon	polyval	volumebounds
diff	int16	polyvalm	voronoi
disp	int2str	pow2	waterfall
display	int32	power	xcorr
divergence	int64	prod	xor
dot	int8	psi	ycbcr2rgb
double	interp1		

To measure the performance of a code running on the GPU, there are two options:

- *gputimeit*: This function takes as input a function handle with no input arguments and returns the execution time of that function. It takes care of benchmarking considerations like repeating the timed operation to get more accurate results, executing the function before measurement to avoid initialization overhead and

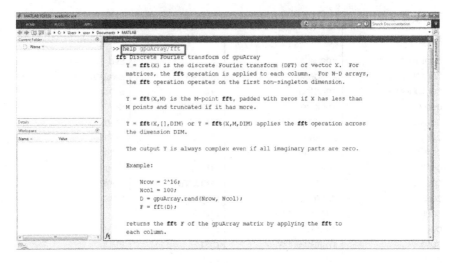

FIG. 4.10

Display documentation of GPU-enabled functions.

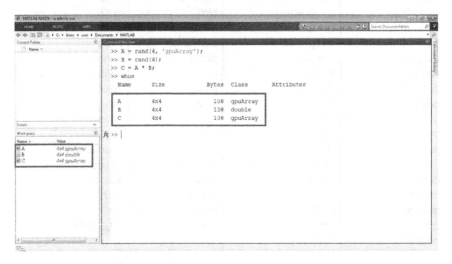

FIG. 4.11

Mixing inputs using *gpuArray* and MATLAB arrays.

subtracting out the overhead of the timing function. Also, *gputimeit* ensures that all operations on the GPU have completed before the final timing. For example, the following code measures the execution time to compute the *fft* of a 1,000 × 1,000 random matrix (Fig. 4.13):

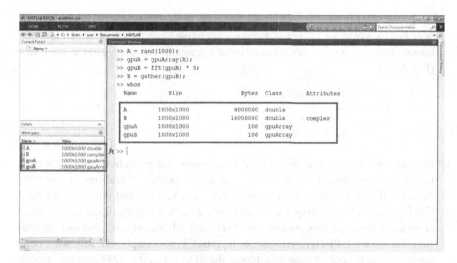

FIG. 4.12

gpuArray objects and arrays on the MATLAB workspace.

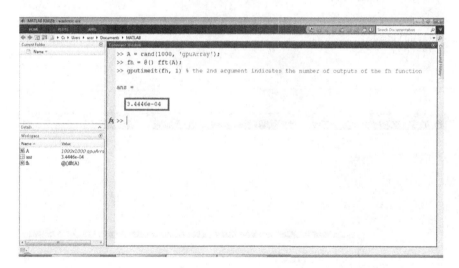

FIG. 4.13

Measuring the execution time of a built-in function using *gputimeit*.

```
>> A = rand(1000, 'gpuArray');
>> fh = @() fft(A);
>> % the 2nd argument indicates the number of outputs of
>> % the fft function
>> gputimeit(fh, 1);
```

If you want to measure a custom function, you can use *gputimeit* in a similar way. For example, let's assume that we want to measure the execution time of the custom function *myFun* that takes as input arguments two arrays of the same size (Fig. 4.14):

```
>> A = rand(1000, 'gpuArray');
>> B = rand(1000, 'gpuArray');
>> fh = @() myFun(A, B);
>> gputimeit(fh, 1);
```

- *tic* and *toc*: We can use *tic* and *toc* to measure the execution time. However, to get accurate timing on the GPU, you must wait for operations to complete before calling *toc*. There are two ways to do this. You can call *gather* on the final GPU output before calling *toc* because this function forces all computations to complete before the time measurement is taken. Alternately, you can use the *wait* function with a *GPUDevice* object as its input. For example, the following code measures the execution time to compute the *fft* of a 1,000 × 1,000 random matrix (Fig. 4.15):

```
>> A = rand(1000, 'gpuArray');
>> gd = gpuDevice();
>> tic;
>> B = fft(A);
>> wait(gd);
>> toc
```

FIG. 4.14

Measuring the execution time of a custom function using *gputimeit*.

FIG. 4.15

Measuring the execution time of a built-in function using *tic* and *toc*.

If you want to measure a custom function, you can also use *tic* and *toc* in a similar way. For example, let's assume that we want to measure the execution time of the custom function *myFun* that takes as input arguments two arrays of the same size (Fig. 4.16):

```
>> A = rand(1000, 'gpuArray');
>> B = rand(1000, 'gpuArray');
>> gd = gpuDevice();
>> tic;
>> C = myFun(A, B);
>> wait(gd);
>> toc
```

As of MATLAB R2015b, there are only a few functions that support sparse *gpuArray* objects. Whenever possible, you should use sparse *gpuArray* objects on your calculations because it will improve your code's performance in cases when your data are sparse. Table 4.4 presents the functions that support sparse *gpuArray* objects:

You can create a sparse *gpuArray* either by calling *sparse* with a *gpuArray* input, or by calling *gpuArray* with a sparse input (Fig. 4.17):

```
>> A = eye(3, 'gpuArray');
>> B = sparse(A);
>> C = sparse(eye(3));
>> D = gpuArray(C);
```

For example, the following code creates two random sparse arrays, transfers them to the GPU, and performs some basic matrix operations (addition, subtraction,

FIG. 4.16

Measuring the execution time of a custom function using *tic* and *toc*.

Table 4.4 MATLAB functions supporting sparse *gpuArray* objects

Function	Function	Function	Function
abs	gmres	length	realsqrt
angle	gpuArray.speye	log1p	round
ceil	imag	minus	sign
classUnderlying	isaUnderlying	mtimes	size
conj	isempty	ndims	sparse
ctranspose	isequal	nextpow2	spfun
deg2rad	isequaln	nnz	spones
end	isfloat	nonzeros	sqrt
expm1	isinteger	numel	sum
find	islogical	nzmax	transpose
fix	isnumeric	plus	uminus
floor	isreal	rad2deg	uplus
full	issparse	real	

multiplication, and transpose). All the calculations are performed on the GPU (Fig. 4.18):

```
>> A = sprand(10000, 10000, 0.1);
>> B = sprand(10000, 10000, 0.1);
>> gpuA = gpuArray(A);
>> gpuB = gpuArray(B);
>> gpuC = gpuA + gpuB;
```

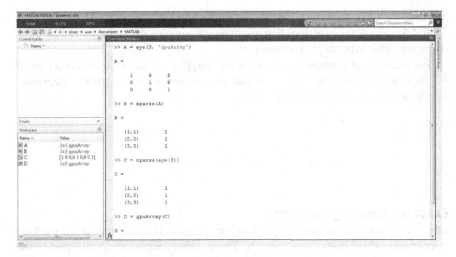

FIG. 4.17

Creating sparse *gpuArray* objects.

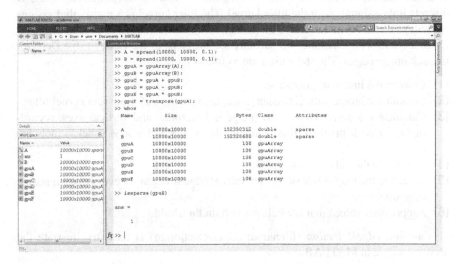

FIG. 4.18

Calculations on sparse *gpuArray* objects.

```
>> gpuD = gpuA - gpuB;
>> gpuE = gpuA * gpuB;
>> gpuF = transpose(gpuA);
```

If the output of a function running on the GPU could potentially be complex, you must explicitly specify its input arguments as complex. This applies to *gpuArray* or to functions called in code run by arrayfun (see Section 4.4). As of MATLAB R2015b, Table 4.5 presents the functions that might return complex data, along with the input range over which the output remains real.

For example, if creating a *gpuArray* that might have negative elements, use *B = gpuArray(complex(A));*. Then you can successfully execute *sqrt(B)*. Otherwise, *sqrt(B)* will generate an error (Fig. 4.19):

```
>> A = [-1 2 3 -4];
>> B = gpuArray(A); % wrong
>> sqrt(B)
>> C = gpuArray(complex(A)); % correct
>> sqrt(C)
```

Example: Image edge detection

Edge detection is a common operation on images. It is a method of tracking discontinuities within the image pixels. These discontinuities may exist due to the morphology of the objects in the image, to shadows, or may be abrupt changes in colors. A simple and efficient way of finding edges is image filtering. Spatial time invariant filtering is achieved by convolving the original signal (in this case the 2-D discrete image signal) with the filter kernel. The filter kernel is a matrix that assigns weights to the terms of the convolution sum.

In the following example, we partially use the steps of the Canny Edge Detector to track image edges. The steps used are as follows:

(1) Convert the image to grayscale.
(2) Smooth the image with Gaussian noise, using a 25 × 25 Gaussian kernel filter.
(3) Calculate the derivatives of the image in horizontal and vertical axes, accordingly, for each pixel. In this example, the 3 × 3 and 9 × 9 Sobel kernels are used.
(4) Normalize the values from step 3.
(5) Calculate the magnitude of the derivative (edge strength) in every pixel ignoring edge direction.
(6) Suppress all values that are below a certain threshold.

Function *edgeDetection* (filename: edgeDetection.m) is used to illustrate the above example in MATLAB.

```
1.   function [imgEdge1, imgEdge2] = edgeDetection(img)
2.   % Filename: edgeDetection.m
3.   % Description: This function detects the edges of an image
4.   % using the 3x3 and 9x9 Sobel kernels
5.   % Authors: Ploskas, N., & Samaras, N.
6.   % Syntax: [imgEdge1, imgEdge2] = edgeDetection(img)
7.   % Input:
8.   %    -- img: the image for which we want to detect the edges
9.   % Output:
10.  %    -- imgEdge1: the image after the edge detection
11.  %       using the 3x3 Sobel kernel
12.  %    -- imgEdge2: the image after the edge detection
```

Table 4.5 MATLAB functions that might return complex data

Function	Input range for real output
acos(x)	$|x| \leq 1$
acosd(x)	$|x| \leq 1$
acosh(x)	$x \geq 1$
acot(x)	$x \in \mathbb{R}$
acotd(x)	$x \in \mathbb{R}$
acoth(x)	$|x| \geq 1$
acsc(x)	$|x| \geq 1$
acscd(x)	$|x| \geq 1$
acsch(x)	$x \in \mathbb{R}$
asec(x)	$|x| \geq 1$
asecd(x)	$|x| \geq 1$
asech(x)	$0 \leq x \leq 1$
asin(x)	$|x| \leq 1$
asind(x)	$|x| \leq 1$
asinh(x)	$x \in \mathbb{R}$
atan(x)	$x \in \mathbb{R}$
atand(x)	$x \in \mathbb{R}$
atanh	$|x| \leq 1$
cos(x)	For purely real values or imaginary values of x
cosd(x)	For purely real values or imaginary values of x
cosh(x)	For purely real values or imaginary values of x
cot(x)	$x \in \mathbb{R}$
cotd(x)	$x \in \mathbb{R}$
coth(x)	$x \in \mathbb{R}$
csc(x)	$x \in \mathbb{R}$
cscd(x)	$x \in \mathbb{R}$
csch(x)	$x \in \mathbb{R}$
log(x)	$x \geq 0$
log1p(x)	$x \geq -1$
log10(x)	$x \geq 0$
log2(x)	$x \geq 0$
power(x,y)	$x \geq 0$
reallog(x)	$x \geq 0$
realsqrt(x)	$x \geq 0$
sin(x)	$x \in \mathbb{R}$
sind(x)	$x \in \mathbb{R}$
sinh(x)	$x \in \mathbb{R}$
sqrt(x)	$x \geq 0$
tan(x)	$x \in \mathbb{R}$
tand(x)	$x \in \mathbb{R}$
tanh(x)	$x \in \mathbb{R}$

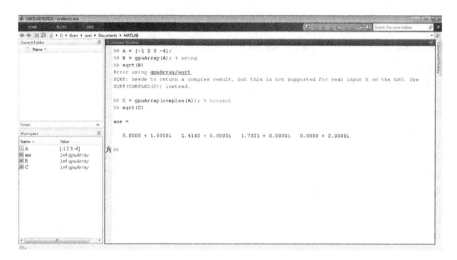

FIG. 4.19

Explicitly specify complex input arguments.

```
13.  %       using the 9x9 Sobel kernel
14.
15.  % convert to grayscale, double precision
16.  imgGray = im2double(rgb2gray(img));
17.  m = 25; n = 25;    % declare the size of the blur kernel
18.  sigma = 10;    % set the sigma parameter of gaussian blur to 10
19.  % create the m x n gaussian blur kernel
20.  [h1, h2] = meshgrid(-(m - 1) / 2:(m - 1) / 2, -(n - 1) / 2:(n - 1) / 2);
21.  hg = exp(-(h1 .^ 2 + h2 .^ 2) / (2 * sigma^2));
22.  gKernel = hg ./ sum(hg(:));
23.  % smooth the grayscale image with the blur kernel
24.  imgBlur = conv2(imgGray, gKernel, 'same');
25.  % create the 3x3 and 9x9 Sobel kernels
26.  sobelF3 = [-1 0 1; -2 0 2; -1 0 1];
27.  sobelF9 = [4 3 2 1 0 -1 -2 -3 -4;
28.  5 4 3 2 0 -2 -3 -4 -5;
29.  6 5 4 3 0 -3 -4 -5 -6;
30.  7 6 5 4 0 -4 -5 -6 -7;
31.  8 7 6 5 0 -5 -6 -7 -8;
32.  7 6 5 4 0 -4 -5 -6 -7;
33.  6 5 4 3 0 -3 -4 -5 -6;
34.  5 4 3 2 0 -2 -3 -4 -5;
35.  4 3 2 1 0 -1 -2 -3 -4];
36.  % 3x3 Sobel kernel
37.  % calculate image derivatives
38.  imgEdgeX1 = conv2(imgBlur, sobelF3', 'same');
39.  imgEdgeY1 = conv2(imgBlur, sobelF3, 'same');
40.  % calculate the magnitude of the derivative
41.  imgEdge1 = sqrt(imgEdgeX1 .^ 2 + imgEdgeY1 .^ 2);
42.  % normalize values
43.  maxV1 = max(imgEdge1(:));
44.  minV1 = min(imgEdge1(:));
45.  range1 = maxV1 - minV1;
```

```
46.     imgEdge1 = (imgEdge1 - minV1) / range1;
47.     % suppress all values which are below a certain threshold (0.5)
48.     imgEdge1(imgEdge1 < 0.05) = 0;
49.     % 9x9 Sobel kernel
50.     % calculate image derivatives
51.     imgEdgeX2 = conv2(imgBlur, sobelF9', 'same');
52.     imgEdgeY2 = conv2(imgBlur, sobelF9, 'same');
53.     % calculate the magnitude of the derivative
54.     imgEdge2 = sqrt(imgEdgeX2 .^ 2 + imgEdgeY2 .^ 2);
55.     % normalize values
56.     maxV2 = max(imgEdge2(:));
57.     minV2 = min(imgEdge2(:));
58.     range2 = maxV2 - minV2;
59.     imgEdge2 = (imgEdge2 - minV2) / range2;
60.     % suppress all values which are below a certain threshold (0.5)
61.     imgEdge2(imgEdge2 < 0.05) = 0;
62.     end
```

Initially, we measure the execution time of this function running on the CPU using a 5,789 × 3,867 jpeg image:

```
>> img = imread('building.jpg');
>> tic; [imgEdge1, imgEdge2] = edgeDetection(img); toc;
Elapsed time is 2.343530 seconds.
```

To execute this function on the GPU, we do not have to perform any changes to the code because all functions and operators used are GPU-enabled. The only difference is that we should pass a *gpuArray* as input to that function. We measure the execution time of this function running on the GPU using the same image:

```
>> img = imread('building.jpg');
>> gd = gpuDevice(); tic; [imgEdge1, imgEdge2] = edgeDetection(gpuArray(img));
wait(gd); toc;
Elapsed time is 0.253540 seconds.
```

Hence, the image edge detection function is running ~9.25× faster on the GPU.

Fig. 4.20 shows the result of the image edge detection function in case of a 3 × 3 and 9 × 9 Sobel filter.

FIG. 4.20

Result of the image edge detection function.

4.4 ELEMENT-WISE MATLAB CODE ON GPUs

Another approach to execute a code on the GPU is to use *arrayfun* and *bsxfun* functions to run your own MATLAB function of element-wise operations on a GPU. The decision on which solution to adopt depends on whether the functions you require are GPU-enabled and the performance impact of transferring data to/from the GPU. Moreover, you can avoid *for-loops*, which can add an overhead to the execution time on a GPU, using these two functions. Functions *arrayfun* and *bsxfun* have the same functionality of the corresponding MATLAB built-in functions, except that the evaluation runs on the GPU. Any required data that is not already present on the GPU, it is automatically transferred to the GPU.

Function *arrayfun* applies a function to each element of an array and has the following syntax:

```
[A, B, ...] = arrayfun(fun, C, ..., Name, Value)
```

where [5]:

- *fun* is a handle to a function. If function *fun* corresponds to more than one function file (that is, if *fun* represents a set of overloaded functions), MATLAB determines which function to call based on the class of the input arguments.
- *C* and any other input are arrays that contain the inputs required for function *fun*. Each array must have the same dimensions. Arrays can be numeric, character, logical, cell, structure, or user-defined object arrays. If any input is a user-defined object array and you overloaded the *subsref* or *size* methods, then *arrayfun* requires that:
  - The *size* method returns an array of type double.
  - The object array supports linear indexing.
  - The product of the sizes returned by the *size* method does not exceed the limit of the array, as defined by linear indexing into the array.
- *Name* and *Value* pairs specify optional comma-separated pairs of *Name, Value* arguments. *Name* is the argument name and *Value* is the corresponding value. *Name* must appear inside single quotes (' '). You can specify several *Name* and *Value* pairs in any order. The options that are available:
  - *'UniformOutput'* is a logical value. A *true (1)* value indicates that for all inputs, each output from function *fun* is a scalar cell array, scalar structure, or scalar value that is always of the same type and size. The *arrayfun* function combines the outputs in the output arrays (A, B, ...). Each output array is of the same type as the individual function outputs. A *false (0)* value indicates that the *arrayfun* function combines the outputs into cell arrays. The outputs of function *fun* can be of any size or type. The default value is *true*.
  - *'ErrorHandler'* is a handle to a function that catches any errors that occur when MATLAB attempts to execute function *fun*. Define this function so that it rethrows the error or returns valid outputs for function *fun*. MATLAB calls the specified error-handling function with two input arguments:

- A structure with the fields: (i) identifier (error identifier), (ii) message (message error), and (iii) index (linear index corresponding to the element of the input cell array at the time of the error).
- The set of input arguments to function *fun* at the time of the error.
- *A, B,* and any other output are arrays that collect the outputs from function *fun*. Each array is of the same size as each of the inputs. Function *fun* can return output arguments of different classes. However, if *UniformOutput* (see below) is *true* (the default), then:
  - The individual outputs from function *fun* must be scalar values (numeric, logical, or character), scalar structures, or scalar cell arrays.
  - The class of a particular output argument must be the same for each set of inputs. The class of the corresponding output array is of the same as the class of the outputs from function *fun*.

For example, assume that we have the following function:

```
function [D, E] = myFun(A, B, C)
D = A .* B + C;
E = A + B .* C + 50.45;
end
```

The function *myFun* performs element-wise operations on three input arrays and returns two arrays as a result. We can use *myFun* with three *gpuArray* objects (Fig. 4.21):

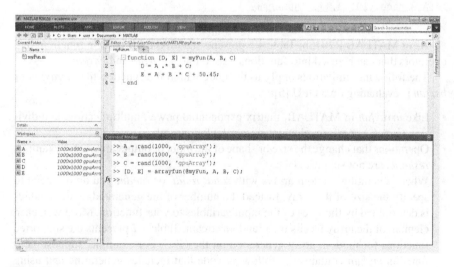

FIG. 4.21

Element-wise operations using *arrayfun.*

```
>> A = rand(1000, 'gpuArray');
>> B = rand(1000, 'gpuArray');
>> C = rand(1000, 'gpuArray');
>> [D, E] = arrayfun(@myFun, A, B, C);
```

Function *bsxfun* applies element-by-element binary operations to two arrays and has the following syntax:

```
C = bsxfun(fun, A, B)
```

where *fun* can be a handle to any binary element-wise function and some built-in functions presented in Table 4.6. A binary element-wise function of the form *C = fun(A, B)* accepts arrays *A* and *B* of arbitrary, but equal size and returns output of the same size. Each element in the output array *C* is the result of an operation on the corresponding elements of *A* and *B* only. *fun* must also support scalar expansion, such that if *A* or *B* is a scalar, then *C* is the result of applying the scalar to every element in the other input array. The corresponding dimensions of *A* and *B* must be equal to each other or equal to one. Whenever a dimension of *A* or *B* is singleton (equal to one), *bsxfun* virtually replicates the array along that dimension to match the other array. In the case where a dimension of *A* or *B* is singleton and the corresponding dimension in the other array is zero, *bsxfun* virtually diminishes the singleton dimension to zero. The size of the output array *C* is equal to *max(size(A), size(B)) .* (size(A) > 0 & size(B) > 0)*.

For example, we can use *bsxfun* to subtract the column maximum element from the corresponding column elements of an array (Fig. 4.22):

```
>> A = randi(10, 3, 4, 'gpuArray')
>> C = bsxfun(@minus, A, max(A))
```

As of MATLAB R2015b, Table 4.6 presents the MATLAB built-in functions and operators that can be used into functions passed into *arrayfun* and *bsxfun*.

The following limitations apply to the code within the function that *arrayfun* or *bsxfun* is evaluating on a GPU [5]:

- Like *arrayfun* in MATLAB, matrix exponential power, multiplication, and division (^, *, /, \) perform element-wise calculations only.
- Operations that change the size or shape of the input or output arrays, for example, *reshape*, are not supported.
- When generating random arrays with *rand*, *randi*, or *randn*, you do not need to specify the size of the array. Instead the number of the generated random values is determined by the sizes of the input variables to your function. Moreover, each element of the array has its own random stream. Table 4.7 presents the supported functions for random array generation on the GPU. For example, suppose your function *myFun* contains the following code that includes generating and using the random matrix *R*:

```
function Y = myFun(X)
    % it will generate an error with arrayfun and a gpuArray input
```

Table 4.6 MATLAB built-in functions and operators that can be used into functions passed into *arrayfun* and *bsxfun*

Function	Function	Function	Special cases
abs	deg2rad	mtimes	Operators:
and	double	NaN	+
acos	eps	ne	-
acosd	eq	nextpow2	.*
acosh	erf	not	./
acot	erfc	nthroot	.\
acotd	erfcinv	or	.^
acoth	erfcx	pi	==
acsc	erfinv	plus	~=
acscd	exp	pow2	<
acsch	expm1	power	<=
and	false	psi	>
angle	fix	rad2deg	>=
asec	floor	rand	&
asecd	gamma	randi	|
asech	gammainc	randn	~
asin	gammaincinv	rdivide	&&
asind	gammaln	real	||
asinh	ge	reallog	
atan	gt	realmax	Scalar expansion
			versions of the following:
atan2	hypot	realmin	*
atan2d	imag	realpow	/
atand	Inf	realsqrt	\
atanh	int8	rem	^
beta	int16	round	
betainc	int32	sec	Branching instructions:
betincinv	int64	secd	break
betaln	intmax	sech	continue
bitand	intmin	sign	else
bitcmp	isfinite	sin	elseif
bitget	isinf	sind	for
bitor	isnan	single	if
bitset	ldivide	sinh	return
bitshift	le	sqrt	while
bitxor	log	tan	
ceil	log2	tand	
complex	log10	tanh	
conj	log1p	times	
cos	logical	true	
cosd	lt	uint8	
cosh	max	uint16	
cot	min	uint32	
cotd	minus	uint64	
coth	mldivide	uminus	
csc	mod	uplus	
cscd	mpower	xor	
csch	mrdivide		

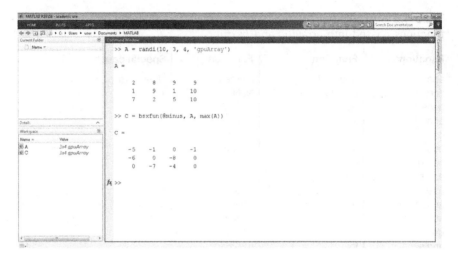

FIG. 4.22

Binary element-wise operations using *bsxfun*.

Table 4.7 Supported functions for random array generation in *arrayfun* and *bsxfun* functions on the GPU

Function	Function
rand	randi
rand()	randi()
rand('single')	randi(IMAX, ...)
rand('double')	randi([IMIN IMAX], ...)
randn	randi(..., 'single')
randn()	randi(..., 'double')
randn('single')	randi(..., 'int32')
randn('double')	randi(..., 'uint32')

```
      R = rand(size(X));
      Y = R .* X;
  end
```

If you call this function without a *gpuArray* object using *arrayfun*, then MATLAB will not generate an error. However, if you use *arrayfun* to run this function with an input variable that is a *gpuArray*, then it will generate an error because the call to *rand* specifies the size of the array (Fig. 4.23). To execute this

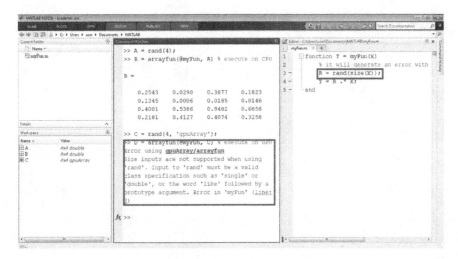

FIG. 4.23

Wrong use of *rand* with *arrayfun*.

function with *arrayfun* on the GPU, the number of the random elements for *R* is determined by the size of *X*, so you should not specify it (Fig. 4.24):

```
function Y = myFun(X)
    R = rand();
    Y = R .* X;
end
```

- *arrayfun* and *bsxfun* support read-only indexing (*subsref*) and access to variables of the parent (outer) function workspace from within nested functions, that is, those variables that exist in the function before the *arrayfun/bsxfun* evaluation on the GPU. *Assignment* or *subsasgn* indexing of these variables from within the nested function is not supported.
- Anonymous functions do not have access to their parent function workspace.
- Overloading the supported functions is not allowed.
- The code cannot call scripts.
- There is no *ans* variable to hold unassigned computation results. Make sure to explicitly assign to variables the results of all calculations that you need to access after your function evaluation.
- The following language features are not supported:
  - **(1)** persistent or global variables
  - **(2)** *parfor*
  - **(3)** *spmd*
  - **(4)** *switch*
  - **(5)** *try/catch*

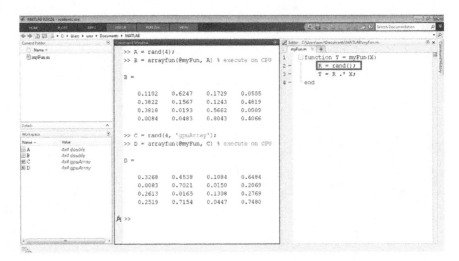

FIG. 4.24

Correct use of *rand* with *arrayfun*.

- P-code files cannot contain a call to *arrayfun* or *bsxfun* with *gpuArray* objects.

Besides *arrayfun* and *bsxfun*, MATLAB offers the *pagefun* function. Function *pagefun* applies a function to each page of an array on GPU and has the following syntax:

```
A = pagefun(fun, B)
A = pagefun(fun, B, C, ...)
[A, B, ...] = pagefun(fun, C, ...)
```

The first *pagefun* variant applies the function specified by *fun* to each page of the *gpuArray B* and returns the results in *gpuArray A*, such that $A(:, :, I, J, \ldots) = fun(B(:, :, I, J, \ldots))$. *fun* is a handle to a function that takes a two-dimensional input argument.

The second *pagefun* variant evaluates *fun* using pages of the arrays *B*, *C*, and so on, as input arguments with scalar expansion enabled. Any of the input page dimensions that are scalar are virtually replicated to match the size of the other arrays in that dimension so that $A(:, :, I, J, \ldots) = fun(B(:, :, I, J, \ldots), C(:, :, I, J, \ldots), \ldots)$. At least one of the inputs *B*, *C*, and so on must be a *gpuArray*. Any other inputs stored in CPU memory are converted to a *gpuArray* before calling the function on the GPU. If an array is to be used in several different *pagefun* calls, it is more efficient to convert that array to a *gpuArray* before your series of *pagefun* calls. The input pages $B(:, :, I, J, \ldots)$, $C(:, :, I, J, \ldots)$, and so on, must satisfy all the input and output requirements of function *fun*.

The third *pagefun* variant applies a function *fun* that returns multiple *gpuArray* objects, each corresponding to one of the output arguments of *fun*. *pagefun* invokes *fun* with as many outputs as there are in the call to *pagefun*. All elements of *A* must be the same class; *B* can be a different class from *A*, but all elements of *B* must be of the same class. *fun* must return values of the same class each time it is called. The order in which *pagefun* computes pages is not specified and should not be relied on.

Generally, *fun* must be a handle to a function that is written in the MATLAB language, that is, not a built-in function or a MEX-function. As of MATLAB R2015b, Table 4.8 presents the supported values for *fun* that can be used in *pagefun*.

Table 4.8 Supported values for *fun* that can be used in *pagefun*

Function	Function	Function	Function
abs	bitshift	ge	power
acos	bitxor	gt	psi
acosd	ceil	hypot	rad2deg
acosh	complex	imag	rdivide
acot	conj	int8	real
acotd	cos	int16	reallog
acoth	cosd	int32	realpow
acsc	cosh	int64	realsqrt
acsch	cot	inv	rem
and	cotd	isfinite	rot90
angle	coth	isinf	round
asec	csc	isnan	sec
asecd	csch	ldivide	secd
asech	ctranspose	le	sech
asin	deg2rad	log	sign
asind	double	log2	sin
asinh	eps	log10	sind
atan	eq	log1p	single
atan2	erf	lt	sinh
atan2d	erfc	max	sqrt
atand	erfcinv	min	tan
atanh	erfcx	minus	tand
besselj	erfinv	mldivide	tanh
bessely	exp	mrdivide	times
beta	expm1	mod	transpose
betainc	fix	mtimes	uint8
betaincinv	fliplr	ne	uint16
betaln	flipud	nextpow2	uint32
bitand	floor	not	uint64
bitcmp	gamma	nthroot	uminus
bitget	gammainc	or	uplus
bitor	gammaincinv	plus	xor
bitset	gammaln	pow2	

For example, we can use *pagefun* to perform multiple matrix multiplications using pages of a *gpuArray*. Let's assume that our first array is an $M \times K$ array and we want to perform a matrix multiplication with a second $K \times N$ array that has multiple pages P. The following code show how to achieve this with and without using *pagefun* (Fig. 4.25):

```
>> M = 3; % output number of rows
>> K = 5; % matrix multiply inner dimension
>> N = 10; % output number of columns
>> P = 2; % number of pages
>> A = rand(M, K, 'gpuArray');
>> B = rand(K,N,P,'gpuArray');
>> % perform matrix multiplication of A and B on every page of B without
>> % using pagefun
>> for i = 1:P
>>    C(:, :, i) = A * B(:, :, i);
>> end
>> % perform matrix multiplication of A and B on every page of B using
>> % pagefun
>> D = pagefun(@mtimes, A, B);
>> C
>> D
```

As expected, the results of the two approaches are the same. Now, let's compare the execution time of the two approaches using large arrays (Fig. 4.26):

```
M = 1000; % output number of rows
K = 2000; % matrix multiply inner dimension
N = 1000; % output number of columns
P = 200; % number of pages
A = rand(M, K, 'gpuArray');
B = rand(K,N,P,'gpuArray');
gd = gpuDevice();
tic;
% perform matrix multiplication of A and B on every page of B without
% using pagefun
for i = 1:P
   C(:, :, i) = A * B(:, :, i);
end
wait(gd);
toc
gd = gpuDevice();
tic;
% perform matrix multiplication of A and B on every page of B using
% pagefun
D = pagefun(@mtimes, A, B);
wait(gd);
toc
Elapsed time is 3.979130 seconds.
Elapsed time is 2.186059 seconds.
```

The second approach using *pagefun* is almost 2× faster than the first approach using the *for-loop*. Now, let's perform one final test to compare the execution time of the two approaches. In the following code, we use small arrays and a large number of pages on the second array (Fig. 4.27):

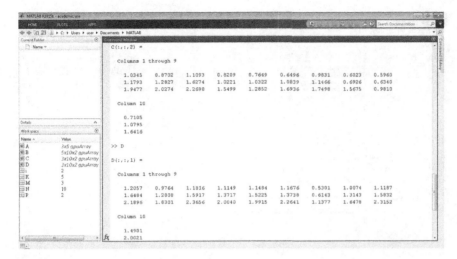

FIG. 4.25

Matrix multiplication of two matrices on multiple pages with and without using *pagefun*.

FIG. 4.26

Matrix multiplication of two large matrices on multiple pages with and without using *pagefun*.

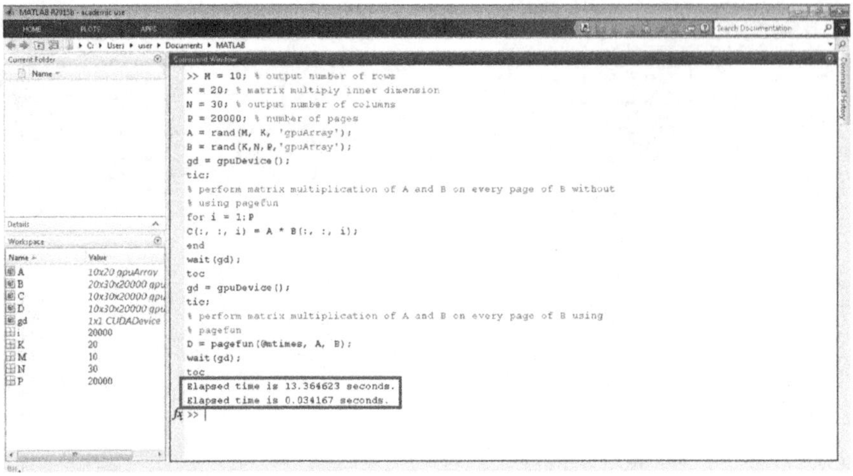

FIG. 4.27

Matrix multiplication of two small matrices on a large number of pages with and without using *pagefun*.

```
M = 10; % output number of rows
K = 20; % matrix multiply inner dimension
N = 30; % output number of columns
P = 20000; % number of pages
A = rand(M, K, 'gpuArray');
B = rand(K,N,P,'gpuArray');
gd = gpuDevice();
tic;
% perform matrix multiplication of A and B on every page of B without
% using pagefun
for i = 1:P
    C(:, :, i) = A * B(:, :, i);
end
wait(gd);
toc
gd = gpuDevice();
tic;
% perform matrix multiplication of A and B on every page of B using
% pagefun
D = pagefun(@mtimes, A, B);
wait(gd);
toc
Elapsed time is 13.496936 seconds.
Elapsed time is 0.026640 seconds.
```

The second approach using *pagefun* is almost 391× faster than the first approach using the *for-loop*. This huge difference in the performance of these two approaches in the second example derives from the many iterations (20,000) that the first approach has to evaluate. Generally speaking, loops, especially those with a large number of iterations, are slower on the GPU. Hence, try to vectorize your code by replacing looped operations with matrix and vector operations or *arrayfun*, *bsxfun*, or *pagefun*.

Example: Filter signal using fast convolution

Fast convolution is a common operation in signal and image processing applications. Fast convolution transforms each column of data from the time domain to the frequency domain, multiplies it by the transform of a filter vector, transforms back to the time domain, and stores the result in an output matrix. In electronic music convolution is the imposition of a spectral or rhythmic structure on a sound. The convolution of two signals is the filtering of one through the other.

In the following example, we perform the fast convolution on the columns of a signal using a low-pass FIR filter. The signal is an audio file that was divided into 1,024 frames.

Function *fastConvolution* (filename: fastConvolution.m) is used to illustrate the preceding example in MATLAB.

```
1.   function filteredData = fastConvolution(data, filter)
2.   % Filename: fastConvolution.m
3.   % Description: This function performs fast convolution on
4.   % the columns of a signal (array data) using a filter
5.   % (vector filter)
6.   % Authors: Ploskas, N., & Samaras, N.
7.   % Syntax: filteredData = fastConvolution(data, filter)
8.   % Input:
9.   %    -- data: the signal (array)
10.  %    -- filter: the filter (vector)
11.  % Output:
12.  %    -- filteredData: the filtered signal (array)
13.
14.  [m, n] = size(data); % get the size of the signal
15.  % pad filter with zeros and calculate its DFT
16.  filterf = fft(filter, m);
17.  % initialize output variable filteredData
18.  filteredData = zeros(m, n, 'like', data);
19.  % transform each column of the signal
20.  for i = 1:n
21.      dataf = fft(data(:, i));
22.      filteredData(:, i) = ifft(dataf .* filterf);
23.  end
24.  end
```

Initially, we measure the execution time of this function running on the CPU using a $1,024 \times 10,336$ signal and a 20×1 filter:

```
>> load fastConvolutionData
>> tic; filteredData = fastConvolution(data, filter); toc
Elapsed time is 0.323660 seconds.
```

To execute this function on the GPU, we do not have to perform any changes to the code because all functions and operators used are GPU-enabled. The only difference is that we should pass a *gpuArray* as input to that function. We measure the execution time of this function running on the GPU using the same data:

```
>> load fastConvolutionData
>> gd = gpuDevice(); tic; filteredData = fastConvolution(gpuArray(data), ...
gpuArray(filter)); wait(gd); toc
Elapsed time is 2.470903 seconds.
```

Hence, the fast convolution function is running ~7.65× faster on the CPU. So, the *for-loop* slows down the GPU because it is executing the FFT, multiplication, and inverse FFT operations on individual columns. However, we can optimize our function by vectorizing the *for-loop* with the use of *bsxfun*. Function *fastConvolutionVectorized* (filename: fastConvolutionVectorized.m) is used to illustrate the use of *bsxfun* on the above example in MATLAB.

```
1.    function filteredData = fastConvolutionVectorized(data, filter)
2.    % Filename: fastConvolutionVectorized.m
3.    % Description: This function performs fast convolution on
4.    % the columns of a signal (array data) using a filter
5.    % (vector filter) (vectorized version using bsxfun)
6.    % Authors: Ploskas, N., & Samaras, N.
7.    % Syntax: filteredData = fastConvolutionVectorized(data, filter)
8.    % Input:
9.    %    -- data: the signal (array)
10.   %    -- filter: the filter (vector)
11.   % Output:
12.   %    -- filteredData: the filtered signal (array)
13.
14.   [m, ~] = size(data); % get the size of the signal
15.   % pad filter with zeros and calculate its DFT
16.   filterf = fft(filter, m);
17.   % transform each column of the signal
18.   dataf = fft(data);
19.   % multiply each column of the signal by the filter and
20.   % compute the inverse transform
21.   filteredData = ifft(bsxfun(@times, dataf, filterf));
22.   end
```

Initially, we measure the execution time of this function running on the CPU using the same data:

```
>> load fastConvolutionData
>> tic; filteredData = fastConvolutionVectorized(data, filter); toc
Elapsed time is 0.216253 seconds.
```

The improved CPU version of the fast convolution function is running ~1.5× faster.

We measure the execution time of this improved function running on the GPU using the same data:

```
>> load fastConvolutionData
>> gd = gpuDevice(); tic; filteredData = ...
fastConvolutionVectorized(gpuArray(data), gpuArray(filter)); wait(gd); toc
Elapsed time is 0.027619 seconds.
```

Hence, the improved GPU version of the fast convolution function is running ~89× faster compared to the initial version running on the GPU. Moreover, the improved GPU version of the fast convolution function is running ~8× faster compared to the improved CPU version. In conclusion, vectorizing the code helps both the CPU and GPU versions to run faster. However, vectorization helps the GPU version much more than the CPU.

4.5 CHAPTER REVIEW

This chapter covered one of the most important topics of this book, the inherent GPU programming features that MATLAB provides. More specifically, this chapter introduced the GPU arrays, arrays that are stored on GPUs. These arrays can be used in computations by built-in MATLAB functions for GPUs and element-wise MATLAB operations. Through a variety of examples, both didactical and real-world examples, we covered many features of GPU programming in MATLAB and presented ideas on how you can use GPU programming to improve the performance on your applications.

To sum up, here are some rules that you should consider before parallelizing your application using a GPU:

(1) If your application contains built-in functions and operators that are GPU-enabled, then you can execute it on a GPU by only transferring your input arguments to the GPU.

(2) If your application contains built-in functions that are not GPU-enabled, then you can change your algorithm to use GPU-enabled functions or write a custom CUDA C/C++ code (see Chapter 7) or a MATLAB MEX file that contains CUDA code (see Chapters 8 and 9) to implement the desired functionality and call that code through MATLAB.

(3) If the amount of data transfer is low in your application, then it is a good candidate to execute it on the GPU. Otherwise, try to minimize the data transfer.

(4) Try to avoid loops and conditional statements because their evaluation is slower on the GPU than the CPU.

(5) Vectorize your code by replacing looped operations with matrix and vector operations or *arrayfun*, *bsxfun*, or *pagefun*.

(6) GPUs are better for numerical computations but cannot handle strings, structs, cell arrays, and other non-primitive MATLAB data types.

(7) The amount of memory of the GPU is smaller than the main memory (although modern GPUs have many Gb of memory).

(8) Profile your applications to find possible bottlenecks (see Chapter 10).

GPU programming on MATLAB toolboxes

5

CHAPTER OBJECTIVES

This Chapter aims to explore GPU-enabled MATLAB functions on several toolboxes other than Parallel Computing Toolbox, like Communications System Toolbox, Image Processing Toolbox, Neural Network Toolbox, Phased Array System Toolbox, Signal Processing Toolbox, and Statistics and Machine Learning Toolbox. This Chapter presents the GPU-enabled functions on these toolboxes with a variety of real-world examples. After reading this Chapter, you should be able to:

- use GPU-based implementations of Communications System Toolbox.
- implement image processing applications on a GPU.
- train and simulate neural networks on a GPU.
- perform clutter simulations on a GPU.
- use GPU-based implementations of Signal Processing Toolbox.
- use GPU-based implementations of Statistics and Machine Learning Toolbox.

5.1 COMMUNICATIONS SYSTEM TOOLBOX

The Communications System Toolbox provides algorithms and applications for the analysis, design, end-to-end simulation, and verification of communications systems. The Communications System Toolbox algorithms, including channel coding, modulation, MIMO, and OFDM, allow users to compose a physical layer model of a system. Users can simulate their models to measure their performance.

The Communications System Toolbox provides constellation and eye diagrams, bit-error-rate, and other analysis tools and scopes for validating user designs. These tools enable users to analyze signals, visualize channel characteristics, and obtain performance metrics such as error vector magnitude. Channel and radio frequency impairment models and compensation algorithms, including carrier and symbol

GPU Programming in MATLAB. http://dx.doi.org/10.1016/B978-0-12-805132-0.00005-9

timing synchronizers, enable you to realistically model your link-level specifications and compensate for the effects of channel degradations.

As of MATLAB R2015b, Communications System Toolbox offers the following GPU-based implementations [14]:

- *comm.gpu.AWGNChannel*: The GPU AWGNChannel object adds white Gaussian noise to an input signal. To do that, you should:

  (1) Define and set up an additive white Gaussian noise channel object.
  (2) Call *step* method to add white Gaussian noise to an input signal according to the properties of *comm.gpu.AWGNChannel*.

  A GPU AWGNChannel object is constructed using the following syntax:

```
H = comm.gpu.AWGNChannel(Name, Value)
```

It creates a GPU-based AWGN channel object, *H*, with the specified property *Name* set to the specified *Value*. You can specify additional name-value pairs in any order. The options that are available:

(1) *NoiseMethod*: Specify the noise level as one of: (i) *Signal to noise ratio (Eb/No)*, (ii) *Signal to noise ratio (Es/No)*, (iii) *Signal to noise ratio (SNR)*, or (iv) *Variance*. The default value is *Signal to noise ratio (Eb/No)*.

(2) *EbNo*: Specify the *Eb/No* ratio in decibels. Set this property to a numeric, real scalar, or row vector with a length equal to the number of channels. This property applies when you set the *NoiseMethod* property to *Signal to noise ratio (Eb/No)*. The default value is 10.

(3) *EsNo*: Specify the *Es/No* ratio in decibels. Set this property to a numeric, real scalar, or row vector with a length equal to the number of channels. This property applies when you set the *NoiseMethod* property to *Signal to noise ratio (Es/No)*. The default value is 10.

(4) *SNR*: Specify the *SNR* value in decibels. Set this property to a numeric, real scalar, or row vector with a length equal to the number of channels. This property applies when you set the *NoiseMethod* property to *Signal to noise ratio (SNR)*. The default value is 10.

(5) *BitsPerSymbol*: Specify the number of bits in each input symbol. You can set this property to a numeric, positive, integer scalar, or row vector with a length equal to the number of channels. This property applies when you set the *NoiseMethod* property to *Signal to noise ratio (Eb/No)*. The default value is 1 bit.

(6) *SignalPower*: Specify the mean square power of the input signal in Watts. Set this property to a numeric, positive, real scalar, or row vector with a length equal to the number of channels. This property applies when you set the *NoiseMethod* property to *Signal to noise ratio (Eb/No)*, *Signal to noise ratio (Es/No)* or *Signal to noise ratio (SNR)*. The default value is 1 Watt. The object assumes a nominal impedance of 1 Ohm.

(7) *SamplesPerSymbol*: Specify the number of samples per symbol. Set this property to a numeric, positive, integer scalar, or row vector with a length equal to the number of channels. This property applies when you set the *NoiseMethod* property to *Signal to noise ratio (Eb/No)* or *Signal to noise ratio (Es/No)*. The default value is 1 sample.

(8) *VarianceSource*: Specify the source of the noise variance as one of: (i) *Property* (specify the noise variance value using the *Variance* property), or (ii) *Input port* (specify the noise variance value via an input to the *step* method). This property applies when you set the *NoiseMethod* property to *Variance*. The default value is *Property*.

(9) *Variance*: Specify the variance of the white Gaussian noise. You can set this property to a numeric, positive, real scalar, or row vector with a length equal to the number of channels. This property applies when you set the *NoiseMethod* property to *Variance* and the *VarianceSource* property to *Property*. The default value is 1.

For example, the following code modulates an 8-PSK signal, adds white Gaussian noise, and plots the signal to observe the effects of noise (Fig. 5.1):

```
>> % create a PSK Modulator System object
>> hPSKMod = comm.PSKModulator;
>> % modulate the signal by calling the step function of the PSK
>> % modulator
>> modData = step(hPSKMod, randi([0 hPSKMod.ModulationOrder - 1], ...
       5000, 1));
>> % add white Gaussian noise to the modulated signal
>> hAWGN = comm.gpu.AWGNChannel('EbNo', 15, 'BitsPerSymbol', ...
       log2(hPSKMod.ModulationOrder));
>> % transmit the signal through the AWGN channel
>> channelOutput = step(hAWGN, modData);
>> % visualize the noiseless and noisy data in scatter plots
>> scatterplot(modData)
>> scatterplot(channelOutput)
```

- *comm.gpu.BlockDeinterleaver*: The BlockDeinterleaver System object restores the original ordering of a sequence that was interleaved using the block interleaver System object. In order to do that, you should:

(1) Define and set up a block deinterleaver object.

(2) Call *step* method to rearrange the elements of the input vector according to the properties of *comm.gpu.BlockDeinterleaver*.

A GPU BlockDeinterleaver object is constructed using the following syntax:

```
H = comm.gpu.BlockDeinterleaver(Name, Value)
H = comm.gpu.BlockDeinterleaver(PERMVEC)
```

The first variant creates a GPU-based block deinterleaver object, *H*, with the specified property *Name* set to the specified *Value*, while the second variant creates a GPU-based block deinterleaver object, *H*, with the *PermutationVector* property set to *PERMVEC*. The only available option for this System object is the

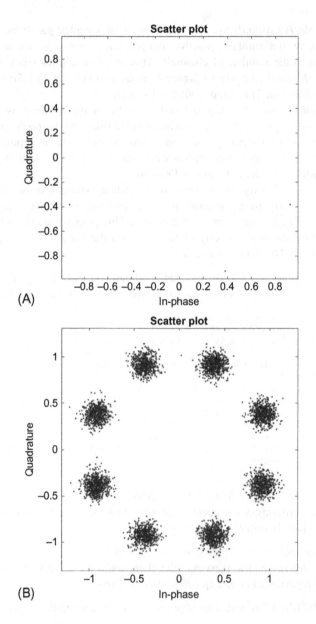

FIG. 5.1

Example using *comm.gpu.AWGNChannel* System object.

PermutationVector option, which specifies the mapping used to permute the input symbols as a column vector of integers. The default is [5; 4; 3; 2; 1]. The mapping is a vector where the number of elements is equal to the length, N, of the input to the *step* method. Each element must be an integer between 1 and N, with no repeated values. An example of this object is presented after the presentation of the *comm.gpu.BlockInterleaver* System object.

- *comm.gpu.BlockInterleaver*: The GPU BlockInterleaver object permutes the symbols in the input signal. To do that, you should:

    (1) Define and set up a block interleaver object.
    (2) Call *step* method to reorder the input symbols according to the properties of *comm.gpu.BlockInterleaver*.

    A GPU BlockInterleaver object is constructed using the following syntax:

```
H = comm.gpu.BlockInterleaver(Name, Value)
H = comm.gpu.BlockInterleaver(PERMVEC)
```

The first variant creates a GPU-based block interleaver object, H, with the specified property *Name* set to the specified *Value*, while the second variant creates a GPU-based block deinterleaver object, H, with the *PermutationVector* property set to *PERMVEC*. As with the GPU-based block deinterleaver object, the only available option for this System object is the *PermutationVector* option, which specifies the mapping used to permute the input symbols as a column vector of integers. The default is [5; 4; 3; 2; 1]. The mapping is a vector where the number of elements is equal to the length, N, of the input to the *step* method. Each element must be an integer between 1 and N, with no repeated values.

For example, the following code interleaves and deinterleaves a random sequence with 5 elements (Fig. 5.2):

```
>> % create a GPU-based block interleaver object
>> hBlockInt = comm.gpu.BlockInterleaver([3 4 1 2 5]');
>> % create a GPU-based block deinterleaver object
>> hBlockDeInt = comm.gpu.BlockDeinterleaver([3 4 1 2 5]');
>> % create a random sequence
>> data = randi(7, 5, 1);
>> % calculate the interleaved sequence
>> interleavedData = step(hBlockInt, data);
>> % calculate the deinterleaved seqeunce
>> deInterleavedData = step(hBlockDeInt, interleavedData);
>> % compare the original, interleaved and restored sequence
>> [data, interleavedData, deInterleavedData]
```

- *comm.gpu.ConvolutionalEncoder*: The GPU ConvolutionalEncoder object encodes a sequence of binary input vectors to produce a sequence of binary output vectors. To do that, you should:

    (1) Define and set up a convolutional encoder object.

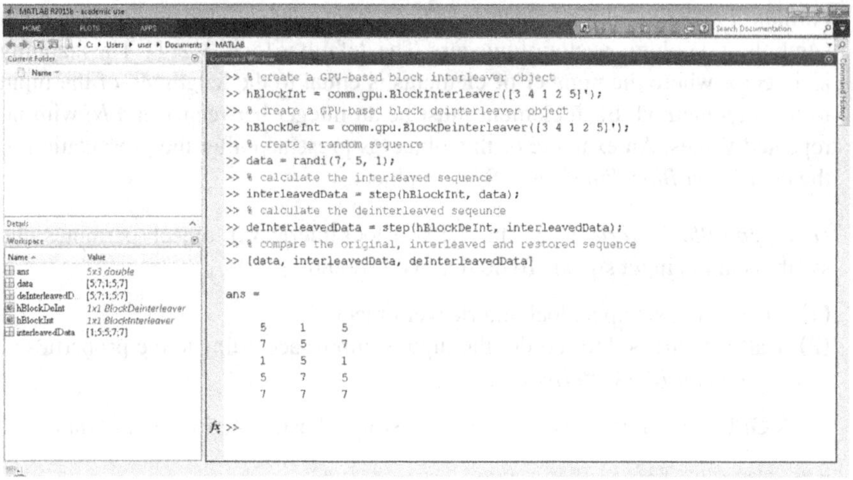

FIG. 5.2

Example using *comm.gpu.BlockInterleaver* and *comm.gpu.BlockDeinterleaver* System objects.

(2) Call *step* method to encode a sequence of binary input vectors to produce a sequence of binary output vectors according to the properties of *comm.gpu.ConvolutionalEncoder*.

A GPU ConvolutionalEncoder object is constructed using the following syntax:

```
H = comm.gpu.ConvolutionalEncoder(Name, Value)
H = comm.gpu.ConvolutionalEncoder(TRELLIS, Name, Value)
```

The first variant creates a convolutional encoder object, *H*, with each specified property *Name* set to the specified *Value*, while the second variant creates a convolutional encoder object, *H*, which has the *TrellisStructure* property set to *TRELLIS* and the other specified properties set to the specified values. The options that are available:

(1) *TrellisStructure*: Specify the trellis as a MATLAB structure that contains the trellis description of the convolutional code. Use the *istrellis* function to check if a structure is a valid trellis structure. The default value is the result of *poly2trellis(7, [171 133])*.

(2) *TerminationMethod*: Specify how the encoded frame is terminated as one of: (i) *Continuous* (the object retains the encoder states at the end of each input vector for use with the next input vector), (ii) *Truncated* (the object treats each input vector independently and resets its states to the all-zeros state), or (iii) *Terminated* (the object treats each input vector independently.

For each input vector, the object uses extra bits to set the encoder states to the all-zeros state at the end of the vector). The default value is *Continuous*.

(3) *PuncturePatternSource*: Specify the source of the puncture pattern as one of: (i) *None* (the object does not apply puncturing), or (ii) *Property* (the object punctures the code). This puncturing is based on the puncture pattern vector that you specify in the *PuncturePattern* property. This property applies when you set the *TerminationMethod* property to *Continuous* or *Truncated*. The default value is *None*.

(4) *PuncturePattern*: Specify the puncture pattern that the object uses to puncture the encoded data as a column vector. The vector contains 1s and 0s, where 0 indicates a punctured, or excluded, bit. This property applies when you set the *TerminationMethod* property to *Continuous* or *Truncated* and the *PuncturePatternSource* property to *Property*. The default value is [1; 1; 0; 1; 0; 1].

(5) *NumFrames*: Specify the number of independent frames contained in a single data input/output vector. The object segments the input vector into *NumFrames* segments and encodes them independently. The output contains *NumFrames* encoded segments. This property is applicable when you set the *TerminationMethod* to *Terminated* or *Truncated*. The default value is 1.

A real-world example using this System object is presented at the end of this section.

- *comm.gpu.ConvolutionalDeinterleaver*: The ConvolutionalDeinterleaver System object recovers a signal that was interleaved using the GPU-based convolutional interleaver object. The parameters in the two blocks should have the same values. To recover an interleaved signal, you should:

  (1) Define and set up your convolutional deinterleaver object.
  (2) Call *step* method to convolutionally deinterleave according to the properties of *comm.gpu.ConvolutionalDeinterleaver*.

A GPU ConvolutionalDeinterleaver object is constructed using the following syntax:

```
H = comm.gpu.ConvolutionalDeinterleaver(Name, Value)
H = comm.gpu.ConvolutionalDeinterleaver(M, B, IC)
```

The first variant creates a GPU-based convolutional deinterleaver System object, *H*, with the specified property *Name* set to the specified *Value*, while the second variant creates a convolutional deinterleaver System object, *H*, with the *NumRegisters* property set to *M*, the *RegisterLengthStep* property set to *B*, and the *InitialConditions* property set to *IC*. *M*, *B*, and *IC* are value-only arguments. To specify a value-only argument, you must also specify all preceding value-only arguments. The options that are available:

(1) *NumRegisters*: Specify the number of internal shift registers as a scalar, positive integer. The default value is 6.

(2) *RegisterLengthStep*: Specify the number of additional symbols that fit in each successive shift register as a positive, scalar integer. The first register holds zero symbols. The default value is 2.

(3) *InitialConditions*: Specify the values that are initially stored in each shift register (except the first shift register, which has zero delay) as a numeric scalar or vector. If you set this property to a scalar, then all shift registers, except the first one, store the same specified value. If you set it to a column vector with length equal to the value of the *NumRegisters* property, then the *i*th shift register stores the *i*th element of the specified vector. The value of the first element of this property is unimportant because the first shift register has zero delay. The default value is 0.

An example of this object is presented after the presentation of the *comm.gpu.ConvolutionalInterleaver* System object.

- *comm.gpu.ConvolutionalInterleaver*: The GPU ConvolutionalInterleaver object permutes the symbols in the input signal. Internally, this class uses a set of shift registers. To permute the symbols in an input signal, you should:

(1) Define and set up your convolutional interleaver object.

(2) Call *step* method to convolutionally interleave according to the properties of *comm.gpu.ConvolutionalInterleaver*.

A GPU ConvolutionalInterleaver object is constructed using the following syntax:

```
H = comm.gpu.ConvolutionalInterleaver(Name, Value)
H = comm.gpu.ConvolutionalInterleaver(M, B, IC)
```

The first variant creates a GPU-based convolutional interleaver System object, *H*, with the specified property *Name* set to the specified *Value*, while the second variant creates a GPU-based convolutional interleaver System object, *H*, with the *NumRegisters* property set to *M*, the *RegisterLengthStep* property set to *B*, and the *InitialConditions* property set to *IC*. *M*, *B*, and *IC* are value-only arguments. To specify a value-only argument, you must also specify all preceding value-only arguments. As with the GPU-based ConvolutionalDeinterleaver object, the options that are available:

(1) *NumRegisters*: Specify the number of internal shift registers as a scalar, positive integer. The default value is 6.

(2) *RegisterLengthStep*: Specify the number of additional symbols that fit in each successive shift register as a positive, scalar integer. The first register holds zero symbols. The default value is 2.

(3) *InitialConditions*: Specify the values that are initially stored in each shift register (except the first shift register, which has zero delay) as a numeric scalar or vector. If you set this property to a scalar, then all shift registers,

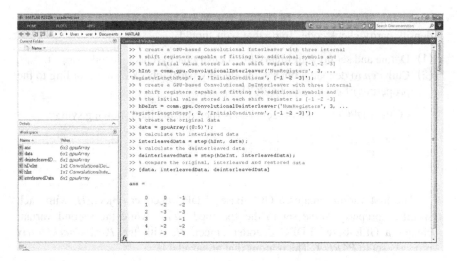

FIG. 5.3

Example using *comm.gpu.ConvolutionalInterleaver* and *comm.gpu.Convolutional Deinterleaver* System objects.

except the first one, store the same specified value. If you set it to a column vector with length equal to the value of the *NumRegisters* property, then the *i*th shift register stores the *i*th element of the specified vector. The value of the first element of this property is unimportant because the first shift register has zero delay. The default value is 0.

For example, the following code interleaves and deinterleaves a random sequence with 5 elements (Fig. 5.3):

```
>> % create a GPU-based Convolutional Interleaver with three internal
>> % shift registers capable of fitting two additional symbols and
>> % the initial value stored in each shift register is [-1 -2 -3]
>> hInt = comm.gpu.ConvolutionalInterleaver('NumRegisters', 3, ...
         'RegisterLengthStep', 2, 'InitialConditions', [-1 -2 -3]');
>> % create a GPU-based Convolutional DeInterleaver with three internal
>> % shift registers capable of fitting two additional symbols and
>> % the initial value stored in each shift register is [-1 -2 -3]
>> hDeInt = comm.gpu.ConvolutionalDeinterleaver('NumRegisters', 3, ...
         'RegisterLengthStep', 2, 'InitialConditions', [-1 -2 -3]');
>> % create the original data
>> data = gpuArray((0:5)');
>> % calculate the interleaved data
>> interleavedData = step(hInt, data);
>> % calculate the deinterleaved data
>> deinterleavedData = step(hDeInt, interleavedData);
>> % compare the original, interleaved and restored data
>> [data, interleavedData, deinterleavedData]
```

- *comm.gpu.LDPCDecoder*: The GPU LDPCDecoder object decodes a binary low-density parity-check code. To do that, you should:

  (1) Define and set up your binary low-density parity-check decoder object.
  (2) Call *step* to decode a binary low-density parity-check code according to the properties of *comm.gpu.LDPCDecoder*.

  A GPU LDPCDecoder object is constructed using the following syntax:

```
H = comm.gpu.LDPCDecoder(Name, Value)
H = comm.gpu.LDPCDecoder(PARITY)
```

The first variant creates a GPU-based LDPC decoder object, *H*, with each specified property *Name* set to the specified *Value*, while the second variant creates a GPU-based LDPC decoder object, *H*, with the *ParityCheckMatrix* property set to *PARITY*. The options that are available:

(1) *ParityCheckMatrix*: Specify the parity-check matrix as a binary valued sparse matrix with dimension (N-by-K) by N, where $N > K > 0$. The last $N - K$ columns in the parity check matrix must be an invertible matrix in GF(2). This property accepts numeric or logical data types. The upper bound for the value of N is $2^{31} - 1$. The default value is the parity-check matrix of the half-rate LDPC code from the DVB-S.2 standard, which is the result of *dvbs2ldpc(1/2)*.

(2) *OutputValue*: Specify the output value format as one of: (i) *Information part* (the output contains only the message bits and is a multiple of K length column vector, assuming an (N-by-K) $\times K$ parity check matrix), or (ii) *Whole codeword* (the output contains the codeword bits and is an N element column vector). The default value is *Information part*.

(3) *DecisionMethod*: Specify the decision method used for decoding as one of: (i) *Hard decision* (the output is decoded bits of logical data type), or (ii) *Soft decision* (the output is log-likelihood ratios of single or double data type). The default value is *Hard decision*.

(4) *IterationTerminationCondition*: Specify the condition to stop the decoding iterations as one of: (i) *Maximum iteration count* (the object will iterate for the number of iterations you specify in the *MaximumIterationCount* property), or (ii) *Parity check satisfied* (the object will determine if the parity checks are satisfied after each iteration and stops if all parity checks are satisfied). The default value is *Maximum iteration count*.

(5) *MaximumIterationCount*: Specify the maximum number of iterations the object uses as an integer valued numeric scalar. This applies when you set the *IterationTerminationCondition* property to *Maximum iteration count*. The default value is 50.

(6) *NumIterationsOutputPort*: Set this property to *true* to output the actual number of iterations the object performed. The default value is *false*.

(7) *FinalParityChecksOutputPort*: Set this property to *true* to output the final parity checks the object calculated. The default value is *false*.

For example, the following code transmits an LDPC-encoded QPSK-modulated bit stream through an AWGN channel, then demodulates it, decodes it, and counts the errors (Fig. 5.4):

```
>> % create an LDPCEncoder System object
>> hLDPCEnc = comm.LDPCEncoder;
>> % create a PSKModulator System object
>> hPSKMod = comm.PSKModulator(4, 'BitInput', true);
>> % create an AWGNChannel System object
>> hAWGNChan = comm.AWGNChannel('NoiseMethod', ...
>>    'Signal to noise ratio (SNR)', 'SNR', 1);
>> % create a PSKDemodulator System object
>> hPSKDemod = comm.PSKDemodulator(4, 'BitOutput', true, ...
      'DecisionMethod', 'Approximate log-likelihood ratio', ...
      'Variance', 1 / 10 ^ (hAWGNChan.SNR / 10));
>> % create a GPU LDPCDecoder System object
>> hLDPCDec = comm.gpu.LDPCDecoder;
>> hError = comm.ErrorRate;
>> for counter = 1:100 % simulate on random data
      % create random data
      data = logical(randi([0 1], 32400, 1));
      encodedData = step(hLDPCEnc, data); % LDPC encoding
      modSignal = step(hPSKMod, encodedData); % PSK modulation
      receivedSignal = step(hAWGNChan, modSignal); % add Gaussian noise
      demodSignal = step(hPSKDemod, receivedSignal); % demodulation
      receivedBits = step(hLDPCDec, demodSignal); % LDPC decoding
      errorStats = step(hError, data, receivedBits); % count errors
   end
>> % print errors
>> fprintf('Error rate = %1.2f\nNumber of errors = %d\n', ...
      errorStats(1), errorStats(2))
```

- *comm.gpu.PSKDemodulator*: The PSKDemodulator object demodulates an input signal using the M-ary phase shift keying (M-PSK) method. To do that, you should:

(1) Define and set up a PSK demodulator object.
(2) Call *step* method to demodulate the signal according to the properties of *comm.gpu.PSKDemodulator*.

A GPU PSKDemodulator object is constructed using the following syntax:

```
H = comm.gpu.PSKDemodulator(Name, Value)
H = comm.gpu.PSKDemodulator(M, PHASE, Name, Value)
```

The first variant creates a GPU-based M-PSK demodulator object, *H*, with the specified property set *Name* to the specified *Value*, while the second variant creates a GPU-based M-PSK demodulator object, *H*, with the *ModulationOrder* property set to *M*, the *PhaseOffset* property set to *PHASE*, and other specified property *Names* set to the specified *Values*. *M* and *PHASE* are value-only

FIG. 5.4

Example using *comm.gpu.LDPCDecoder* System object.

arguments. To specify a value-only argument, you must also specify all preceding value-only arguments. The options that are available:

(1) *ModulationOrder*: Specify the number of points in the signal constellation as a positive, integer scalar. The default value is 8.

(2) *PhaseOffset*: Specify the phase offset of the zeroth point of the constellation, in radians, as a real scalar. The default value is $\frac{\pi}{8}$.

(3) *BitOutput*: Specify whether the output consists of groups of bits or integer symbol values. When you set this property to *true*, the *step* method outputs a column vector of bit values with length equal to *log2(ModulationOrder)* times the number of demodulated symbols. When you set this property to *false*, the *step* method outputs a column vector, with a length equal to the input data vector that contains integer symbol values between 0 and *ModulationOrder* − 1. The default value is *false*.

(4) *SymbolMapping*: Specify how the object maps an integer or group of *log2(ModulationOrder)* bits to the corresponding symbol as: (i) *Binary* (the integer *m*, where $0 \leq m \leq ModulationOrder − 1$, maps to the complex value; this value is represented as *exp(j * PhaseOffset + j * 2 * π * m / ModulationOrder)*), (ii) *Gray* (the object uses a Gray-encoded signal constellation), or (iii) *Custom* (the object uses the signal constellation defined in the *CustomSymbolMapping* property). The default value is *Gray*.

(5) *CustomSymbolMapping*: Specify a custom constellation symbol mapping vector. This property must be a row or a column vector of size *ModulationOrder* with unique integer values in the range [0, *ModulationOrder* − 1].

The values must be of data type double. The first element of this vector corresponds to the constellation point at an angle of $0 + PhaseOffset$, with subsequent elements running counterclockwise. The last element corresponds to the constellation point at an angle of $-\pi/ModulationOrder + PhaseOffset$. This property applies when you set the *SymbolMapping* property to *Custom*. The default value is $0 : 7$.

(6) *DecisionMethod*: Specify the decision method that the object uses as one of: (i) *Hard decision*, (ii) *Log-likelihood ratio*, or (iii) *Approximate log-likelihood ratio*. When you set *DecisionMethod* to false, the object always performs hard decision demodulation. This property applies when you set the *BitOutput* property to *true*. The default value is *Hard decision*.

(7) *VarianceSource*: Specify the source of the noise variance as one of: (i) *Property*, or (ii) *Input port*. This property applies when you set the *BitOutput* property to *true* and the *DecisionMethod* property to *Log-likelihood ratio* or *Approximate log-likelihood ratio*. The default value is *Property*.

(8) *Variance*: Specify the variance of the noise as a positive, real scalar. If this value is very small, that is, SNR is very high, then log-likelihood ratio (LLR) computations may yield *Inf* or *-Inf*. In such cases, approximate LLR is recommended because its algorithm does not compute exponentials. This property applies when you set the *BitOutput* property to *true*, the *DecisionMethod* property to *Log-likelihood ratio* or *Approximate log-likelihood ratio*, and the *VarianceSource* property to *Property*. The default value is 1.

(9) *OutputDataType*: When you set this property to *Full precision*, the output signal inherits its data type from the input signal.

An example of this object is presented after the presentation of the *comm.gpu.PSKModulator* System object.

- *comm.gpu.PSKModulator*: The GPU PSKModulator object modulates a signal using the M-ary phase shift keying method. The input is a baseband representation of the modulated signal. The input and output for this object are discrete-time signals. This object accepts a scalar-valued or column vector input signal. To modulate a signal, you should:

(1) Define and set up a PSK modulator object.

(2) Call *step* to modulate the signal according to the properties of *comm.gpu.PSK-Modulator*.

A GPU PSKModulator object is constructed using the following syntax:

```
H = comm.gpu.PSKModulator(Name, Value)
H = comm.gpu.PSKModulator(M, PHASE, Name, Value)
```

The first variant creates a GPU-based M-PSK modulator object, *H*, with the specified property *Name* set to the specified *Value*, while the second variant creates a GPU-based M-PSK modulator object, *H*, with the *ModulationOrder* property set to *M*, the *PhaseOffset* property set to *PHASE*, and other specified property *Names* set to the specified *Values*. *M* and *PHASE* are value-only arguments. The options that are available:

(1) *ModulationOrder*: Specify the number of points in the signal constellation as a positive, integer scalar. The default value is 8.
(2) *PhaseOffset*: Specify the phase offset of the zeroth point of the constellation, in radians, as a real scalar. The default value is $\frac{\pi}{8}$.
(3) *BitInput*: Specify whether the input is bits or integers. When you set this property to *true*, the *step* method input must be a column vector of bit values whose length is an integer multiple of *log2(ModulationOrder)*. This vector contains bit representations of integers between 0 and *ModulationOrder* − 1. The input data type can be numeric or logical. When you set the *BitInput* property to *false*, the *step* method input must be a column vector of integer symbol values between 0 and *ModulationOrder* − 1. The data type of the input must be numeric. The default value is *false*.
(4) *SymbolMapping*: Specify how the object maps an integer or group of *log2(ModulationOrder)* bits to the corresponding symbol as: (i) *Binary* (the integer *m*, where $0 \leq m \leq ModulationOrder - 1$, maps to the complex value; this value is represented as *exp(j * PhaseOffset + j * 2 * π * m / ModulationOrder)*), (ii) *Gray* (the object uses a Gray-encoded signal constellation), or (iii) *Custom* (the object uses the signal constellation defined in the *CustomSymbolMapping* property). The default value is *Gray*.
(5) *CustomSymbolMapping*: Specify a custom constellation symbol mapping vector. This property must be a row or a column vector of size *ModulationOrder* with unique integer values in the range [0, *ModulationOrder* − 1]. The values must be of data type double. The first element of this vector corresponds to the constellation point at an angle of 0 + *PhaseOffset*, with subsequent elements running counterclockwise. The last element corresponds to the constellation point at an angle of −π/*ModulationOrder* + *PhaseOffset*. This property applies when you set the *SymbolMapping* property to *Custom*. The default value is 0 : 7.
(6) *OutputDataType*: Specify the output data type as one of: (i) *double*, or (ii) *single*. The default value is *double*.

For example, the following code transmits an LDPC-encoded QPSK-modulated bit stream through an AWGN channel, then demodulates it, decodes it and counts the errors (Fig. 5.5):

```
>> % create a PSKModulator System object
>> hPSKMod = comm.gpu.PSKModulator(32, 'PhaseOffset', pi / 32);
>> % create an AWGNChannel System object
>> hAWGNChan = comm.gpu.AWGNChannel('NoiseMethod', ...
      'Signal to noise ratio (SNR)', 'SNR', 15);
>> % create a PSKDemodulator System object
```

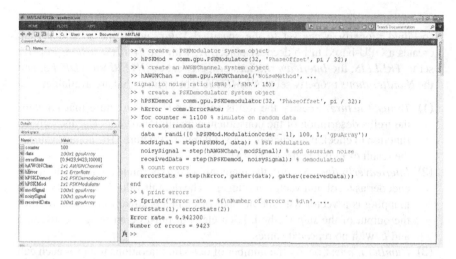

FIG. 5.5

Example using *comm.gpu.PSKModulator* and *comm.gpu.PSKDemodulator* System objects.

```
>> hPSKDemod = comm.gpu.PSKDemodulator(32, 'PhaseOffset', pi / 32);
>> hError = comm.ErrorRate;
>> for counter = 1:100 % simulate on random data
        % create random data
        data = randi([0 hPSKMod.ModulationOrder - 1], 100, 1, 'gpuArray');
        modSignal = step(hPSKMod, data); % PSK modulation
        noisySignal = step(hAWGNChan, modSignal); % add Gaussian noise
        receivedData = step(hPSKDemod, noisySignal); % demodulation
        % count errors
        errorStats = step(hError, gather(data), gather(receivedData));
    end
>> % print errors
>> fprintf('Error rate = %f\nNumber of errors = %d\n', ...
        errorStats(1), errorStats(2))
```

- *comm.gpu.TurboDecoder*: The GPU TurboDecoder object decodes the input signal using a parallel concatenated decoding scheme. This scheme uses the a-posteriori probability (APP) decoder as the constituent decoder. In order to decode an input signal, you should:

  (1) Define and set up your turbo decoder object.
  (2) Call *step* method to decode a binary signal according to the properties of *comm.gpu.TurboDecoder*.

A GPU TurboDecoder object is constructed using the following syntax:

```
H = comm.gpu.TurboDecoder(Name, Value)
H = comm.gpu.TurboDecoder(TRELLIS, INTERLVRINDICES, NUMITER)
```

The first variant creates a GPU-based turbo decoder object, *H*, with the specified property *Name* set to the specified *Value*, while the second variant creates a GPU-based turbo decoder object, *H*, with the *TrellisStructure* property set to *TRELLIS*, the *InterleaverIndices* property set to *INTERLVRINDICES*, and the *NumIterations* property set to *NUMITER*. The options that are available:

(1) *TrellisStructure*: Specify the trellis as a MATLAB structure that contains the trellis description of the constituent convolutional code. Use the *istrellis* function to check if a structure is a valid trellis structure. The default value is the result of *poly2trellis(4, [13 15], 13)*.

(2) *InterleaverIndices*: Specify the mapping used to permute the input bits at the encoder as a column vector of integers. The default value is *(64:-1:1).'*. This mapping is a vector with the number of elements equal to the length, *L*, of the output of the *step* method. Each element must be an integer between 1 and *L*, with no repeated values.

(3) *NumIterations*: Specify the number of decoding iterations used for each call to the *step* method. The object iterates and provides updates to the log-likelihood ratios (LLR) of the uncoded output bits. The output of the *step* method is the hard-decision output of the final LLR update. The default value is 6.

(4) *NumFrames*: Specify the number of independent frames that a single data input/output vector contains. This object segments the input vector into *NumFrames* segments and decodes the segments independently. The output contains *NumFrames* decoded segments. The default value is 1.

For example, the following code transmits turbo-encoded blocks of data over a BPSK-modulated AWGN channel, then decodes it using an iterative turbo decoder and counts the errors (Fig. 5.6):

```
>> % establish a frame length of 512
>> interleaverIndices = randperm(512);
>> % create a Turbo Encoder System object
>> hTurboEnc = comm.TurboEncoder('TrellisStructure', poly2trellis(4, ...
     [13 15 17], 13), 'InterleaverIndices', interleaverIndices);
>> % create a BPSK Modulator System object
>> hBPSKMod = comm.BPSKModulator;
>> % Create an AWGN Channel System object
>> hAWGNChan = comm.AWGNChannel('NoiseMethod', 'Variance', 'Variance', ...
     15);
>> % create a GPU-Based Turbo Decoder System object
>> hTurboDec = comm.gpu.TurboDecoder('TrellisStructure', poly2trellis(4, ...
     [13 15 17], 13), 'InterleaverIndices', interleaverIndices, ...
     'NumIterations', 10);
>> hError = comm.ErrorRate;
>> for i = 1:100 % simulate on random data
     % create random data
     data = randi([0 1], 512, 1);
     encodedData = step(hTurboEnc, data); % Turbo encoding
     modSignal = step(hBPSKMod, encodedData); % BPSK modulation
     receivedSignal = step(hAWGNChan, modSignal); % add Gaussian noise
```

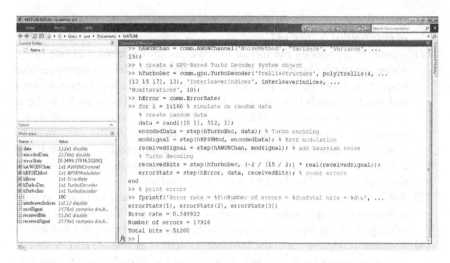

FIG. 5.6

Example using *comm.gpu.TurboDecoder* System object.

```
    % Turbo decoding
    receivedBits  = step(hTurboDec, (-2 / (15 / 2)) * real(receivedSignal));
    errorStats = step(hError, data, receivedBits); % count errors
  end
>> % print errors
>> fprintf('Error rate = %f\nNumber of errors = %d\nTotal bits = %d\n', ...
     errorStats(1), errorStats(2), errorStats(3))
```

- *comm.gpu.ViterbiDecoder*: The GPU ViterbiDecoder object decodes input symbols to produce binary output symbols. This object processes variable-size signals; however, variable-size signals cannot be applied for erasure inputs. To decode input symbols, you should:

  (1) Define and set up a Viterbi decoder object.
  (2) Call *step* method to decode input symbols according to the properties of *comm.gpu.ViterbiDecoder*.

  A GPU ViterbiDecoder object is constructed using the following syntax:

```
H = comm.gpu.ViterbiDecoder(Name, Value)
H = comm.gpu.ViterbiDecoder(TRELLIS, Name, Value)
```

  The first variant creates a Viterbi decoder object, *H*, with the specified property *Name* set to the specified *Value*, while the second variant creates a Viterbi decoder object, *H*, with the *TrellisStructure* property set to *TRELLIS*, and other specified property *Names* set to the specified *Values*. The options that are available:

  (1) *TrellisStructure*: Specify the trellis as a MATLAB structure that contains the trellis description of the convolutional code. Use the *istrellis* function to check if a structure is a valid trellis structure. The default value is the result of *poly2trellis(7, [171 133])*.

(2) *InputFormat*: Specify the format of the input to the decoder as one of: (i) *Unquantized* (the input must be a real vector of double- or single-precision unquantized soft values. The object considers negative numbers to be ones and positive numbers to be zeros), (ii) *Hard* (the input must be a vector of hard decision values, which are zeros or ones. The data type of the inputs can be double- or single precision), or (iii) *Soft* (the input must be a vector of quantized soft values represented as integers between 0 and 2^SoftInputWordLength - 1. The data type of the inputs can be double- or single precision). The default value is *Unquantized*.

(3) *SoftInputWordLength*: Specify the number of bits used to represent each quantized soft input value as a positive, integer scalar. This property applies when you set the *InputFormat* property to *Soft*. The default value is 4 bits.

(4) *TerminationMethod*: Specify *TerminationMethod* as one of: (i) *Continuous* (the object saves its internal state metric at the end of each frame for use with the next frame and the object treats each traceback path independently. Select this option value mode when the input signal contains only one symbol), (ii) *Truncated* (the object treats each frame independently and the traceback path starts at the state with the best metric and always ends in the all-zeros state), or (iii) *Terminated* (the object treats each frame independently and the traceback path always starts and ends in the all-zeros state). The default value is *Continuous*.

(5) *TracebackDepth*: Specify the number of trellis branches used to construct each traceback path as a positive, integer scalar less than or equal to 256. The traceback depth influences the decoding accuracy and delay. The number of zero symbols that precede the first decoded symbol in the output represent a decoding delay. When you set the *TerminationMethod* property to *Continuous*, the decoding delay consists of *TracebackDepth* zero symbols or *TracebackDepth* zero bits for a rate $1/N$ convolutional code. When you set the *TerminationMethod* property to *Truncated* or *Terminated*, there is no output delay and *TracebackDepth* must be less than or equal to the number of symbols in each input. If the code rate is 1/2, a typical traceback depth value is about five times the constraint length of the code. The default value is 34.

(6) *ResetInputPort*: Set this property to *true* to enable an additional *step* method input. When the reset input is a nonzero value, the object resets the internal states of the decoder to the initial conditions. This property applies when you set the *TerminationMethod* property to *Continuous*. The default value is *false*.

(7) *PuncturePatternSource*: Specify the source of the puncture pattern as one of: (i) *None* (the object assumes no puncturing), or (ii) *Property* (if you want to decode punctured codewords based on a puncture pattern vector specified via the *PuncturePattern* property). The default value is *None*.

(8) *PuncturePattern*: Specify puncture pattern used to puncture the encoded data. The puncture pattern is a column vector of ones and zeros, where the zeros indicate where to insert dummy bits. The puncture pattern must match the puncture pattern used by the encoder. This property applies when you set the *PuncturePatternSource* property to *Property*. The default is [1; 1; 0; 1; 0; 1].

(9) *NumFrames*: Specify the number of independent frames contained in a single data input/output vector. The input vector will be segmented into *NumFrames* segments and decoded independently. The output will contain *NumFrames* decoded segments. This property is applied when the *TerminationMethod* is set to *Terminated* or *Truncated*. The default value is 1.

A real-world example using this System object is presented at the end of this section.

The preceding System objects accept MATLAB arrays or objects that were created using the *gpuArray* class as inputs to the *step* method. The input signals can be either double- or single-precision data types. The output signals inherit their datatype from the input signals. If you pass a MATLAB array as an argument to this System object (not a *gpuArray*), then the output signal will be also a MATLAB array; the System object automatically transfers data between the CPU and GPU. On the other hand, if the input signal is a *gpuArray*, then the output signal will be also a *gpuArray*. In this case, the data remains on the GPU and no transfer occurs between the CPU and the GPU. Calling the *step* method with *gpuArray* input arguments provides increased performance by reducing the simulation time.

Example: Convolutional coding

Convolutional coding is a general category of codes with great use in today's wireless and satellite communications. In convolutional coding, the original message is not transmitted but only the parity bits calculated from it. Instead of splitting the message into blocks, there is a window that slides over the original message, so the parity bits are calculated over overlapping windows. The size of the window is called the constraint length. By increasing the constraint length, the system is less prone to bit errors.

The process of decoding is the estimation of the most probable original message transmitted (or in the case of a trellis representation is finding the most likely path). The most well-known decoding algorithm of convolutional codes over noisy links is the Viterbi decoder.

In the following example, we simulate the transmission of a binary sequence over a noisy channel and the decoding of the received signal to the original. The steps are as follows:

(1) Calculate the convolutionally encoded data (parity bits) from the original message. We create a code generator matrix and a corresponding trellis structure description. The trellis has 1 input, 7 shift registers and 4 outputs, so the rate of the feedforward encoder is $\frac{1}{4}$.

(2) Modulate the data with the BPSK modulator in order to be transmitted.

(3) Add white noise to the signal (noise from the transmission link).

(4) Demodulate the signal.

(5) Decode the signal with the Viterbi decoder.

Function *convolutionalCodingCPU* (filename: convolutionalCodingCPU.m) is used to illustrate the above example in MATLAB.

```
1.    function convolutionalCodingCPU(data, N)
2.    % Filename: convolutionalCodingCPU.m
3.    % Description: This function simulates the transmission
4.    % of a binary sequence over a noisy channel and the
5.    % decoding of the received signal to the original
6.    % (execution on CPU)
7.    % Authors: Ploskas, N., & Samaras, N.
8.    % Syntax: convolutionalCodingCPU(data, N)
9.    % Input:
10.   %   -- data: the original message (array)
11.   %   -- N: the number of blocks
12.   % Output: simmulation of the transmission of a binary
13.   % sequence over a noisy channel and the decoding of
14.   % the received signal to the original
15.
16.   % set the octal numbers for the code generator of the encoder
17.   trellisGen = [322 234 147 271];
18.   % convert the convolutional code polynomial to trellis description
19.   p = poly2trellis(8, trellisGen);
20.   % create the Convolutional Encoder System object
21.   hConEnc = comm.ConvolutionalEncoder('TrellisStructure', p);
22.   % create the binary PSK Modulator System object
23.   hPSKMod = comm.PSKModulator('BitInput', true, 'ModulationOrder', 2);
24.   % create the Additive White Gaussian Noise channel System object
25.   hAWGNChannel = comm.AWGNChannel('NoiseMethod', ...
26.       'Signal to noise ratio (SNR)', 'SNR', 5);
27.   % create the binary PSK Demodulator System object
28.   hPSKDemod = comm.PSKDemodulator(2);
29.   % create the Viterbi Decoder System object
30.   hVitDecod = comm.ViterbiDecoder('InputFormat', 'Hard', ...
31.       'TrellisStructure', p);
32.   for i = 1:N % simulate convolutional coding on input data
33.       encodedData = step(hConEnc, data{i}); % convolutional encoding
34.       modSignal = step(hPSKMod, encodedData); % PSK modulation
35.       receivedSignal = step(hAWGNChannel, modSignal); % add Gaussian noise
36.       demodSignal = step(hPSKDemod, receivedSignal); % demodulation
37.       receivedBits = step(hVitDecod, demodSignal); % Viterbi decoding
38.   end
39.   end
```

Initially, we measure the execution time of this function running on the CPU using 100 blocks of 50,000 bits per block:

```
>> for i = 1:100
     data{i} = randi([0 1], [50000 1]);
   end
>> tic; convolutionalCodingCPU(data, 100); toc
Elapsed time is 7.341227 seconds.
```

To execute this function on the GPU, we should perform some changes to the code. First of all, we should change all System objects to the equivalent GPU-enabled ones, for example, from *comm.ConvolutionalEncoder* to *comm.gpu.Convolutional Encoder*. Moreover, we should pass a *gpuArray* as input to that function.

Function *convolutionalCodingGPU* (filename: convolutionalCodingGPU.m) is used to illustrate the preceding example in MATLAB running on the GPU.

```
1.    function convolutionalCodingGPU(data, N)
2.    % Filename: convolutionalCodingGPU.m
3.    % Description: This function simulates the transmission
4.    % of a binary sequence over a noisy channel and the
5.    % decoding of the received signal to the original
6.    % (execution on GPU)
7.    % Authors: Ploskas, N., & Samaras, N.
8.    % Syntax: convolutionalCodingGPU(data, N)
9.    % Input:
10.   %   -- data: the original message (array)
11.   %   -- N: the number of blocks
12.   % Output: simmulation of the transmission of a binary
13.   % sequence over a noisy channel and the decoding of
14.   % the received signal to the original
15.
16.   % set the octal numbers for the code generator of the encoder
17.   trellisGen = [322 234 147 271];
18.   % convert the convolutional code polynomial to trellis description
19.   p = poly2trellis(8, trellisGen);
20.   % create the Convolutional Encoder System object
21.   hConEnc = comm.gpu.ConvolutionalEncoder('TrellisStructure', p);
22.   % create the binary PSK Modulator System object
23.   hPSKMod = comm.gpu.PSKModulator('BitInput', true, 'ModulationOrder', 2);
24.   % create the Additive White Gaussian Noise channel System object
25.   hAWGNChannel = comm.gpu.AWGNChannel('NoiseMethod', ...
26.       'Signal to noise ratio (SNR)', 'SNR', 5);
27.   % create the binary PSK Demodulator System object
28.   hPSKDemod = comm.gpu.PSKDemodulator(2);
29.   % create the Viterbi Decoder System object
30.   hVitDecod = comm.gpu.ViterbiDecoder('InputFormat', 'Hard', ...
31.       'TrellisStructure', p);
32.   for i = 1:N % simulate convolutional coding on input data
33.       encodedData = step(hConEnc, data{i}); % convolutional encoding
34.       modSignal = step(hPSKMod, encodedData); % PSK modulation
35.       receivedSignal = step(hAWGNChannel, modSignal); % add Gaussian noise
36.       demodSignal = step(hPSKDemod, receivedSignal); % demodulation
37.       receivedBits = step(hVitDecod, demodSignal); % Viterbi decoding
38.   end
39.   end
```

We measure the execution time of this function running on the GPU using the same data:

```
>> for i = 1:100
    data{i} = gpuArray(data{i});
   end
>> gd = gpuDevice(); tic; convolutionalCodingGPU(data, 100); wait(gd); toc
Elapsed time is 0.936665 seconds.
```

Hence, the convolutional coding function is running $\sim 8\times$ faster on the GPU.

5.2 IMAGE PROCESSING TOOLBOX

The Image Processing Toolbox provides a set of functions and applications for image processing, analysis, and visualization. There are many functions available for image analysis, image segmentation, image enhancement, noise reduction, geometric transformations, and image registration. Moreover, many functions support multicore and multiprocessor CPUs, and GPUs.

The Image Processing Toolbox supports a wide variety of image types, including high dynamic range, gigapixel resolution, embedded ICC profile, and tomographic. Visualization functions allow users to explore images and videos, examine a region of pixels, adjust color and contrast, create contours or histograms, and manipulate regions of interest.

The Image Processing Toolbox provides many GPU-enabled functions. To perform an image processing operation on a GPU, you can apply the following steps:

- Transfer data, for example, an image, from the CPU to the GPU by creating *gpuArray* objects.
- Perform the image processing operation on the GPU either by using the GPU-enabled functions that accept a *gpuArray* object or by performing element-wise or pixel-based operations on a GPU using *arrayfun* and *bsxfun*.
- Transfer data back to the CPU from the GPU using the *gather* function.

As of MATLAB R2015b, Table 5.1 lists all the Image Processing Toolbox functions that have been enabled to run on a GPU. Most functions support the same syntax and operate the same on the CPU and GPU, but in some cases there are some limitations when evaluating them on the GPU. The third column of Table 5.1 lists these limitations.

Example: Computed tomography image reconstruction

The inverse Radon transform is mostly applied in image reconstruction from an object's back projections. The projections are commonly generated by cross-sectional scans of the object. Computed tomography scans are an example of the aforementioned method, where X-rays are used to project the body structures, which block or attenuate the beams.

On the contrary, the Radon transform creates the objects, back projections, by integrating a function, called indicator or characteristic function, over straight lines. In computed tomography scans, the indicator function is the attenuation coefficient's function.

In the following example, we obtain the back projections of an image in specific angles, and then we try to reconstruct the original image. The steps used are as follows:

Table 5.1 GPU-enabled functions on the Image Processing Toolbox

Function	Description	Remarks/Limitations
bwdist	Compute the distance transform of a binary image.	Inputs must be 2-D and have less than $2^{32} - 1$ elements. Euclidean is the only distance metric supported.
bwlabel	Calculate label connected components on a 2-D binary image.	–
bwlookup	Perform nonlinear filtering using lookup tables.	–
bwmorph	Apply morphological operations on a binary image.	–
corr2	Calculate the 2-D correlation coefficient of two arrays.	–
edge	Find edges in an intensity image.	Canny method is not supported on the GPU.
histeq	Enhance contrast using histogram equalization.	–
im2double	Convert image to double precision.	–
im2single	Convert image to single precision.	–
im2uint8	Convert image to 8-bit unsigned integers.	–
im2uint16	Convert image to 16-bit unsigned integers.	–
imabsdiff	Compute the absolute difference of two images.	Only single and double are supported.
imadjust	Adjust image intensity values or colormap.	–
imbothat	Perform morphological bottom-hat filtering.	*gpuArray* input must be of type uint8 or logical and the structuring element must be flat and two-dimensional.
imclose	Perform morphological closing on an image.	*gpuArray* input must be of type uint8 or logical and the structuring element must be flat and two-dimensional.
imcomplement	Compute the complement of an image.	–
imdilate	Dilate an image.	*gpuArray* input must be of type uint8 or logical and the structuring element must be flat and two-dimensional. The PACKOPT syntaxes are not supported on the GPU.

Continued

Table 5.1 GPU-enabled functions on the Image Processing Toolbox—cont'd

Function	Description	Remarks/Limitations
imerode	Erode an image.	*gpuArray* input must be of type uint8 or logical and the structuring element must be flat and two-dimensional. The PACKOPT syntaxes are not supported on the GPU.
imfill	Fill image regions and holes.	Inputs must be 2-D, supporting only the 2-D connectivities, 4 and 8. Does not support the interactive hole filling syntax.
imfilter	Filter multidimensional images.	Input kernel must be 2-D.
imgradient	Calculate the gradient magnitude and direction of an image.	–
imgradientxy	Compute the directional gradients of an image.	–
imhist	Calculate the histogram of an image.	When running on a GPU, imhist does not display the histogram. To display the histogram, use stem(X,counts).
imlincomb	Computes the linear combination of images.	–
imnoise	Add noise to an image.	–
ycbcr2rgb	Convert YCbCr color values to RGB color space.	–
imopen	Perform morphological opening on an image.	*gpuArray* input must be of type uint8 or logical and the structuring element must be flat and two-dimensional.
imreconstruct	Perform morphological reconstruction of an image.	–
imregdemons	Estimate the displacement field that aligns two 2-D or 3-D images.	The parameter 'PyramidLevels' is not supported on the GPU.
imresize	Resize an image.	Only cubic interpolation is supported on GPU, and function always performs antialiasing.
imrotate	Rotate an image.	The 'bicubic' interpolation mode used in the GPU implementation of this function differs from the default (CPU) bicubic mode. The GPU and CPU versions of this function are expected to give slightly different results.
imshow	Display an image.	–

Table 5.1 GPU-enabled functions on the Image Processing Toolbox—cont'd

Function	Description	Remarks/Limitations
imtophat	Perform morphological top-hat filtering.	*gpuArray* input must be of type uint8 or logical and the structuring element must be flat and two-dimensional.
iradon	Perform the inverse Radon transform.	The GPU implementation of this function supports only Nearest-neighbor and linear interpolation methods.
mat2gray	Convert a matrix to a grayscale image.	–
mean2	Compute the average or mean of matrix elements.	–
medfilt2	Perform 2-D median filtering.	Padding options are not supported on the GPU.
normxcorr2	Compute the normalized 2-D cross-correlation of two arrays.	–
padarray	Pad an array.	–
radon	Perform the Radon transform.	–
rgb2gray	Convert an RGB image or colormap to grayscale.	–
rgb2ycbcr	Convert RGB color values to YCbCr color space.	–
std2	Calculate the standard deviation of matrix elements.	–
stdfilt	Compute the local standard deviation of an image.	–
stretchlim	Find the limits to a contrast stretching image.	–

(1) Calculate back projections, 1 per degree, for half a circle, using the Radon transform.

(2) Calculate back projections, 1 per 15 degrees, for half a circle, using the Radon transform.

(3) Calculate the inverse Radon transform for both cases. We use a Hann window to avoid the blurriness of the reconstructed image.

Function *ctImageReconstruction* (filename: ctImageReconstruction.M) is used to illustrate the preceding example in MATLAB.

```
1.    function [ir1, ir15] = ctImageReconstruction(img)
2.    % Filename: ctImageReconstruction.m
3.    % Description: This function obtains the back
4.    % projections of an image in specific angles and then
5.    % it tries to reconstruct the original image
```

```
6.    % Authors: Ploskas, N., & Samaras, N.
7.    % Syntax: [ir1, ir15] = ctImageReconstruction(img)
8.    % Input:
9.    %   -- img: the image for which we want to obtain the
10.   %      back projections in specific angles and then
11.   %      reconstruct the original image
12.   % Output:
13.   %   -- ir1: the reconstructed image using theta = 1 degree
14.   %   -- ir15: the reconstructed image using theta = 15 degrees
15.
16.   % reconstruct image - theta = 1 degree
17.   % define the angle steps for half the circle - 1 degree
18.   th1 = 0:1:179;
19.   % calculate back projections
20.   r1 = radon(img, th1);
21.   % reconstruct image from back projections
22.   ir1 = iradon(r1, th1, 'hann');
23.   % reconstruct image - theta = 15 degrees
24.   % define the angle steps for half the circle - 15 degrees
25.   th15 = 0:15:179;
26.   % calculate back projections
27.   r15 = radon(img, th15);
28.   % reconstruct image from back projections
29.   ir15 = iradon(r15, th15, 'hann');
30.   end
```

Initially, we measure the execution time of this function running on the CPU using a $2,000 \times 2,000$ phantom image:

```
>> img = phantom(2000);
>> tic; [ir1, ir15] = ctImageReconstruction(img); toc
Elapsed time is 6.126523 seconds.
```

To execute this function on the GPU, we do not have to perform any changes to the code because all functions and operators used are GPU-enabled. The only difference is that we should pass a *gpuArray* as input to that function. We measure the execution time of this function running on the GPU using the same image:

```
>> gd = gpuDevice(); tic; [ir1, ir15] = ctImageReconstruction(gpuArray(img));
wait(gd); toc
Elapsed time is 0.497152 seconds.
```

Hence, the computed tomography image reconstruction function is running ~12.30× faster on the GPU.

Fig. 5.7 shows the result of the computed tomography image reconstruction function for the two different angle steps theta = 1 degree and theta = 15 degrees.

5.3 NEURAL NETWORK TOOLBOX

The Neural Network Toolbox provides functions and applications for modeling complex nonlinear systems that are not easily modeled with a closed-form equation.

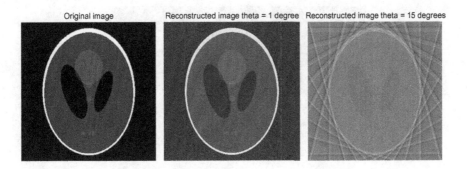

FIG. 5.7

Result of the computed tomography image reconstruction function.

The Neural Network Toolbox supports supervised learning with feedforward, radial basis, and dynamic networks. It also supports unsupervised learning with self-organizing maps and competitive layers. With the Neural Network Toolbox you can design, train, visualize, and simulate neural networks. The Neural Network Toolbox can be used to solve many types of applications such as data fitting, pattern recognition, clustering, time-series prediction, and dynamic system modeling and control.

To speed up training and handle large data sets, the Neural Network Toolbox can distribute computations and data across multicore and multiprocessor CPUs, GPUs and computer clusters using the Parallel Computing Toolbox.

To train and simulate a neural network in MATLAB, you have to follow the steps below:

- Prepare the input and target data.
- Create a neural network using the *feedforwardnet* function.
- Configure the neural network with the input and target data using the *configure* function.
- Train the neural network using the *train* function.
- Simulate the neural network using the implicit call to the *sim* function (where the network *net* is called as a function).

To illustrate this process, execute the following commands:

```
>> [x, t] = house_dataset; % prepare the input and target data
>> net = feedforwardnet(10); % create a neural network
>> net = configure(net, x, t); % configure the neural network
>> [net, tr] = train(net, x, t); % train the neural network
>> y = net(x); % simulate the neural network
```

The training window will appear during training (Fig. 5.8). Note that if you do not want to have this window displayed during training, you can set the parameter *net.trainParam.showWindow* to *false*. If you want training information displayed in

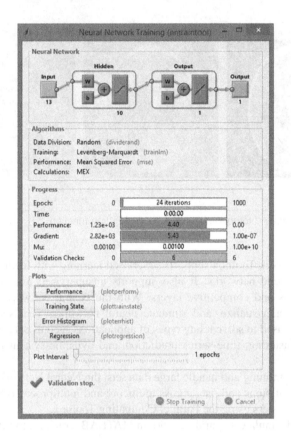

FIG. 5.8

Training window.

the command line, you can set the parameter *net.trainParam.showCommandLine* to *true*.

The training window (Fig. 5.8) displays all the available information from the training and simulation of a neural network. More specifically, it shows:

- the structure of your neural network (in the previous example, a two-layer neural network was created with 13 inputs, 10 nodes in the hidden layer and 1 output).
- the method with which the data is divided (in the previous example, the data has been divided using the *dividerand* function).
- the training method (in the previous example, the Levenberg-Marquardt (*trainlm*) training method has been used).

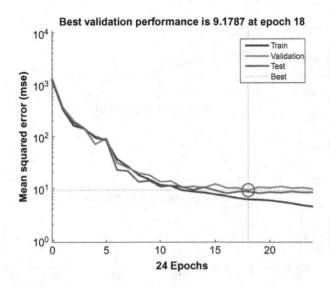

FIG. 5.9

Performance plot.

- the performance function (in the previous example, the mean squared error performance function has been used).
- the training computation mode (in the previous example, the training computations were performed through a compiled MEX algorithm).
- the number of epochs (in the previous example, 24 iterations were performed).
- the training time (in the previous example, the training time is almost zero).
- the performance (in the previous example, the best performance is 9.1787 and is obtained at epoch 18).
- the magnitude of the gradient of performance (in the previous example, the magnitude of the gradient of performance is 5.4251 at epoch 24)
- the mu factor (in the previous example, the mu factor is 0.001 at epoch 24).
- the number of validation checks (in the previous example, 6 successful validation checks were performed at epoch 24, so the algorithm terminated).
- the performance plot (Fig. 5.9).
- the training state plot (Fig. 5.10).
- the error histogram (Fig. 5.11).
- the regression plot (Fig. 5.12).

In the previous example, six successful validation checks were performed at epoch 24, so the algorithm terminated. There are other criteria that can be used to stop network training:

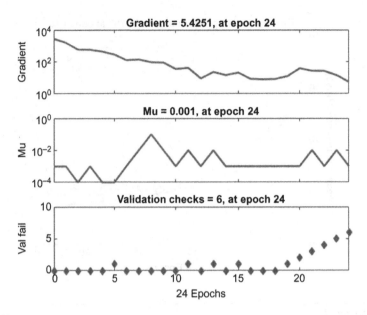

FIG. 5.10

Training state plot.

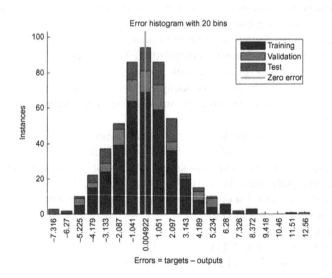

FIG. 5.11

Error histogram.

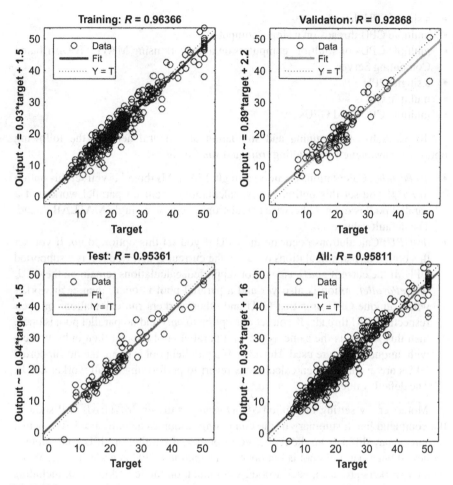

FIG. 5.12

Regression plot.

- The maximum number of epochs (iterations) is reached.
- The maximum amount of time is exceeded.
- Performance is minimized to the goal.
- The performance gradient falls below *min_grad*.
- *mu* factor exceeds *mu_max*.
- Validation performance has increased more than *max_fail* times since the last time it decreased.

In the previous example, the two steps you can parallelize are the call to *train* method and the implicit call to *sim* (where the network net is called as a function). The Parallel Computing Toolbox allows neural network training and simulation to run on:

- a single CPU thread
- multiple CPU threads on a single computer
- multiple CPUs on multiple computers on a network using MATLAB Distributed Computing Server
- a single GPU
- multiple GPUs
- multiple CPUs and GPUs

To parallelize the training and simulation of a neural network the following options are available when calling *train* and *sim* functions:

- *useParallel*: Calculations occur on a single MATLAB thread if you set this option to *no*. If you set this option to *yes*, calculations occur on parallel workers if a parallel pool is open. Otherwise calculations occur on a single MATLAB thread. The default value is *no*.
- *useGPU*: Calculations occur on the CPU if you set this option to *no*. If you set this option to *yes*, calculations occur on the current *gpuDevice* if it is a supported GPU. If the current *gpuDevice* is not supported, calculations remain on the CPU. If *useParallel* option is also *yes* and a parallel pool is open, then each worker with a unique GPU uses that GPU and other workers run calculations on their respective CPU threads. If you set this option to *only* and no parallel pool is open, then this setting is the same as *yes*. If a parallel pool is open then only workers with unique GPUs are used. However, if a parallel pool is open, but no supported GPUs are available, then calculations revert to performing on all worker CPUs. The default value is *no*.

Moreover, by setting the option *ShowResources* to *yes*, MATLAB will show at the command line a summary of the computing resources actually used. The actual resources may differ from the requested resources, if parallel or GPU computing is requested but a parallel pool is not open or a supported GPU is not available. When parallel workers are used, each worker's computation mode is described, including workers in the pool that are not used.

Some other features that you should consider before training and simulating a neural network on the GPU are the following:

- If the neural network has the default training function *trainlm*, you see a warning that GPU calculations do not support Jacobian training, but only gradient training. So, the training function is automatically changed to the gradient training function *trainscg*. To avoid the warning, you can specify the function before training and simulating: *net1.trainFcn = 'trainscg'*.
- To verify that the training and simulation occur on the GPU device, request that the computer resources be shown (set option *ShowResources* to *yes*).
- You can call *train* and *sim* functions either with regular MATLAB arrays or *gpuArray* objects. Regardless of your choice, if you set the *useGPU* to *yes* or *only* and the current *gpuDevice* is supported, MATLAB will automatically transfer the data from the CPU on the GPU and execute the training and simulation on

the GPU. However, for neural networks trained and simulated on the GPU, it may sometimes be more efficient to use *nndata2gpu* prior to the training and simulation of the neural network: *gpuX = nndata2gpu(x);*. *nndata2gpu* formats neural data for efficient GPU training or simulation. After the training and simulation of the neural network, you can use the *gpu2nndata* function to reformat and transfer back to the CPU the results.

- On GPUs, it is often the case that the exponential function *exp* is not implemented with hardware, but with a software library. This can slow down neural networks that use the tansig sigmoid transfer function. An alternative function is the Elliot sigmoid function whose expression does not include a call to any higher order functions. Before training the neural network, the network's *tansig* layers can be converted to *elliotsig* layers as follows:

```
for i = 1:net.numLayers
    if strcmp(net.layers{i}.transferFcn, 'tansig')
        net.layers{i}.transferFcn = 'elliotsig';
    end
end
```

- Distributed GPU computing can benefit from manually creating Composite values (see Section 3.3 for more information on Composite objects). Defining the Composite values manually, lets you indicate which workers to use, how many samples to assign to each worker, and which workers use GPUs. For example, let's assume that we have open a parallel pool with four workers and only two

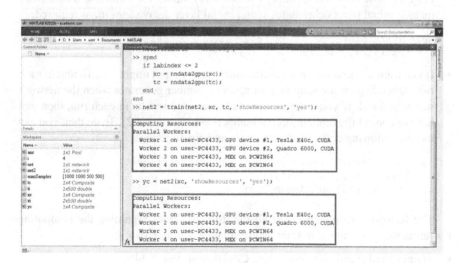

FIG. 5.13

Train and simulate neural networks on multiple CPU threads and GPUs with Composite objects.

GPUs are available and supported. We can define larger datasets for the GPU workers (Fig. 5.13):

```
>> parpool('local', 4);
>> numSamples = [1000 1000 500 500];
>> xc = Composite;
>> tc = Composite;
>> for i = 1:4
      xi = rand(2, numSamples(i));
      ti = xi(1, :) .^ 2 + 3 * xi(2, :);
      xc{i} = xi;
      tc{i} = ti;
   end
>> net = feedforwardnet(10);
>> net2 = configure(net, xc{1}, tc{1});
>> net2.trainFcn = 'trainscg';
>> spmd
      if labindex <= 2
          xc = nndata2gpu(xc);
          tc = nndata2gpu(tc);
      end
   end
>> net2 = train(net2, xc, tc, 'showResources', 'yes');
>> yc = net2(xc, 'showResources', 'yes');
```

• Ensure that each GPU is used by only one worker, so that the computations are more efficient. If multiple workers assign *gpuArray* data on the same GPU, the computation will still work but will be slower.

• For time series networks, simply use cell array values for *x* and *t*, and optionally include initial input delay states *xi* and initial layer delay states *ai*, as required.

```
net2 = train(net, x, t, xi, ai, 'useGPU', 'yes');
y = net2(x, xi, ai, 'useGPU', 'yes');
```

• If you train a neural network several times, your output might be different in each run, depending on the state of your random number generator when the network was initialized. If you want to reproduce the same results in each run, then you have to control the random stream numbers (see Section 4.2). To do that, you can use the following code prior to the *train* and *sim* functions:

```
rs = RandStream('CombRecursive', 'NormalTransform', ...
    'Inversion', 'Seed', 4);
RandStream.setGlobalStream(rs);
```

The following examples cover all the different cases regarding the computing resources that you can use to train and simulate a neural network:

• Training and simulation on a single CPU thread (Fig. 5.14):

```
>> [x, t] = house_dataset;
>> net = feedforwardnet(10);
>> net = configure(net, x, t);
```

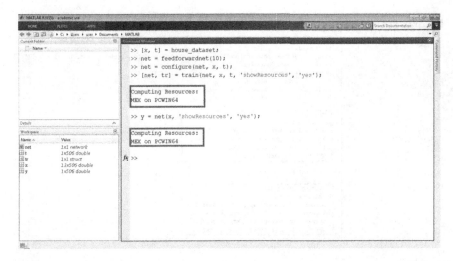

FIG. 5.14

Train and simulate neural networks on a single CPU thread.

```
>> [net, tr] = train(net, x, t, 'showResources', 'yes');
>> y = net(x, 'showResources', 'yes');
```

- Training and simulation on multiple CPU threads (Fig. 5.15):

```
>> parpool('local', 4);
>> [x, t] = house_dataset;
>> net = feedforwardnet(10);
>> net = configure(net, x, t);
>> [net, tr] = train(net, x, t, 'useParallel', 'yes', ...
      'showResources', 'yes');
>> y = net(x, 'useParallel', 'yes', 'showResources', 'yes');
```

- Training and simulation on a single GPU (Fig. 5.16):

```
>> [x, t] = house_dataset;
>> net = feedforwardnet(10);
>> net = configure(net, x, t);
>> net.trainFcn = 'trainscg';
>> [net, tr] = train(net, x, t, 'useGPU', 'yes', ...
      'showResources', 'yes');
>> y = net(x, 'useGPU', 'yes', 'showResources', 'yes');
```

- Training and simulation on multiple GPUs (Fig. 5.17):

```
>> parpool('local', 4);
>> [x, t] = house_dataset;
>> net = feedforwardnet(10);
>> net = configure(net, x, t);
>> net.trainFcn = 'trainscg';
```

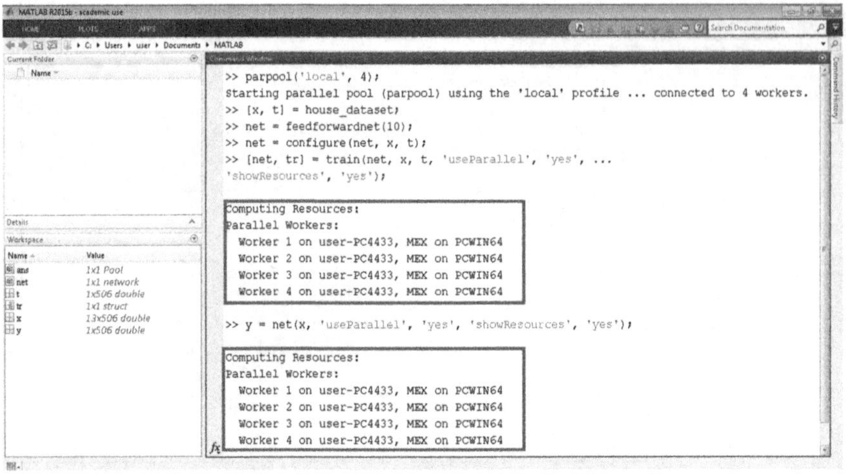

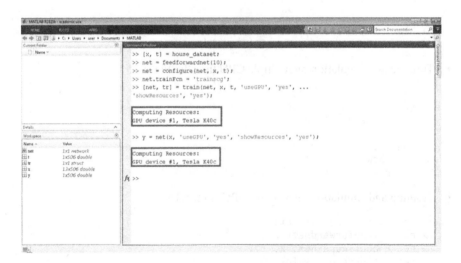

FIG. 5.15

Train and simulate neural networks on multiple CPU threads.

FIG. 5.16

Train and simulate neural networks on a single GPU.

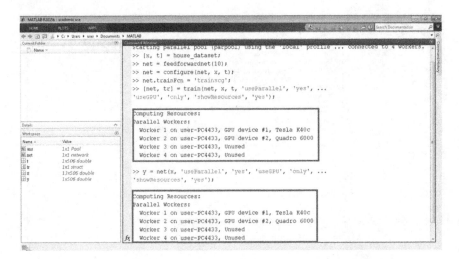

FIG. 5.17

Train and simulate neural networks on multiple GPUs.

```
>> [net, tr] = train(net, x, t, 'useParallel', 'yes', ...
    'useGPU', 'only', 'showResources', 'yes');
>> y = net(x, 'useParallel', 'yes', 'useGPU', 'only', ...
    'showResources', 'yes');
```

- Training and simulation on multiple CPU threads and GPUs (Fig. 5.18):

```
>> parpool('local', 4);
>> [x, t] = house_dataset;
>> net = feedforwardnet(10);
>> net = configure(net, x, t);
>> net.trainFcn = 'trainscg';
>> [net, tr] = train(net, x, t, 'useParallel', 'yes', ...
    'useGPU', 'yes', 'showResources', 'yes');
>> y = net(x, 'useParallel', 'yes', 'useGPU', 'yes', ...
    'showResources', 'yes');
```

Example: Neural network training and simulation on chemical dataset

Function fitting is the process of training a neural network on a set of inputs to estimate the set of target outputs. After training the neural network, it can be used to generate outputs for inputs that it was not trained on.

In the following example, we train and simulate a neural network to estimate the MP4 energy of different chemical configurations of vinyl bromide. The vinyl dataset is derived from physical simulations relating to electron energies in molecules [15]. The vinyl dataset includes two variables:

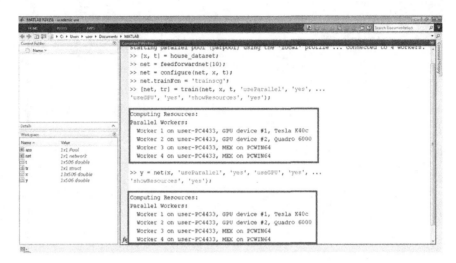

FIG. 5.18

Train and simulate neural networks on multiple CPU threads and GPUs.

- vinylInputs: a $16 \times 68,308$ array defining 16 attributes of 68,308 different chemical configurations of vinyl bromide. The first 15 attributes are bond distances defining the geometry of the chemical configuration, while that last attribute is the HF energy for the chemical configuration.
- vinylTargets: a $1 \times 68,308$ vector of each configuration's MP4 energy.

Function *trainNetworkSingleCPU1* (filename: trainNetworkSingleCPU1.m) is used to illustrate the preceding example in MATLAB. Note that we control the random number stream to reproduce the computations on all different versions of this function and thus make the comparisons fair. For the same reason, we use the scaled conjugate gradient method as the network training function because it is available both on the CPU and GPU implementations.

```
1.    function y = trainNetworkSingleCPU1(x, t)
2.    % Filename: trainNetworkSingleCPU1.m
3.    % Description: This function trains and simulates a neural
4.    % network (version where only one CPU thread is used)
5.    % Authors: Ploskas, N., & Samaras, N.
6.    % Syntax: y = trainNetworkSingleCPU1(x, t)
7.    % Input:
8.    %    -- x: network inputs (array)
9.    %    -- t: network targets (vector)
10.   % Output:
11.   %    -- y: network output (vector)
12.
13.   % control random number stream
14.   rs = RandStream('CombRecursive', 'NormalTransform', ...
```

```
15.        'Inversion', 'Seed', 4);
16.    RandStream.setGlobalStream(rs);
17.    % create a network using 100 nodes in the hidden layer
18.    net = feedforwardnet(100);
19.    % configure network inputs and outputs
20.    net = configure(net, x, t);
21.    % use the scaled conjugate gradient method
22.    net.trainFcn = 'trainscg';
23.    % train the neural network using only one CPU thread
24.    net = train(net, x, t);
25.    % simulate the neural network using only one CPU thread
26.    y = net(x);
27.    end
```

Initially, we measure the execution time of this function running on a single CPU thread:

```
>> [x, t] = vinyl_dataset;
>> tic; y = trainNetworkSingleCPU1(x, t); toc
Elapsed time is 87.876858 seconds.
```

To execute this function on the GPU, we should perform some changes to the code. We should set the *useGPU* option to *only* to execute the training and simulation of the neural network on the GPU.

Function *trainNetworkSingleGPU1* (filename: trainNetworkSingleGPU1.m) is used to illustrate the preceding example in MATLAB running on a single GPU.

```
1.     function y = trainNetworkSingleGPU1(x, t)
2.     % Filename: trainNetworkSingleGPU1.m
3.     % Description: This function trains and simulates a neural
4.     % network (version where only one GPU is used)
5.     % Authors: Ploskas, N., & Samaras, N.
6.     % Syntax: y = trainNetworkSingleGPU1(x, t)
7.     % Input:
8.     %    -- x: network inputs (array)
9.     %    -- t: network targets (vector)
10.    % Output:
11.    %    -- y: network output (vector)
12.
13.    % control random number stream
14.    rs = RandStream('CombRecursive', 'NormalTransform', ...
15.        'Inversion', 'Seed', 4);
16.    RandStream.setGlobalStream(rs);
17.    % create a network using 100 nodes in the hidden layer
18.    net = feedforwardnet(100);
19.    % configure network inputs and outputs
20.    net2 = configure(net, x, t);
21.    % use the scaled conjugate gradient method
22.    net2.trainFcn = 'trainscg';
23.    % train the neural network using only one GPU
24.    net2 = train(net2, x, t, 'useGPU','only');
25.    % simulate the neural network using only one GPU
```

```
26.   y = net2(x, 'useGPU', 'only');
27.   end
```

We measure the execution time of this function running on a single GPU:

```
>> [x, t] = vinyl_dataset;
>> gd = gpuDevice(); tic; y = trainNetworkSingleGPU1(x, t); wait(gd); toc
Elapsed time is 15.722446 seconds.
```

Hence, the neural network training and simulation function is running $\sim 5.60\times$ faster on the GPU.

Note that in the previous function the neural network data is automatically transferred on the GPU. Another option that may increase the performance of the neural network training and simulation is to transfer manually the data on the GPU using the *nndata2gpu* function, train and simulate the neural network without defining the *useGPU* option, and finally transfer the output back to the local workspace using the *gpu2nndata* function. Function *trainNetworkSingleGPU2* (filename: trainNetworkSingleGPU2.m) is used to illustrate this option running on a single GPU.

```
1.    function y = trainNetworkSingleGPU2(x, t)
2.    % Filename: trainNetworkSingleGPU2.m
3.    % Description: This function trains and simulates a neural
4.    % network (version where only one GPU is used and the data
5.    % is transferred back and forth between the main memory
6.    % and the GPU device using nndata2gpu and gpu2nndata functions)
7.    % Authors: Ploskas, N., & Samaras, N.
8.    % Syntax: y = trainNetworkSingleGPU2(x, t)
9.    % Input:
10.   %   -- x: network inputs (array)
11.   %   -- t: network targets (vector)
12.   % Output:
13.   %   -- y: network output (vector)
14.
15.   % control random number stream
16.   rs = RandStream('CombRecursive', 'NormalTransform', ...
17.       'Inversion', 'Seed', 4);
18.   RandStream.setGlobalStream(rs);
19.   % create a network using 100 nodes in the hidden layer
20.   net = feedforwardnet(100);
21.   % move data to the GPU
22.   gpuX = nndata2gpu(x);
23.   gpuT = nndata2gpu(t);
24.   % configure network inputs and outputs
25.   net2 = configure(net, x, t);
26.   % use the scaled conjugate gradient method
27.   net2.trainFcn = 'trainscg';
28.   % train the neural network using only one GPU
29.   net2 = train(net2, gpuX, gpuT);
30.   % simulate the neural network using only one GPU
31.   gpuY = net2(gpuX);
32.   % transfer output to local workspace
```

```
33.    y = gpu2nndata(gpuY);
34.    end
```

We measure the execution time of this function running on a single GPU:

```
>> [x, t] = vinyl_dataset;
>> gd = gpuDevice(); tic; y = trainNetworkSingleGPU2(x, t); wait(gd); toc
Elapsed time is 47.020221 seconds.
```

The neural network training and simulation function is running $\sim$3$\times$ slower on a single GPU by transferring manually the neural network data. So, it is not a good option on the specific dataset.

Another option that may increase the performance of the neural network training and simulation is to use the Elliot symmetric sigmoid transfer function. On GPUs and other hardware, it is often the case that the exponential function *exp* is not implemented with hardware, but with a software library. This can slow down neural networks that use the tansig sigmoid transfer function. Function *trainNetworkSingleCPU2* (filename: trainNetworkSingleCPU2.m) is used to illustrate this option running on a single CPU thread, while function *trainNetworkSingleGPU3* (filename: trainNetworkSingleGPU3.m) is used to illustrate this option running on a single GPU.

```
1.     function y = trainNetworkSingleCPU2(x, t)
2.     % Filename: trainNetworkSingleCPU2.m
3.     % Description: This function trains and simulates a neural
4.     % network (version where only one CPU thread is used and the
5.     % Elliot symmetric sigmoid transfer function is utilized)
6.     % Authors: Ploskas, N., & Samaras, N.
7.     % Syntax: y = trainNetworkSingleCPU2(x, t)
8.     % Input:
9.     %    -- x: network inputs (array)
10.    %    -- t: network targets (vector)
11.    % Output:
12.    %    -- y: network output (vector)
13.
14.    % control random number stream
15.    rs = RandStream('CombRecursive', 'NormalTransform', ...
16.        'Inversion', 'Seed', 4);
17.    RandStream.setGlobalStream(rs);
18.    % create a network using 100 nodes in the hidden layer
19.    net = feedforwardnet(100);
20.    % configure network inputs and outputs
21.    net = configure(net, x, t);
22.    % use the Elliot symmetric sigmoid transfer function
23.    for i = 1:net.numLayers
24.        if strcmp(net.layers{i}.transferFcn, 'tansig')
25.            net.layers{i}.transferFcn = 'elliotsig';
26.        end
27.    end
28.    % use the scaled conjugate gradient method
29.    net.trainFcn = 'trainscg';
30.    % train the neural network using only one CPU thread
```

```
31.  net = train(net, x, t);
32.  % simulate the neural network using only one CPU thread
33.  y = net(x);
34.  end
```

```
1.   function y = trainNetworkSingleGPU3(x, t)
2.   % Filename: trainNetworkSingleGPU3.m
3.   % Description: This function trains and simulates a neural
4.   % network (version where only one GPU is used and the
5.   % Elliot symmetric sigmoid transfer function is utilized)
6.   % Authors: Ploskas, N., & Samaras, N.
7.   % Syntax: y = trainNetworkSingleGPU3(x, t)
8.   % Input:
9.   %    -- x: network inputs (array)
10.  %    -- t: network targets (vector)
11.  % Output:
12.  %    -- y: network output (vector)
13.
14.  % control random number stream
15.  rs = RandStream('CombRecursive', 'NormalTransform', ...
16.      'Inversion', 'Seed', 4);
17.  RandStream.setGlobalStream(rs);
18.  % create a network using 100 nodes in the hidden layer
19.  net = feedforwardnet(100);
20.  % configure network inputs and outputs
21.  net2 = configure(net, x, t);
22.  % use the Elliot symmetric sigmoid transfer function
23.  for i = 1:net2.numLayers
24.      if strcmp(net2.layers{i}.transferFcn, 'tansig')
25.          net2.layers{i}.transferFcn = 'elliotsig';
26.      end
27.  end
28.  % use the scaled conjugate gradient method
29.  net2.trainFcn = 'trainscg';
30.  % train the neural network using only one GPU
31.  net2 = train(net2, x, t, 'useGPU','only');
32.  % simulate the neural network using only one GPU
33.  y = net2(x, 'useGPU', 'only');
34.  end
```

We measure the execution time of this function running on a single CPU thread:

```
>> [x, t] = vinyl_dataset;
>> tic; y = trainNetworkSingleCPU2(x, t); toc
Elapsed time is 51.591612 seconds.
```

The neural network training and simulation function is running ~1.70× faster on a single CPU thread by using the Elliot symmetric sigmoid transfer function. So, it is a good option on the specific dataset when executing the function on the CPU.

Let's also execute the function trainNetworkSingleGPU3 on a single GPU:

```
>> [x, t] = vinyl_dataset;
>> gd = gpuDevice(); tic; y = trainNetworkSingleGPU3(x, t); wait(gd); toc
Elapsed time is 13.381036 seconds.
```

The neural network training and simulation function is running ~1.20× faster on a single GPU by using the Elliot symmetric sigmoid transfer function. This function is also ~3.85× faster on a single GPU compared to the corresponding function running on a single CPU thread. So, it is a good option on the specific dataset when executing the function on the GPU.

Another option that may increase the performance of the neural network training and simulation is to use multiple GPUs. We implement the three versions of this example executed on a single GPU (*trainNetworkSingleGPU1*, *trainNetworkSingleGPU2*, and *trainNetworkSingleGPU3*). Function *trainNetwork-MultipleGPUs1* (filename: trainNetworkMultipleGPUs1.m) is equivalent to function *trainNetworkSingleGPU1*, function *trainNetworkMultipleGPUs2* (filename: train-NetworkMultipleGPUs2.m) is equivalent to function *trainNetworkSingleGPU2*, and function *trainNetworkMultipleGPUs3* (filename: trainNetworkMultipleGPUs3.m) is equivalent to function *trainNetworkSingleGPU3*. To execute these methods on multiple GPUs, we will open a parallel pool.

```
1.  function y = trainNetworkMultipleGPUs1(x, t)
2.  % Filename: trainNetworkMultipleGPUs1.m
3.  % Description: This function trains and simulates a neural
4.  % network (version where multiple GPUs are used)
5.  % Authors: Ploskas, N., & Samaras, N.
6.  % Syntax: y = trainNetworkMultipleGPUs1(x, t)
7.  % Input:
8.  %   -- x: network inputs (array)
9.  %   -- t: network targets (vector)
10. % Output:
11. %   -- y: network output (vector)
12.
13. % control random number stream
14. rs = RandStream('CombRecursive', 'NormalTransform', ...
15.     'Inversion', 'Seed', 4);
16. RandStream.setGlobalStream(rs);
17. % create a network using 100 nodes in the hidden layer
18. net = feedforwardnet(100);
19. % configure network inputs and outputs
20. net2 = configure(net, x, t);
21. % use the scaled conjugate gradient method
22. net2.trainFcn = 'trainscg';
23. % train the neural network using multiple GPUs
24. net2 = train(net2, x, t, 'useParallel', 'yes', 'useGPU', 'only');
25. % simulate the neural network using multiple GPUs
26. y = net2(x, 'useParallel', 'yes', 'useGPU', 'only');
27. end


1.  function y = trainNetworkMultipleGPUs2(x, t)
2.  % Filename: trainNetworkMultipleGPUs2.m
3.  % Description: This function trains and simulates a neural
4.  % network (version where multiple GPUs are used and the data
5.  % is transferred back and forth between the main memory
6.  % and the GPU device using nndata2gpu and gpu2nndata functions)
7.  % Authors: Ploskas, N., & Samaras, N.
8.  % Syntax: y = trainNetworkMultipleGPUs2(x, t)
9.  % Input:
```

```
10.  %    -- x: network inputs (array)
11.  %    -- t: network targets (vector)
12.  % Output:
13.  %    -- y: network output (vector)
14.
15.  % control random number stream
16.  rs = RandStream('CombRecursive', 'NormalTransform', ...
17.      'Inversion', 'Seed', 4);
18.  RandStream.setGlobalStream(rs);
19.  % create a network using 100 nodes in the hidden layer
20.  net = feedforwardnet(100);
21.  % move data to the GPU
22.  gpuX = Composite;
23.  gpuT = Composite;
24.  spmd
25.      if labindex <= 2
26.          gpuX = nndata2gpu(x);
27.          gpuT = nndata2gpu(t);
28.      end
29.  end
30.  % configure network inputs and outputs
31.  net2 = configure(net, x, t);
32.  % use the scaled conjugate gradient method
33.  net2.trainFcn = 'trainscg';
34.  % simulate the neural network using multiple GPUs
35.  net2 = train(net2, gpuX, gpuT, 'useParallel', 'yes', 'useGPU', 'only');
36.  % simulate the neural network using multiple GPUs
37.  gpuY = net2(gpuX, 'useParallel', 'yes', 'useGPU', 'only');
38.  % transfer output to local workspace
39.  y = gather(gpuY);
40.  end
```

```
1.   function y = trainNetworkMultipleGPUs3(x, t)
2.   % Filename: trainNetworkMultipleGPUs3.m
3.   % Description: This function trains and simulates a neural
4.   % network (version where multiple GPUs are used and the
5.   % Elliot symmetric sigmoid transfer function is utilized)
6.   % Authors: Ploskas, N., & Samaras, N.
7.   % Syntax: y = trainNetworkMultipleGPUs3(x, t)
8.   % Input:
9.   %    -- x: network inputs (array)
10.  %    -- t: network targets (vector)
11.  % Output:
12.  %    -- y: network output (vector)
13.
14.  % control random number stream
15.  rs = RandStream('CombRecursive', 'NormalTransform', ...
16.      'Inversion', 'Seed', 4);
17.  RandStream.setGlobalStream(rs);
18.  % create a network using 100 nodes in the hidden layer
19.  net = feedforwardnet(100);
20.  % configure network inputs and outputs
21.  net2 = configure(net, x, t);
22.  % use the Elliot symmetric sigmoid transfer function
23.  for i = 1:net2.numLayers
24.      if strcmp(net2.layers{i}.transferFcn, 'tansig')
```

```
25.          net2.layers{i}.transferFcn = 'elliotsig';
26.      end
27.  end
28.  % use the scaled conjugate gradient method
29.  net2.trainFcn = 'trainscg';
30.  % simulate the neural network using multiple GPUs
31.  net2 = train(net2, x, t, 'useParallel', 'yes', 'useGPU', 'only');
32.  % transfer output to local workspace using multiple GPUs
33.  y = net2(x, 'useParallel', 'yes', 'useGPU', 'only');
34.  end
```

We measure the execution time of these three functions running on two GPUs:

```
>> parpool('local', 2);
>> [x, t] = vinyl_dataset;
>> gd1 = gpuDevice(1); gd2 = gpuDevice(2); tic;
y = trainNetworkMultipleGPUs1(x, t); wait(gd1); wait(gd2); toc
Elapsed time is 12.232389 seconds.
>>
>> gd1 = gpuDevice(1); gd2 = gpuDevice(2); tic;
y = trainNetworkMultipleGPUs2(x, t); wait(gd1); wait(gd2); toc
Elapsed time is 91.731001 seconds.
>>
>> gd1 = gpuDevice(1); gd2 = gpuDevice(2); tic;
y = trainNetworkMultipleGPUs3(x, t); wait(gd1); wait(gd2); toc
Elapsed time is 11.670318 seconds.
```

Functions *trainNetworkMultipleGPUs1* and *trainNetworkMultipleGPUs3* are faster than the equivalent running on a single GPU (*trainNetworkSingleGPU1* and *trainNetworkSingleGPU3*), while function *trainNetworkMultipleGPUs2* is slower than function *trainNetworkSingleGPU2*.

Let's also measure the performance of the neural network training and simulation using multiple CPU threads and multiple GPUs. We implement the three versions of this example executed on a single GPU or multiple GPUs. Function *trainNetwork-MultipleCPUsGPUs1* (filename: trainNetworkMultipleCPUsGPUs1.m) is equivalent to function *trainNetworkSingleGPU1*, function *trainNetworkMultipleCPUsGPUs2* (filename: trainNetworkMultipleCPUsGPUs2.m) is equivalent to function *train-NetworkSingleGPU2*, and function *trainNetworkMultipleCPUsGPUs3* (filename: trainNetworkMultipleCPUsGPUs3.m) is equivalent to function *trainNetworkSin-gleGPU3*. To execute these methods on multiple CPU threads and multiple GPUs, we will open a parallel pool.

```
1.   function y = trainNetworkMultipleCPUsGPUs1(x, t)
2.   % Filename: trainNetworkMultipleCPUsGPUs1.m
3.   % Description: This function trains and simulates a neural
4.   % network (version where multiple CPU threads and GPUs
5.   % are used)
6.   % Authors: Ploskas, N., & Samaras, N.
7.   % Syntax: y = trainNetworkMultipleCPUsGPUs1(x, t)
8.   % Input:
9.   %    -- x: network inputs (array)
10.  %    -- t: network targets (vector)
```

```
11.  % Output:
12.  %   -- y: network output (vector)
13.
14.  % control random number stream
15.  rs = RandStream('CombRecursive', 'NormalTransform', ...
16.       'Inversion', 'Seed', 4);
17.  RandStream.setGlobalStream(rs);
18.  % create a network using 100 nodes in the hidden layer
19.  net = feedforwardnet(100);
20.  % configure network inputs and outputs
21.  net2 = configure(net, x, t);
22.  % use the scaled conjugate gradient method
23.  net2.trainFcn = 'trainscg';
24.  % train the neural network using multiple CPU threads and GPUs
25.  net2 = train(net2, x, t, 'useParallel', 'yes', 'useGPU', 'yes');
26.  % transfer output to local workspace using multiple CPU threads and GPUs
27.  y = net2(x, 'useParallel', 'yes', 'useGPU', 'yes');
28.  end


1.   function y = trainNetworkMultipleCPUsGPUs2(x, t)
2.   % Filename: trainNetworkMultipleCPUsGPUs2.m
3.   % Description: This function trains and simulates a neural
4.   % network (version where multiple CPU threads and GPUs
5.   % are used and the data is transferred back and forth
6.   % between the main memory and the GPU device using
7.   % nndata2gpu and gpu2nndata functions)
8.   % Authors: Ploskas, N., & Samaras, N.
9.   % Syntax: y = trainNetworkMultipleCPUsGPUs2(x, t)
10.  % Input:
11.  %   -- x: network inputs (array)
12.  %   -- t: network targets (vector)
13.  % Output:
14.  %   -- y: network output (vector)
15.
16.  % control random number stream
17.  rs = RandStream('CombRecursive', 'NormalTransform', ...
18.       'Inversion', 'Seed', 4);
19.  RandStream.setGlobalStream(rs);
20.  % create a network using 100 nodes in the hidden layer
21.  net = feedforwardnet(100);
22.  % move data to the GPU
23.  gpuX = Composite;
24.  gpuT = Composite;
25.  spmd
26.      if labindex <= 2
27.          gpuX = nndata2gpu(x);
28.          gpuT = nndata2gpu(t);
29.      end
30.  end
31.  % configure network inputs and outputs
32.  net2 = configure(net, x, t);
33.  % use the scaled conjugate gradient method
34.  net2.trainFcn = 'trainscg';
35.  % train the neural network using multiple CPU threads and GPUs
36.  net2 = train(net2, x, t, 'useParallel', 'yes', 'useGPU', 'yes');
37.  % transfer output to local workspace using multiple CPU threads and GPUs
38.  gpuY = net2(x, 'useParallel', 'yes', 'useGPU', 'yes');
39.  % transfer output to local workspace
```

```
40.   y = gather(gpuY);
41.   end

1.    function y = trainNetworkMultipleCPUsGPUs3(x, t)
2.    % Filename: trainNetworkMultipleCPUsGPUs3.m
3.    % Description: This function trains and simulates a neural
4.    % network (version where multiple CPU threads and GPUs
5.    % are used and the Elliot symmetric sigmoid transfer
6.    % function is utilized)
7.    % Authors: Ploskas, N., & Samaras, N.
8.    % Syntax: trainNetworkMultipleCPUsGPUs3(x, t)
9.    % Input:
10.   %  -- x: network inputs (array)
11.   %  -- t: network targets (vector)
12.   % Output:
13.   %  -- y: network output (vector)
14.
15.   % control random number stream
16.   rs = RandStream('CombRecursive', 'NormalTransform', ...
17.       'Inversion', 'Seed', 4);
18.   RandStream.setGlobalStream(rs);
19.   % create a network using 100 nodes in the hidden layer
20.   net = feedforwardnet(100);
21.   % configure network inputs and outputs
22.   net2 = configure(net, x, t);
23.   % use the Elliot symmetric sigmoid transfer function
24.   for i = 1:net2.numLayers
25.       if strcmp(net2.layers{i}.transferFcn, 'tansig')
26.           net2.layers{i}.transferFcn = 'elliotsig';
27.       end
28.   end
29.   % use the scaled conjugate gradient method
30.   net2.trainFcn = 'trainscg';
31.   % train the neural network using multiple CPU threads and GPUs
32.   net2 = train(net2, x, t, 'useParallel', 'yes', 'useGPU', 'yes');
33.   % transfer output to local workspace using multiple CPU threads and GPUs
34.   y = net2(x, 'useParallel', 'yes', 'useGPU', 'yes');
35.   end
```

We measure the execution time of these three functions running on two CPU threads and two GPUs:

```
>> parpool('local', 4);
>> [x, t] = vinyl_dataset;
>> gd1 = gpuDevice(1); gd2 = gpuDevice(2); tic;
y = trainNetworkMultipleCPUsGPUs1(x, t); wait(gd1); wait(gd2); toc
Elapsed time is 29.563011 seconds.
>>
>> gd1 = gpuDevice(1); gd2 = gpuDevice(2); tic;
y = trainNetworkMultipleCPUsGPUs2(x, t); wait(gd1); wait(gd2); toc
Elapsed time is 30.136026 seconds.
>>
>> gd1 = gpuDevice(1); gd2 = gpuDevice(2); tic;
y = trainNetworkMultipleCPUsGPUs3(x, t); wait(gd1); wait(gd2); toc
Elapsed time is 13.594115 seconds.
```

Functions *trainNetworkMultipleCPUsGPUs1* and *trainNetworkMultipleCPUs GPUs3* are slower than the equivalent running on a single GPU (*train-NetworkSingleGPU1* and *trainNetworkSingleGPU3*) or on multiple GPUs (*trainNetworkMultipleGPUs1* and *trainNetworkMultipleGPUs3*), while function *trainNetworkMultipleCPUsGPUs2* is faster than functions *trainNetworkSingleGPU2* and *trainNetworkMultipleGPUs2*.

To conclude, we started with using one CPU thread to train and simulate a large neural network and explored various alternatives to improve the performance using a single GPU, multiple GPUs, and multiple CPU threads and GPUs. The initial version of this function (*trainNetworkSingleCPU1* using one single CPU thread) was executed on 87.876858 seconds, while the best version of this function (*trainNetworkMultipleGPUs3* using multiple GPUs and the Elliot symmetric sigmoid transfer function) was executed on 11.670318 seconds. Hence, we achieved a speedup of ~7.50×.

5.4 PHASED ARRAY SYSTEM TOOLBOX

The Phased Array System Toolbox provides algorithms and applications for the design, simulation, and analysis of sensor array systems in radar, sonar, wireless communications, and medical imaging applications. It includes pulsed and continuous waveforms and signal processing algorithms for beamforming, matched filtering, direction of arrival estimation, and target detection. It also includes models for transmitters and receivers, propagation, targets, jammers, and clutter.

The Phased Array System Toolbox lets users model the dynamics of ground-based, airborne, or ship-borne multifunction radar systems with moving targets and platforms. Users can design end-to-end phased array systems and analyze their performance under different scenarios using synthetic or acquired data.

The Phased Array System Toolbox provides the ConstantGammaClutter System object that can perform constant gamma clutter simulation both on the CPU (using the *phased.ConstantGammaClutter* System object) and on the GPU (using the *phased.gpu.ConstantGammaClutter* System object). To compute the clutter return, you should:

(1) Define and set up a clutter simulator.
(2) Call *step* to simulate the clutter return for your system according to the properties of *phased.gpu.ConstantGammaClutter*.

The clutter simulation is based on the following assumptions [16]:

(1) The radar system is monostatic.
(2) The propagation is in free space.
(3) The terrain is homogeneous.
(4) The clutter patch is stationary during the coherence time. Coherence time indicates how frequently the software changes the set of random numbers in the clutter simulation.

(5) The signal is narrowband. Thus, the spatial response can be approximated by a phase shift. Similarly, the Doppler shift can be approximated by a phase shift.

(6) The radar system maintains a constant height during simulation.

(7) The radar system maintains a constant speed during simulation.

A GPU ConstantGammaClutter object is constructed using the following syntax:

```
H = phased.gpu.ConstantGammaClutter
H = phased.gpu.ConstantGammaClutter(Name, Value)
```

The first variant creates a constant gamma clutter simulation System object, *H*, which simulates the clutter return of a monostatic radar system using the constant gamma model, while the second variant creates a constant gamma clutter simulation object, *H*, with additional options specified by one or more *Name, Value* pairs. The options that are available:

(1) *Sensor*: Specify the sensor as an antenna element object or as an array object whose *Element* property value is an antenna element object. If the sensor is an array, it can contain subarrays. The default value is a *phased.ULA* System object with default property values.

(2) *PropagationSpeed*: Specify the propagation speed of the signal, in meters per second, as a positive scalar. The default value is the speed of light.

(3) *OperatingFrequency*: Specify the operating frequency of the system in hertz as a positive scalar. The default value is 300 MHz ($3e8$).

(4) *SampleRate*: Specify the sample rate, in hertz, as a positive scalar. The default value is 1 MHz ($1e6$).

(5) *PRF*: Specify the pulse repetition frequency in hertz as a positive scalar or a row vector. When PRF is a vector, it represents a staggered PRF. In this case, the output pulses use elements in the vector as their PRFs, one after another, in a cycle. The default value is 10 kHz ($1e4$).

(6) *Gamma*: Specify the γ value used in the constant γ clutter model, as a scalar in decibels. The γ value depends on both terrain type and the operating frequency. The default value is 0.

(7) *EarthModel*: Specify the earth model used in clutter simulation as one of: (i) *Flat* (the earth is assumed to be a flat plane), or (ii) *Curved* (the earth is assumed to be a sphere). The default value is *Flat*.

(8) *PlatformHeight*: Specify the radar platform height in meters measured upward from the surface as a nonnegative scalar. The default value is 300.

(9) *PlatformSpeed*: Specify the radar platform speed as a nonnegative scalar in meters per second. The default value is 300.

(10) *PlatformDirection*: Specify the direction of the radar platform motion as a 2-by-1 vector in the form *[AzimuthAngle; ElevationAngle]* in degrees. The default value is *[90; 0]* and indicates that the platform moves perpendicular to the radar antenna array's broadside. Both azimuth and elevation angles are measured in the local coordinate system of the radar antenna or antenna array.

Azimuth angle must be between −180 and 180 degrees and elevation angle must be between −90 and 90 degrees.

(11) *BroadsideDepressionAngle*: Specify the depression angle in degrees of the broadside of the radar antenna array. This value is a scalar. The broadside is defined as zero degrees azimuth and zero degrees elevation. The depression angle is measured downward from horizontal. The default value is 0.

(12) *MaximumRange*: Specify the maximum range in meters for the clutter simulation as a positive scalar. The maximum range must be greater than the value specified in the *PlatformHeight* property. The default value is 5000.

(13) *AzimuthCoverage*: Specify the azimuth coverage in degrees as a positive scalar. The clutter simulation covers a region having the specified azimuth span, symmetric to 0 degrees azimuth. Typically, all clutter patches have their azimuth centers within the region, but the *PatchAzimuthWidth* value can cause some patches to extend beyond the region. The default value is 60.

(14) *PatchAzimuthWidth*: Specify the azimuth span of each clutter patch in degrees as a positive scalar. The default value is 1.

(15) *TransmitSignalInputPort*: Set this property to *true* to add input to specify the transmit signal in the *step* function. Set this property to *false* to omit the transmit signal in the *step* function. The *false* option is less computationally expensive; to use this option, you must also specify the *TransmitERP* property. The default value is *false*.

(16) *TransmitERP*: Specify the transmitted effective radiated power of the radar system in watts as a positive scalar. This property applies only when you set the *TransmitSignalInputPort* property to *false*. The default value is 5000.

(17) *CoherenceTime*: Specify the coherence time in seconds for the clutter simulation as a positive scalar. After the coherence time elapses, the *step* method updates the random numbers it uses for the clutter simulation at the next pulse. A value of *Inf* means the random numbers are never updated. The default value is *Inf*.

(18) *OutputFormat*: Specify the format of the output signal as one of: (i) *Pulses* (the output of the *step* method is in the form of multiple pulses and the number of pulses is the value of the *NumPulses* property), or (ii) *Samples* (the output of the *step* method is in the form of multiple samples and the number of samples is the value of the *NumSamples* property). In staggered PRF applications, you might find the *Samples* option more convenient because the *step* output always has the same matrix size. The default value is *Pulses*.

(19) *NumPulses*: Specify the number of pulses in the output of the *step* method as a positive integer. This property applies only when you set the *OutputFormat* property equal to *Pulses*. The default value is 1.

(20) *NumSamples*: Specify the number of samples in the output of the *step* method as a positive integer. Typically, you use the number of samples in one pulse.

This property applies only when you set the *OutputFormat* property equal to *Samples*. The default value is 100.

(21) *SeedSource*: Specify how the object generates random numbers as one of: (i) *Auto* (random numbers come from the global GPU random number stream), or (ii) *Property* (random numbers come from a private stream of random numbers). The default value is *Auto*.

(22) *Seed*: Specify the seed for the random number generator as a scalar integer between 0 and $2^{32} - 1$. This property applies when you set the *SeedSource* property equal to *Property*. The default value is 0.

Example: Clutter simulation of a radar system

Surface clutter refers to reflections of a radar signal from land, sea, or the land-sea interface. For a radar system, clutter refers to the received echoes from environmental scatters other than targets, such as land, sea, or rain. Clutter echoes can be many orders of magnitude larger than target echoes.

In the following example, we simulate the clutter return from terrain with a gamma value of 0 dB of a radar system with known power (5 kw). The radar system has a 4-element Uniform Linear Array (ULA). The sample rate is 1 MHz, and the Pulse Repetition Frequency (PRF) is 10 kHz. The propagation speed is 300,000 km/s, and the operating frequency is 300 MHz. The radar platform is flying 2 km above the ground with a path parallel to the ground along the array axis. The platform speed is 1,000 m/s. The mainlobe has a depression angle of 30 degrees. The configuration assumes that the earth is flat. The maximum clutter range of interest is 10 km, and the maximum azimuth coverage is $+/-60$ degrees. Finally, we simulate the clutter return for 1,000 pulses.

Function *constantGammaClutterCPU* (filename: constantGammaClutterCPU.m) is used to illustrate the preceding example in MATLAB.

```
1.   function constantGammaClutterCPU
2.   % Filename: constantGammaClutterCPU.m
3.   % Description: This function simulates the clutter return
4.   % of a system with known power using the constant gamma model
5.   % (version where the CPU is used)
6.   % Authors: Ploskas, N., & Samaras, N.
7.   % Syntax: constantGammaClutterCPU
8.   % Input: none
9.   % Output: a figure with the angle-Doppler response of the clutter
10.
11.  % set up the characteristics of the radar system
12.  nOfElements = 4; % number of elements
13.  propSpeed = 3e8; % propagation speed
14.  opFreq = 3e8; % operating frequency
15.  % create the uniform linear array with the above attributes
16.  ula = phased.ULA('NumElements', nOfElements, 'ElementSpacing', ...
17.      (propSpeed / opFreq) / 2);
18.  sampleRate = 1e6; % sample rate
19.  prf = 10e3; % pulse repetition frequency
20.  height = 2000; % radar platform height from surface
21.  direction = [90; 0]; % direction of radar platform motion
```

```
22.   speed = 1000; % radar platform speed
23.   depAngle = 30; % depression angle of array broadside
24.   rMax = 10000; % maximum range for clutter simulation
25.   azCov = 120; % azimuth coverage for clutter simulation
26.   terGamma = 0; % terrain gamma value
27.   tPower = 5000; % effective transmitted power
28.   % create the clutter simulation object
29.   clutter = phased.ConstantGammaClutter('Sensor', ula, ...
30.       'PropagationSpeed', propSpeed, 'OperatingFrequency', opFreq, ...
31.       'PRF', prf, 'SampleRate', sampleRate, 'Gamma', terGamma, ...
32.       'EarthModel', 'Flat', 'TransmitERP', tPower, ...
33.       'PlatformHeight', height, 'PlatformSpeed', speed, ...
34.       'PlatformDirection', direction, ...
35.       'BroadsideDepressionAngle', depAngle, 'MaximumRange', rMax, ...
36.       'AzimuthCoverage', azCov, 'SeedSource', 'Property', 'Seed', 10000);
37.   % simulate the clutter return for 1000 pulses
38.   nOfSamples = sampleRate / prf; % number of samples
39.   nOfPulses = 1000; % number of pulses
40.   % initialize collected clutter return
41.   y = zeros(nOfSamples, nOfElements, nOfPulses);
42.   % compute the collected clutter return for each pulse
43.   for m = 1:nOfPulses
44.       y(:, :, m) = step(clutter);
45.   end
46.   % plot the angle-Doppler response of the clutter at the 20th range bin
47.   hresp = phased.AngleDopplerResponse('SensorArray', ula, ...
48.       'OperatingFrequency', opFreq, 'PropagationSpeed', propSpeed, ...
49.       'PRF', prf);
50.   plotResponse(hresp, shiftdim(y(20, :, :)), 'NormalizeDoppler', true);
51.   end
```

Initially, we measure the execution time of this function running on the CPU:

```
>> tic; constantGammaClutterCPU; toc
Elapsed time is 28.728894 seconds.
```

To execute this function on the GPU, we should perform only one change to the code. The clutter simulation object is created with the *phased.gpu.ConstantGamma Clutter* system object.

Function *constantGammaClutterGPU* (filename: constantGammaClutterGPU.m) is used to illustrate the preceding example in MATLAB running on the GPU.

```
1.    function constantGammaClutterGPU
2.    % Filename: constantGammaClutterGPU.m
3.    % Description: This function simulates the clutter return
4.    % of a system with known power using the constant gamma model
5.    % (version where the GPU is used)
6.    % Authors: Ploskas, N., & Samaras, N.
7.    % Syntax: constantGammaClutterGPU
8.    % Input: none
9.    % Output: a figure with the angle-Doppler response of the clutter
10.
11.   % set up the characteristics of the radar system
12.   nOfElements = 4; % number of elements
13.   propSpeed = 3e8; % propagation speed
14.   opFreq = 3e8; % operating frequency
15.   % create the uniform linear array with the above attributes
```

```
16.  ula = phased.ULA('NumElements', nOfElements, 'ElementSpacing', ...
17.      (propSpeed / opFreq) / 2);
18.  sampleRate = 1e6; % sample rate
19.  prf = 10e3; % pulse repetition frequency
20.  height = 2000; % radar platform height from surface
21.  direction = [90; 0]; % direction of radar platform motion
22.  speed = 1000; % radar platform speed
23.  depAngle = 30; % depression angle of array broadside
24.  rMax = 10000; % maximum range for clutter simulation
25.  azCov = 120; % azimuth coverage for clutter simulation
26.  terGamma = 0; % terrain gamma value
27.  tPower = 5000; % effective transmitted power
28.  % create the clutter simulation object
29.  clutter = phased.gpu.ConstantGammaClutter('Sensor', ula, ...
30.      'PropagationSpeed', propSpeed, 'OperatingFrequency', opFreq, ...
31.      'PRF', prf, 'SampleRate', sampleRate, 'Gamma', terGamma, ...
32.      'EarthModel', 'Flat', 'TransmitERP', tPower, ...
33.      'PlatformHeight', height, 'PlatformSpeed', speed, ...
34.      'PlatformDirection', direction, ...
35.      'BroadsideDepressionAngle', depAngle, 'MaximumRange', rMax, ...
36.      'AzimuthCoverage', azCov, 'SeedSource', 'Property', 'Seed', 10000);
37.  % simulate the clutter return for 1000 pulses
38.  nOfSamples = sampleRate / prf; % number of samples
39.  nOfPulses = 1000; % number of pulses
40.  % initialize collected clutter return
41.  y = zeros(nOfSamples, nOfElements, nOfPulses);
42.  % compute the collected clutter return for each pulse
43.  for m = 1:nOfPulses
44.      y(:, :, m) = step(clutter);
45.  end
46.  % plot the angle-Doppler response of the clutter at the 20th range bin
47.  hresp = phased.AngleDopplerResponse('SensorArray', ula, ...
48.      'OperatingFrequency', opFreq, 'PropagationSpeed', propSpeed, ...
49.      'PRF', prf);
50.  plotResponse(hresp, shiftdim(y(20, :, :)), 'NormalizeDoppler', true);
51.  end
```

We measure the execution time of this function running on the GPU:

```
>> gd = gpuDevice(); tic; constantGammaClutterGPU; wait(gd); toc
Elapsed time is 5.212692 seconds.
```

Hence, the clutter simulation function is running $\sim 5.50\times$ faster on the GPU.

Fig. 5.19 shows the result of the clutter simulation function, that is, the angle-Doppler response of the clutter at the 20th range bin.

5.5 SIGNAL PROCESSING TOOLBOX

The Signal Processing Toolbox provides functions and applications to generate, measure, transform, filter, and visualize signals. The Signal Processing Toolbox includes algorithms for resampling, smoothing and synchronizing signals, designing and analyzing filters, estimating power spectra, and measuring peaks, bandwidth, and distortion. The Signal Processing Toolbox also includes parametric and linear

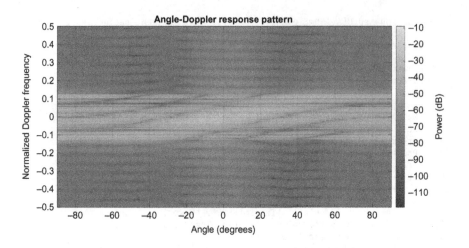

FIG. 5.19

Result of the clutter simulation function.

predictive modeling algorithms. Users can use the Signal Processing Toolbox to analyze and compare signals in time, frequency, and time-frequency domains; identify patterns and trends; extract features; and develop and validate custom algorithms to gain insight into their data.

The Signal Processing Toolbox provides some GPU-enabled functions. To use these functions on a GPU, you can apply the following steps:

- Transfer data, for example, a signal, from the CPU to the GPU by creating *gpuArray* objects.
- Perform the corresponding operation on the GPU by using the GPU-enabled functions that accept a *gpuArray* object.
- Transfer data back to the CPU from the GPU using the *gather* function.

As of MATLAB R2015b, Table 5.2 lists all the Signal Processing Toolbox functions that have been enabled to run on a GPU.

Example: Filter signal using circular convolution

Convolution is a mathematical operation on two functions, producing a third one that is typically viewed as a modified version of one of the original functions. Convolution is a common operation in signal and image processing applications. In electronic music, convolution is the imposition of a spectral or rhythmic structure on a sound. The convolution of two signals is the filtering of one through the other.

In the following example, we perform linear convolution using the *cconv* method (circular convolution) on a signal using a low-pass FIR filter. The signal is an audio file with 10,584,064 samples.

Table 5.2 GPU-enabled functions on the Signal Processing Toolbox

Function	Description
xcorr	Calculate the autocorrelation sequence of a discrete-time sequence or the cross-correlation of two discrete-time sequences.
xcorr2	Compute the cross-correlation of two matrices.
fftfilt	Filter data using the efficient FFT-based method of overlap-add.
xcov	Calculate the autocovariance sequence of a discrete-time sequence or the cross-covariance of two discrete-time sequences.
cconv	Convolve two discrete Fourier transform sequences.

Function *circularConvolution* (filename: circularConvolution.m) is used to illustrate the preceding example in MATLAB.

```
1.    function filteredData = circularConvolution(data, filter)
2.    % Filename: circularConvolution.m
3.    % Description: This function performs linear convolution
4.    % using the cconv method (circular convolution) on a signal
5.    % (array data) using a filter (vector filter)
6.    % Authors: Ploskas, N., & Samaras, N.
7.    % Syntax: filteredData = circularConvolution(data, filter)
8.    % Input:
9.    %    -- data: the signal (array)
10.   %    -- filter: the filter (vector)
11.   % Output:
12.   %    -- filteredData: the filtered signal (array)
13.
14.   filteredData = cconv(data, filter, length(data) + length(filter) -1);
15.   end
```

Initially, we measure the execution time of this function running on the CPU using a 10,584,064 × 1 signal and a 20 × 1 filter:

```
>> load circularConvolutionData
>> tic; filteredData = circularConvolution(data, filter); toc
Elapsed time is 2.334759 seconds.
```

To execute this function on the GPU, we do not have to perform any changes to the code because all functions and operators used are GPU-enabled. The only difference is that we should pass a *gpuArray* as input to that function. We measure the execution time of this function running on the GPU using the same data:

```
>> load circularConvolutionData
>> tic; filteredData = circularConvolution(gpuArray(data), gpuArray(filter));
wait(gd); toc
Elapsed time is 0.156799 seconds.
```

Hence, the circular convolution function is running ~15× faster on the GPU.

5.6 STATISTICS AND MACHINE LEARNING TOOLBOX

The Statistics and Machine Learning Toolbox provides functions and applications to describe, analyze, and model data using statistics and machine learning. You can use descriptive statistics and plots for exploratory data analysis, fit probability distributions to data, generate random numbers for Monte Carlo simulations, and perform hypothesis tests. Regression and classification algorithms let you draw inferences from data and build predictive models.

For analyzing multidimensional data, the Statistics and Machine Learning Toolbox lets users identify key variables or features that impact their model with sequential feature selection, stepwise regression, principal component analysis, regularization, and other dimensionality reduction methods. The Statistics and Machine Learning Toolbox provides supervised and unsupervised machine learning algorithms, including support vector machines (SVMs), boosted and bagged decision trees, k-nearest neighbor, k-means, k-medoids, hierarchical clustering, Gaussian mixture models, and hidden Markov models.

The Statistics and Machine Learning Toolbox provides many GPU-enabled functions. To use these functions on a GPU, you can apply the following steps:

- Transfer data from the CPU to the GPU by creating *gpuArray* objects.
- Perform the corresponding operation on the GPU by using the GPU-enabled functions that accept a *gpuArray* object.
- Transfer data back to the CPU from the GPU using the *gather* function.

As of MATLAB R2015b, Table 5.3 lists all the Statistics and Machine Learning Toolbox functions that have been enabled to run on a GPU.

Example: Estimation of descriptive statistics measures using the Monte Carlo method

The Monte Carlo method is a numerical integration method using sampling, which can be used to determine the descriptive statistics measures of a random variable, such as the mean, standard deviation, skewness, kurtosis, and percentiles. We can generate random numbers from a probability distribution and estimate the descriptive statistics measures of a variable. By the law of large numbers, their convergence to the real values is assured as the sample size tends to infinity.

In the following example, we use the Monte Carlo method to estimate the descriptive statistics measures (mean, standard deviation, skewness, kurtosis, and percentiles) of the random variable r knowing that $r = 2 \times x + y \times z - w$ and that x, y, z, and w are distributed lognormally with $\mu_x = 20$, $\delta_x = 0.2$, $\mu_y = 30$, $\delta_y = 0.3$, $\mu_z = 40$, $\delta_z = 0.4$, $\mu_w = 50$, and $\delta_w = 0.5$.

Function *statistics* (filename: statistics.m) is used to illustrate the preceding example in MATLAB.

```
1.   function [m, s, sk, k, p50, p95] = statistics(n, mux, sigmax, ...
2.      muy, sigmay, muz, sigmaz, muw, sigmaw)
3.   % Filename: statistics.m
```

Table 5.3 GPU-enabled functions on the Statistics and Machine Learning Toolbox

Function	Description
betacdf	Perform the beta cumulative distribution function at each of the values in a vector.
betainv	Compute the inverse of the beta cumulative distribution function.
betapdf	Perform the beta probability density function at each of the values in a vector.
betastat	Calculate the mean of and variance for the beta distribution.
binofit	Compute a maximum likelihood estimate of the probability of success in a given binomial trial based on the number of successes observed in independent trials.
binoinv	Calculate the smallest integer such that the binomial cumulative distribution function evaluated is equal to or exceeds a given number.
binopdf	Compute the binomial probability density function at each of the values in a vector.
binornd	Generate random numbers from the binomial distribution.
binostat	Calculate the mean of and variance for the binomial distribution.
chi2cdf	Perform the chi-square cumulative distribution function at each of the values in a vector.
chi2gof	Compute a test decision for the null hypothesis that the data in a vector comes from a normal distribution with a mean and variance estimated from the vector, using the chi-square goodness-of-fit test.
chi2inv	Compute the inverse of the chi-square cumulative distribution function.
chi2stat	Calculate the mean of and variance for the chi-square distribution.
cholcov	Perform Cholesky-like covariance decomposition.
corrcov	Convert a covariance matrix to a correlation matrix.
expcdf	Perform the exponential cumulative distribution function at each of the values in a vector.
expfit	Estimate the mean of an exponentially distributed sample.
expinv	Compute the inverse of the exponential cumulative distribution function.
explike	Calculate the negative of the log-likelihood for the exponential distribution.
exppdf	Compute the probability density function of the exponential distribution.
exprnd	Generate random numbers from the exponential distribution.
expstat	Calculate the mean of and variance for the exponential distribution.
fcdf	Perform the F cumulative distribution function at each of the values in a vector.
finv	Compute the inverse of the F cumulative distribution function.
fstat	Calculate the mean of and variance for the exponential distribution.
gamcdf	Perform the gamma distribution function at each of the values in a vector.
gaminv	Compute the inverse of the gamma cumulative distribution function.
gamlike	Calculate the negative of the log-likelihood for the gamma distribution.
gampdf	Compute the probability density function of the gamma distribution.
gamstat	Calculate the mean of and variance for the gamma distribution.

Continued

Table 5.3 GPU-enabled functions on the Statistics and Machine Learning Toolbox—cont'd

Function	Description
geocdf	Perform the geometric cumulative distribution function at each of the values in a vector.
geoinv	Compute the inverse of the geometric cumulative distribution function.
geomean	Calculate the geometric mean of a sample.
geopdf	Compute the probability density function of the geometric distribution.
geornd	Generate random numbers from the geometric distribution.
geostat	Calculate the mean of and variance for the geometric distribution.
harmmean	Calculate the harmonic mean of a sample.
iqr	Compute the interquartile range for a ProbDistUnivKernel object.
kurtosis	Calculate the sample kurtosis.
logncdf	Perform the lognormal cumulative distribution function at each of the values in a vector.
lognfit	Calculate a vector of maximum likelihood estimates for a lognormal distribution fitting data.
logninv	Compute the inverse of the lognormal cumulative distribution function.
lognlike	Calculate the negative of the log-likelihood for the lognormal distribution.
lognpdf	Compute the probability density function of the lognormal distribution.
lognrnd	Generate random numbers from the lognormal distribution.
lognstat	Calculate the mean of and variance for the lognormal distribution.
mad	Find the mean absolute deviation of the values in a vector or array.
moment	Compute the central sample moment of a vector or array.
mvncdf	Compute the cumulative probability of the multivariate normal distribution with zero mean and identity covariance matrix, evaluated at each row of a matrix.
mvnpdf	Compute the probability density function of the multivariate normal distribution.
mvnrnd	Generate random numbers from the multivariate normal distribution.
nanmax	Find the maximum element after removing NaN values.
nanmean	Calculate the mean of a sample after removing NaN values.
nanmedian	Compute the median of a sample after removing NaN values.
nanmin	Find the minimum element after removing NaN values.
nanstd	Calculate the standard deviation of a sample after removing NaN values.
nansum	Compute the sum of a sample after removing NaN values.
nanvar	Calculate the variance of a sample after removing NaN values.
normcdf	Perform the standard normal cumulative distribution function at each of the values in a vector.
norminv	Compute the inverse of the normal cumulative distribution function.
normlike	Calculate the negative of the log-likelihood for the normal distribution.
normpdf	Compute the probability density function of the normal distribution.
normrnd	Generate random numbers from the normal distribution.

Table 5.3 GPU-enabled functions on the Statistics and Machine Learning Toolbox—cont'd

Function	Description
normstat	Calculate the mean of and variance for the normal distribution.
poisscdf	Perform the Poisson cumulative distribution function at each of the values in a vector.
poissinv	Calculate the smallest integer such that the Poisson cumulative distribution function evaluated is equal to or exceeds a given number.
poisspdf	Compute the probability density function of the Poisson distribution.
poisstat	Calculate the mean of and variance for the Poisson distribution.
prctile	Compute percentiles of the values in a data vector or matrix.
quantile	Calculate quantiles of the values in a data vector or matrix.
range	Compute the difference between the maximum and the minimum of a sample.
raylcdf	Perform the Rayleigh cumulative distribution function at each of the values in a vector.
raylfit	Calculate the maximum likelihood estimates of the parameter of the Rayleigh distribution given the data in a vector.
raylinv	Compute the inverse of the Rayleigh cumulative distribution function.
raylpdf	Compute the probability density function of the Rayleigh distribution.
raylrnd	Generate random numbers from the Rayleigh distribution.
raylstat	Calculate the mean of and variance for the Rayleigh distribution.
skewness	Compute the sample skewness of a vector or array.
tcdf	Perform the student's t cumulative distribution function at each of the values in a vector.
tinv	Compute the inverse of the student's t cumulative distribution function.
tpdf	Compute the probability density function of the student's t distribution.
tstat	Calculate the mean of and variance for the student's t distribution.
ttest	Perform the one-sample and paired-sample t-test.
ttest2	Perform the two-sample t-test.
trimmean	Calculate the trimmed mean of a sample.
unidcdf	Perform the discrete uniform cumulative distribution function at each of the values in a vector.
unidinv	Calculate the smallest integer such that the discrete uniform cumulative distribution function evaluated is equal to or exceeds a given number.
unidpdf	Compute the probability density function of the discrete uniform distribution.
unidrnd	Generate random numbers from the discrete uniform distribution.
unidstat	Calculate the mean of and variance for the discrete uniform distribution.
unifinv	Compute the inverse of the uniform cumulative distribution function.
unifrnd	Generate random numbers from the continuous uniform distribution.
unifstat	Calculate the mean of and variance for the continuous uniform distribution.
vartest	Perform the chi-square variance test.
vartest2	Perform the two-sample F-test for equal variances.
zscore	Compute the standardized z-scores.
ztest	Perform the z-test.

```
4.    % Description: This function creates four random variables
5.    % (x, y, z, w) from the lognormal distribution and calculates the
6.    % mean, standard deviation, skewness, kurtosis, 50th and 95th
7.    % percentiles of r = 2 * x + y .* z - w
8.    % Authors: Ploskas, N., & Samaras, N.
9.    % Syntax: [m, s, sk, k, p50, p95] = statistics(n, mux, sigmax, ...
10.   %    muy, sigmay, muz, sigmaz, muw, sigmaw)
11.   % Input:
12.   %    -- n: the number of random elements for each variable
13.   %    -- mux: the mean of variable x
14.   %    -- sigmax: the standard deviation of variable x
15.   %    -- muy: the mean of variable y
16.   %    -- sigmay: the standard deviation of variable y
17.   %    -- muz: the mean of variable z
18.   %    -- sigmaz: the standard deviation of variable z
19.   %    -- muw: the mean of variable w
20.   %    -- sigmaw: the standard deviation of variable w
21.   % Output:
22.   %    -- m: the mean of variable r
23.   %    -- s: the standard deviation of variable r
24.   %    -- sk: the skewness of variable r
25.   %    -- k: the kurtosis of variable r
26.   %    -- p50: the 50th percentile of variable r
27.   %    -- p95: the 95th percentile of variable r
28.
29.   % calculate the mean and variance of the associated
30.   % normal distribution for variable x
31.   mux1 = log((mux ^ 2) / sqrt(sigmax + mux ^ 2));
32.   sigmax1 = sqrt(log(sigmax / (mux ^ 2) + 1));
33.   x = lognrnd(mux1, sigmax1, n, 1);
34.   % calculate the mean and variance of the associated
35.   % normal distribution for variable y
36.   muy1 = log((muy ^ 2) / sqrt(sigmay + muy ^ 2));
37.   sigmay1 = sqrt(log(sigmay / (muy ^ 2) + 1));
38.   y = lognrnd(muy1, sigmay1, n, 1);
39.   % calculate the mean and variance of the associated
40.   % normal distribution for variable z
41.   muz1 = log((muz ^ 2) / sqrt(sigmaz + muz ^ 2));
42.   sigmaz1 = sqrt(log(sigmaz / (muz ^ 2) + 1));
43.   z = lognrnd(muz1, sigmaz1, n, 1);
44.   % calculate the mean and variance of the associated
45.   % normal distribution for variable w
46.   muw1 = log((muw ^ 2) / sqrt(sigmaw + muw ^ 2));
47.   sigmaw1 = sqrt(log(sigmaw / (muw ^ 2) + 1));
48.   w = lognrnd(muw, sigmaw, n, 1);
49.   % calculate variable r
50.   r = 2 * x + y + z - w;
51.   m = mean(r); % calculate mean
52.   s = std(r); % calculate standard deviation
53.   sk = skewness(r); % calculate skewness
54.   k = kurtosis(r); % calculate kurtosis
55.   p50 = prctile(r, 50); % calculate 50th percentile
56.   p95 = prctile(r, 95); % calculate 95th percentile
57.   end
```

Initially, we measure the execution time of this function running on the CPU generating $10,000,000 \times 1$ random values for variables x, y, z, and w:

```
>> mux = 20; sigmax = 0.2;
>> muy = 30; sigmay = 0.3;
>> muz = 40; sigmaz = 0.4;
>> muw = 50; sigmaw = 0.5;
>> tic; [m, s, sk, k, p50, p95] = statistics(10000000, mux, sigmax, ...
   muy, sigmay, muz, sigmaz, muw, sigmaw); toc
Elapsed time is 2.439921 seconds.
```

To execute this function on the GPU, we do not have to perform any changes to the code because all functions and operators used are GPU-enabled. The only difference is that we should pass a *gpuArray* as input to that function. We measure the execution time of this function running on the GPU using the same data:

```
>> mux = 20; sigmax = 0.2;
>> mux = gpuArray(mux); sigmax = gpuArray(sigmax);
>> muy = 30; sigmay = 0.3;
>> muy = gpuArray(muy); sigmay = gpuArray(sigmay);
>> muz = 40; sigmaz = 0.4;
>> muz = gpuArray(muz); sigmaz = gpuArray(sigmaz);
>> muw = 50; sigmaw = 0.5;
>> muw = gpuArray(muw); sigmaw = gpuArray(sigmaw);
>> tic; [m, s, sk, k, p50, p95] = statistics(10000000, mux, sigmax, ...
    muy, sigmay, muz, sigmaz, muw, sigmaw); toc
Elapsed time is 0.125056 seconds.
```

Hence, the Monte Carlo function is running $\sim$20$\times$ faster on the GPU.

5.7 **CHAPTER REVIEW**

This chapter introduced the GPU-enabled MATLAB functions on several toolboxes other than the Parallel Computing Toolbox, like the Communications System Toolbox, Image Processing Toolbox, Neural Network Toolbox, Phased Array System Toolbox, Signal Processing Toolbox, and Statistics and Machine Learning Toolbox. This chapter presented the GPU-enabled functions on these toolboxes with a variety of real-world examples.

To sum up, if the Parallel Computing Toolbox and the previously mentioned toolboxes are installed, then you can:

- use GPU-based implementations of the Communications System Toolbox objects for source coding, channel coding, interleaving, modulation, and channel modeling.
- implement image processing applications on a GPU to improve the performance of your codes.
- train and simulate neural networks on multiple CPUs and GPUs.
- perform clutter simulations on a GPU.
- use GPU-based implementations of the Signal Processing Toolbox in applications that you want to estimate one- and two-dimensional cross-correlation, filter a

signal with an FIR filter using the overlap/add method, compute cross-covariance sequences, and circularly convolve vectors.

- use GPU-based implementations of the Statistics and Machine Learning Toolbox to compute descriptive statistics from sample data, fit probability distributions to sample data, evaluate probability functions, generate random numbers, and perform hypothesis tests.

Multiple GPUs

6

CHAPTER OBJECTIVES

This Chapter covers a hot topic about utilizing multiple GPUs. In this Chapter, we present the use of multiple GPUs both on a multicore machine and on different machines. Multiple GPUs are used in order to improve the performance on task-parallel or data-parallel codes, and when working with data that cannot fit in the memory of a single GPU. This Chapter includes a variety of examples, both didactical and real-world examples. After reading this Chapter, you should be able to:

* understand MATLAB's GPU programming features for utilizing multiple GPUs.
* execute the same code on different GPUs.
* use multiple GPUs to execute codes when working with data that cannot fit in the memory of a single GPU.
* utilize multiple GPUs to improve the performance on task-parallel codes.
* utilize multiple GPUs to improve the performance on data-parallel codes.
* partition the data between the GPUs to improve the performance of a code.

6.1 IDENTIFY AND RUN CODE ON A SPECIFIC GPU DEVICE

If you have only one GPU in your computer, that GPU is the default. If you have more than one GPU device in your computer, you can use the following functions to identify and select which device you want to use:

* *gpuDeviceCount*: Display the number of GPU devices in your computer.
* *gpuDevice*: Select which device to use or display which device is selected and view its properties. If you type the command "gpuDevice" in MATLAB, the following properties of the selected GPU will be displayed (Fig. 6.1):

    (1) *Name*: the name/type of the GPU device, for example, NVIDIA Tesla K40c.
    (2) *Index*: the index of the GPU device. If there are many GPUs available in a computer, then each GPU device has a different index number, which can be used to select a GPU device.

GPU Programming in MATLAB. http://dx.doi.org/10.1016/B978-0-12-805132-0.00006-0

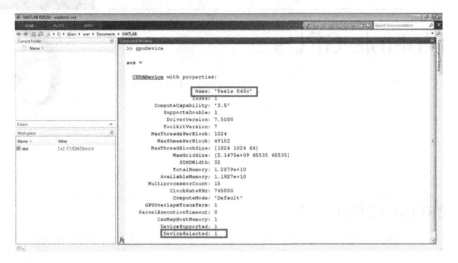

FIG. 6.1

Display the properties of the selected GPU device.

(3) *ComputeCapability*: the computational capability of the GPU device. As already explained in Section 2.1, MATLAB supports CUDA-capable GPUs with compute capability 2.0 or higher (as of MATLAB R2015b). NVIDIA maintains a list of all CUDA-capable GPUs [10].

(4) *SupportsDouble*: 1 if the GPU supports double-precision arithmetic or 0 if supports single-precision arithmetic. Note that if your GPU supports only single-precision, you can improve the performance of your codes using the GPU, but the solution will not be accurate on applications with strict precision requirements (in some cases, no solution will be reported).

(5) *DriverVersion*: The CUDA toolkit version installed on your computer (see Chapter 2). You should always update to the newest version of the CUDA toolkit as many improvements are released in each version.

(6) *MaxThreadsPerBlock*: Maximum supported number of threads per block during CUDAKernel execution.

(7) *MaxShmemPerBlock*: Maximum supported amount of shared memory that can be used by a thread block during CUDAKernel execution.

(8) *MaxThreadBlockSize*: Maximum size in each dimension for thread block.

(9) *MaxGridSize*: Maximum size of grid of thread blocks.

(10) *SIMDWidth*: Number of simultaneously executing threads.

(11) *TotalMemory*: Total memory (in bytes) on the device.

(12) *AvailableMemory*: Total amount of memory (in bytes) available for data.

(13) *MultiprocessorCount*: The number of vector processors present on the device.

(14) *ClockRateKHz*: Peak clock rate of the GPU in kHz.

(15) *ComputeMode*: The compute mode of the device can be one of: (i) *Default* (the device is not restricted and can be used by multiple applications simultaneously. MATLAB can share the device with other applications, including other MATLAB sessions or workers), and (ii) *Exclusive thread* (the device can be used by only one application at a time. While the device is selected in MATLAB, it cannot be used by other applications, including other MATLAB sessions or workers), (iii) *Exclusive process* (the device can be used by only one application at a time. While the device is selected in MATLAB, it cannot be used by other applications, including other MATLAB sessions or workers), and (iv) *Prohibited* (the device cannot be used).

(16) *GPUOverlapsTransfers*: Indicates if the device supports overlapped transfers.

(17) *KernelExecutionTimeout*: Indicates if the device can abort long-running kernels. If *true*, the operating system places an upper bound on the time allowed for the CUDA kernel to execute, after which the CUDA driver times out the kernel and returns an error.

(18) *CanMapHostMemory*: Indicates if the device supports mapping host memory into the CUDA address space.

(19) *DeviceSupported*: Indicates if MATLAB can use this device. Not all devices are supported (see Chapter 2).

(20) *DeviceSelected*: Indicates if this is the currently selected device.

To use another device, call the *gpuDevice* with the index of the other device, and display its properties to verify that it is the one you wanted to select. For example, the command *gpuDevice(2)* chooses the second device and displays its properties (Fig. 6.2). The following code generates a random 100,000,000 × 1 vector, executes function *myFun1* on both available GPUs, and measures their performance (Fig. 6.3).

```
>> A = rand(100000000, 1);
>> gd = gpuDevice(1);
>> fprintf('%s - %s\n', gd.Name, gd.ComputeCapability);
Tesla K40c - 3.5
>> gpuA = gpuArray(A);
>> tic; maximum1 = myFun1(gpuA); wait(gd); toc
Elapsed time is 0.004967 seconds.
>> maximum1 = gather(maximum1);
>> gd = gpuDevice(2);
>> fprintf('%s - %s\n', gd.Name, gd.ComputeCapability);
Quadro 6000 - 2.0
```

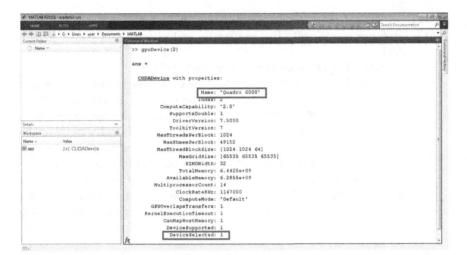

FIG. 6.2

Select and display the properties of the second GPU device.

FIG. 6.3

Execute code on multiple GPUs.

```
>> gpuA = gpuArray(A);
>> tic; maximum2 = myFun1(gpuA); wait(gd); toc
Elapsed time is 0.008626 seconds.
>> maximum2 = gather(maximum2);
>> maximum1 - maximum2
```

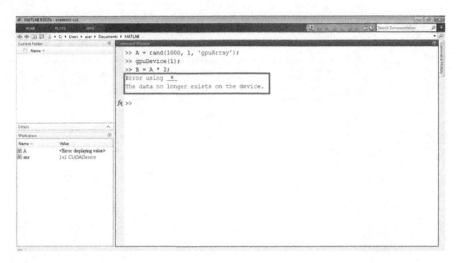

FIG. 6.4

Error while accessing a variable after calling the *gpuDevice* function.

Note that when using the *gpuDevice* function, then the variables stored in the GPU memory are cleared. If you try to access a variable that you have created before calling the *gpuDevice*, then MATLAB generates an error (Fig. 6.4).

To utilize multiple GPUs, you should use an *spmd* statement (see Section 3.3). Open a parallel pool and try the following code that outputs the name of the selected GPU device in each worker (Fig. 6.5):

```
>> parpool('local', 2);
>> spmd
      gd = gpuDevice;
      gd.Name
   end
```

MATLAB automatically assigns a GPU device to each worker. It is possible for multiple workers to share the same GPU device, if the GPU is in *Default* compute mode. In this case, the GPU driver serializes the accesses to the device. You should be aware that there will be a performance degradation due to the serialization.

So, you can use an *spmd* statement to utilize multiple GPUs on your codes. There are two options when using multiple GPUs inside an *spmd* statement:

- *Execute the same task using different data*: The following code shows how to use multiple GPUs when you want to execute the same task, for example, function *myFun1* using different data, for example, two different vectors (Fig. 6.6).

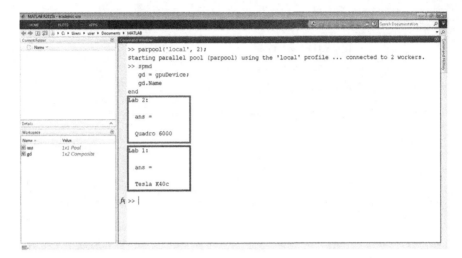

FIG. 6.5

Use of *spmd* statement to display information of the selected GPU in each worker.

FIG. 6.6

Execute the same task on multiple GPUs using different data.

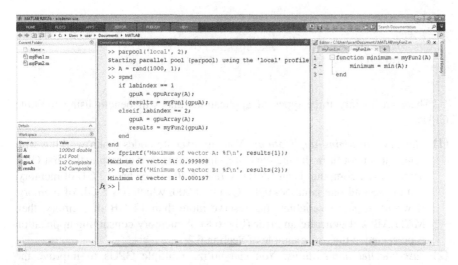

FIG. 6.7

Execute different tasks on multiple GPUs using the same data.

```
>> parpool('local', 2);
>> A = rand(1000, 1);
>> B = rand(1000, 1);
>> spmd
      if labindex == 1
          gpuA = gpuArray(A);
          maximum = myFun1(gpuA);
      elseif labindex == 2;
          gpuB = gpuArray(B);
          maximum = myFun1(gpuB);
      end
   end
   >>fprintf('Maximum of vector A: %f\n', maximum{1});
   >>fprintf('Maximum of vector B: %f\n', maximum{2});
```

• *Execute different tasks using the same data*: The following code shows how to use multiple GPUs when you want to execute different tasks, for example, functions *myFun1* and *myFun2*, using the same data, for example, one vector (Fig. 6.7).

```
>> parpool('local', 2);
>> A = rand(1000, 1);
>> spmd
      if labindex == 1
          gpuA = gpuArray(A);
          results = myFun1(gpuA);
      elseif labindex == 2;
          gpuA = gpuArray(A);
          results = myFun2(gpuA);
```

```
    end
  end
>>fprintf('Maximum of vector A: %f\n', results{1});
>>fprintf('Minimum of vector B: %f\n', results{2});
```

There are mainly three types of applications that will benefit using multiple GPUs:

(1) *Memory consuming applications*: You can execute codes when working with data that cannot fit in the memory of a single GPU. For example, the first GPU device in our computer is an NVIDIA Tesla K40, which has 12 GB of memory, and the second one is an NVIDIA Quadro 6000, which has 6 GB of memory. If we try to store variables that reserve more than 12 GB of memory, then MATLAB will generate an error (Fig. 6.8). A memory consuming application is presented in the first example of Section 6.2.

(2) *Task-parallel applications*: You can utilize multiple GPUs to improve the performance on task-parallel codes. When an application has different tasks that should be executed, then each GPU can evaluate a portion of them. A task-parallel application is presented in the second example of Section 6.2.

(3) *Data-parallel applications*: You can utilize multiple GPUs to improve the performance on data-parallel codes. When an application executes the same task on different data, then each GPU can execute this task on a portion of the data. A data-parallel application is presented in the third example of Section 6.2.

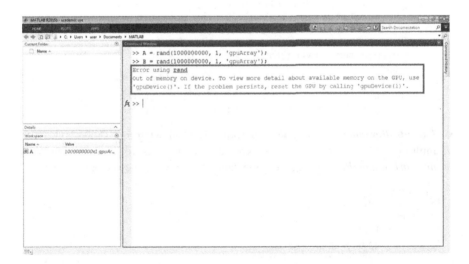

FIG. 6.8

Out of memory on GPU device.

Note that it is not always possible to obtain a speedup of n when using n GPUs for the following reasons:

- *Communication cost*: In some applications, the different GPUs should communicate to transfer data between them. If the communication cost is large, then a linear speedup cannot be obtained.
- *Memory utilization*: Using multiple GPUs means that you will distribute the application's data on different GPUs. A different memory utilization can sometimes reduce the performance.
- *Heterogeneous devices*: If you are using heterogeneous devices, that is, devices with different capabilities, you cannot expect to obtain a linear speedup.

Note that sometimes it is possible to obtain a super-linear speedup, that is, a speedup of more than n when using n GPUs. A super-linear speedup can be obtained mainly due to better memory utilization. A super-linear speedup is obtained in the second example of Section 6.2.

When your GPU devices are heterogeneous, then you should consider assigning more tasks or a larger portion of data to the faster device. We exploit this case in the first example of Section 6.3.

6.2 EXAMPLES USING MULTIPLE GPUs

Three real-world examples are presented in this section:

- In the first example, we approximate the area of a definite integral using the Monte Carlo method. This application is memory consuming and we use two GPUs to improve its performance. We also consider the number of iterations that each GPU will evaluate to achieve the best possible performance.
- In the second example, we estimate some descriptive statistic measures using the Monte Carlo method. This is a task-parallel application, and each GPU executes a different task on the same data.
- In the third example, we track image edges on multiple images. This is a data-parallel application and each GPU executes the same task on different data.

Example 1: Monte Carlo simulation to approximate the area of a figure

Let's consider again the example presented in Section 3.2. A Monte Carlo simulation was used to approximate the area of the following definite integral:

$$\int_0^2 x(x-2)^6 dx$$

In Section 3.2, we presented various ways to compute the area of the preceding definite integral using one or multiple CPU threads. The fastest code without using

Parallel Computing Toolbox was the vectorized function. Function *monteCarloVectorized* (filename: monteCarloVectorized.m) presents this vectorized code.

```
1.    function area = monteCarloVectorized(n)
2.    % Filename: monteCarloVectorized.m
3.    % Description: This function computes the area of the
4.    % definite integral int(x * (x - 2) ^ 6, x = 0..2)
5.    % (vectorized version)
6.    % Authors: Ploskas, N., & Samaras, N.
7.    % Syntax: area = monteCarloVectorized(n)
8.    % Input:
9.    %    -- n: the number of random points to generate
10.   % Output:
11.   %    -- area: the area of the integral
12.
13.   x = 2 * rand(n, 1);
14.   y = 8 * rand(n, 1);
15.   counter = sum(y < (x .* (x - 2) .^ 6));
16.   area = counter / n * 2 * 8;
17.   end
```

The *monteCarloVectorized* function runs in 56.45 seconds and requires 16 Gb to create and store variables *x* and *y*. In Sections 3.2 and 3.3, we also proposed a faster code that uses the Parallel Computing Toolbox and requires a small amount of memory. Function *monteCarloMultiCPU* (filename: monteCarloMultiCPU.m) presents this code using 8 MATLAB workers.

```
1.    function area = monteCarloMultiCPU(n)
2.    % Filename: monteCarloMultiCPU.m
3.    % Description: This function computes the area of the
4.    % definite integral int(x * (x - 2) ^ 6, x = 0..2)
5.    % (multi-threaded semi-vectorized version using spmd)
6.    % Authors: Ploskas, N., & Samaras, N.
7.    % Syntax: area = monteCarloMultiCPU(n)
8.    % Input:
9.    %    -- n: the number of random points to generate
10.   % Output:
11.   %    -- area: the area of the integral
12.
13.   n = n / 100;
14.   spmd(8)
15.      iterations = floor(100 / 8);
16.      if labindex <= mod(100, 8)
17.         iterations = iterations + 1;
18.      end
19.      counter = 0;
20.      for i = 1:iterations
21.         x = 2 * rand(n, 1);
22.         y = 8 * rand(n, 1);
23.         counter = counter + sum(y < (x .* (x - 2) .^6 ));
24.      end
25.   end
```

```
26.    counterStruct = gplus(counter);
27.    counter = 0;
28.    for i = 1:8
29.        counter = counter + counterStruct{i};
30.    end
31.    area = counter / (n * 100) * 2 * 8;
32.    end
```

The *monteCarloMultiCPU* function runs in 25.79 seconds using 8 MATLAB workers, a ~2.19× speedup compared to the *monteCarloVectorized* function.

Now, let's change these functions to calculate the area of the definite integral on the GPU. Initially, we make the appropriate changes to the *monteCarloVectorized* function to execute it on the GPU. Function *monteCarloVectorizedGPU* (filename: monteCarloVectorizedGPU.m) presents this version.

```
1.    function area = monteCarloVectorizedGPU(n)
2.    % Filename: monteCarloVectorizedGPU.m
3.    % Description: This function computes the area of the
4.    % definite integral int(x * (x - 2) ^ 6, x = 0..2)
5.    % (vectorized version running on the GPU)
6.    % Authors: Ploskas, N., & Samaras, N.
7.    % Syntax: area = monteCarloVectorizedGPU(n)
8.    % Input:
9.    %    -- n: the number of random points to generate
10.   % Output:
11.   %    -- area: the area of the integral
12.
13.   x = 2 * rand(n, 1, 'gpuArray');
14.   y = 8 * rand(n, 1, 'gpuArray');
15.   counter = sum(y < (x .* (x - 2) .^ 6));
16.   gpuArea = counter / n * 2 * 8;
17.   area = gather(gpuArea);
18.   end
```

Try to execute the *monteCarloVectorizedGPU* function with $n = 1,000,000,000$. MATLAB generates an error that the GPU is out of memory (Fig. 6.9). As already mentioned, executing this function with $n = 1,000,000,000$ requires 16 Gb to create and store variables x and y. As of 2015, the only CUDA-capable GPU with more than 16 Gb of memory is NVIDIA Tesla K80. We use for our experiments an NVIDIA Tesla K40 that has 12 Gb of memory. So, we cannot straightforward implement the vectorized version of this code on the GPU using so many random points. (Note that if we execute the *monteCarloVectorizedGPU* function with $n = 100,000,000$, then the *monteCarloVectorizedGPU* function is faster ~46× than the *monteCarloVectorized* function and ~27× than the *monteCarloMultiCPU* (Fig. 6.10).)

We can try to minimize the amount of memory used on the GPU by modifying the *monteCarloVectorizedGPU*. Instead of generating vectors x and y with 1,000,000,000 values, we will generate them with 10,000,000 values and perform the for-loop 100 times (a similar approach on the CPU is function *test2* that

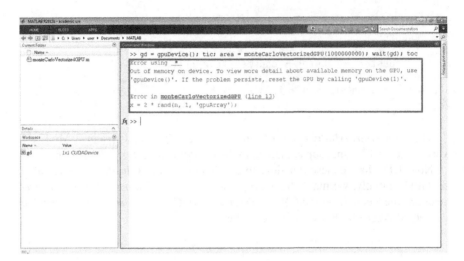

FIG. 6.9

Error while executing *monteCarloVectorizedGPU* function with $n = 1,000,000,000$.

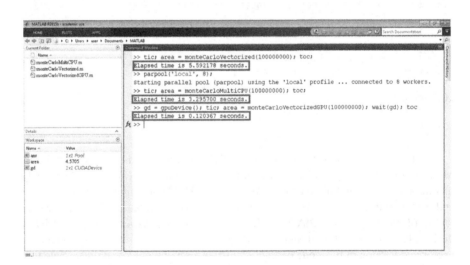

FIG. 6.10

Executing *monteCarloVectorizedGPU* function with $n = 100,000,000$.

was presented in Section 3.2). Function *monteCarloSemiVectorizedGPU* (filename: monteCarloSemiVectorizedGPU.m) presents this version.

```
1.    function area = monteCarloSemiVectorizedGPU(n)
2.    % Filename: monteCarloSemiVectorizedGPU.m
3.    % Description: This function computes the area of the
4.    % definite integral int(x * (x - 2) ^ 6, x = 0..2)
5.    % (semi-vectorized version running on the GPU)
6.    % Authors: Ploskas, N., & Samaras, N.
7.    % Syntax: area = monteCarloSemiVectorizedGPU(n)
8.    % Input:
9.    %    -- n: the number of random points to generate
10.   % Output:
11.   %    -- area: the area of the integral
12.
13.   n = n / 100;
14.   counter = 0;
15.   for i = 1:100
16.       x = 2 * rand(n, 1, 'gpuArray');
17.       y = 8 * rand(n, 1, 'gpuArray');
18.       counter = counter + sum(y < (x .* (x - 2) .^ 6));
19.   end
20.   gpuArea = counter / n * 2 * 8;
21.   area = gather(gpuArea);
21.   end
```

The *monteCarloSemiVectorizedGPU* function runs in 1.29 seconds and is faster ~44× than the *monteCarloVectorized* function and ~20× than the *monteCarlo-MultiCPU*. Note that this execution time was reported by executing the *monteCarloSemiVectorizedGPU* function on an NVIDIA Tesla K40. Running the same function using the same data on an NVIDIA Quadro 6000, the execution time is 1.84 seconds (Fig. 6.11).

The *monteCarloSemiVectorizedGPU* function offered a significant reduction on the execution time compared to the functions that are evaluated on the CPU. Now, let's try to improve the execution time by utilizing both GPUs that are present on our system. Function *monteCarloMultiGPUs* (filename: monteCarloMultiGPUs.m) is equivalent to the *monteCarloMultiCPU* function but utilizes multiple GPUs (two on the specific example).

```
1.    function area = monteCarloMultiGPUs(n)
2.    % Filename: monteCarloMultiGPUs.m
3.    % Description: This function computes the area of the
4.    % definite integral int(x * (x - 2) ^ 6, x = 0..2)
5.    % (semi-vectorized version running on multiple GPUs)
6.    % Authors: Ploskas, N., & Samaras, N.
7.    % Syntax: area = monteCarloMultiGPUs(n)
8.    % Input:
9.    %    -- n: the number of random points to generate
10.   % Output:
11.   %    -- area: the area of the integral
12.
```

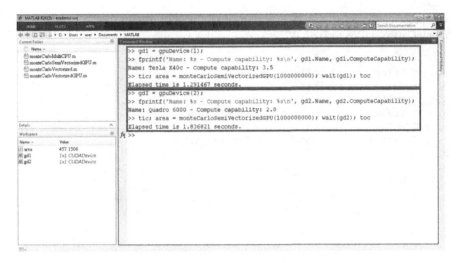

FIG. 6.11

Executing *monteCarloSemiVectorizedGPU* function on an NVIDIA Tesla K40 and on an NVIDIA Quadro 6000.

```
13.   n = n / 100;
14.   spmd(2)
15.      iterations = floor(100 / 2);
16.      if labindex <= mod(100, 2)
17.         iterations = iterations + 1;
18.      end
19.      counter = 0;
20.      for i = 1:iterations
21.         x = 2 * rand(n, 1, 'gpuArray');
22.         y = 8 * rand(n, 1, 'gpuArray');
23.         counter = counter + sum(y < (x .* (x - 2) .^6 ));
24.      end
25.   end
26.   counterStruct = gplus(counter);
27.   counter = 0;
28.   for i = 1:2
29.      counter = counter + counterStruct{i};
30.   end
31.   gpuArea = counter / (n * 100) * 2 * 8;
32.   area = gather(gpuArea);
33.   end
```

The *monteCarloMultiGPUs* function runs in 0.95 seconds and is faster ~1.36× than *monteCarloSemiVectorizedGPU* function when executed on the NVIDIA Tesla K40. We cannot achieve a linear speedup of 2× due to the communication cost and mainly due to the heterogeneous speed of the GPUs. Moreover, the *monteCarloMulti-*

GPUs function is faster ~59× than the *monteCarloVectorized* function and ~27× than the *monteCarloMultiCPU*.

Due to the different capabilities of our GPUs, let's try to optimize in *monteCarloMultiGPUs* function the number of iterations that each GPU evaluates. In *monteCarloMultiGPUs* function, each GPU evaluates 50 iterations. We should increase the number of iterations that the NVIDIA Tesla K40 evaluates because it is more powerful than the NVIDIA Quadro 6000. After some tuning and experimenting with various partitions, we found that the NVIDIA Tesla K40 should evaluate 60 iterations ($\frac{3}{5}$ of the iterations) and the NVIDIA Quadro 6000 should evaluate 40 iterations ($\frac{2}{5}$ of the iterations). Function *monteCarloMultiGPUsIterationsOptimization* (filename: monteCarloMultiGPUIterationsOptimization.m) presents this optimized version.

```
1.   function area = monteCarloMultiGPUsIterationsOptimization(n)
2.   % Filename: monteCarloMultiGPUsIterationsOptimization.m
3.   % Description: This function computes the area of the
4.   % definite integral int(x * (x - 2) ^ 6, x = 0..2)
5.   % (semi-vectorized version running on multiple GPUs. Each
6.   % GPU evaluates a different number of iterations)
7.   % Authors: Ploskas, N., & Samaras, N.
8.   % Syntax: area = monteCarloMultiGPUsIterationsOptimization(n)
9.   % Input:
10.  %    -- n: the number of random points to generate
11.  % Output:
12.  %    -- area: the area of the integral
13.
14.  n = n / 100;
15.  spmd(2)
16.     if labindex == 1
17.        iterations = 3 * floor(100 / 5) + mod(100, 5);
18.     elseif labindex == 2
19.        iterations = 2 * floor(100 / 5);
20.     end
21.     counter = 0;
22.     for i = 1:iterations
23.        x = 2 * rand(n, 1, 'gpuArray');
24.        y = 8 * rand(n, 1, 'gpuArray');
25.        counter = counter + sum(y < (x .* (x - 2) .^6 ));
26.     end
27.  end
28.  counterStruct = gplus(counter);
29.  counter = 0;
30.  for i = 1:2
31.     counter = counter + counterStruct{i};
32.  end
33.  gpuArea = counter / (n * 100) * 2 * 8;
34.  area = gather(gpuArea);
35.  end
```

The *monteCarloMultiGPUsIterationsOptimization* function runs in 0.81 seconds and is faster ~1.17× than *monteCarloMultiGPUs* function.

To conclude, we started with an optimized code running on multiple CPU threads and explored various alternatives to improve the performance using a single GPU and multiple GPUs. The optimized version of this code running on 8 CPU threads (*monteCarloMultiGPUsIterationsOptimization*) was executed in 25.79 seconds, while the best version of this function running on two GPUs (*monteCarloMultiGPUsIterationsOptimization*) was executed in 0.81 seconds. Hence, we achieved a speedup of ~32×.

Example 2: Estimation of descriptive statistics measures using the Monte Carlo method

The Monte Carlo method is a numerical integration method using sampling, which can be used to determine the descriptive statistics measures of a random variable, such as the mean, standard deviation, skewness, kurtosis, and percentiles. We can generate random numbers from a probability distribution and estimate the descriptive statistics measures of a variable. By the law of large numbers, their convergence to the real values is assured as the sample size tends to infinity.

We will extend the example presented in Section 5.6 to use the Monte Carlo method to estimate the descriptive statistics measures (mean, standard deviation, skewness, kurtosis, and percentiles) of the random variable r knowing that $r = 2 \times x + y \times z - w$ and that x, y, z, and w are distributed either lognormally or normally with $\mu_x = 1, \delta_x = 0.1, \mu_y = 2, \delta_y = 0.2, \mu_z = 3, \delta_z = 0.4, \mu_w = 4$, and $\delta_w = 0.4$. Note that the mean parameter μ and the standard deviation parameter δ are referring to the normal distribution.

Function *distributionStatistics* (filename: distributionStatistics.m) is used to illustrate the preceding example in MATLAB.

```
1.   function [lognm, logns, lognsk, lognk, lognp50, lognp95, ...
2.       normalm, normals, normalsk, normalk, normalp50, ...
3.       normalp95] = distributionStatistics(n, mux, sigmax, ...
4.       muy, sigmay, muz, sigmaz, muw, sigmaw)
5.   % Filename: distributionStatistics.m
6.   % Description: This function creates four random variables
7.   % (x, y, z, w) from the lognormal and normal distribution and
8.   % calculates the mean, standard deviation, skewness, kurtosis,
9.   % 50th and 95th percentiles of r = 2 * x + y .* z - w (version
10.  % running on the CPU or on a single GPU)
11.  % Authors: Ploskas, N., & Samaras, N.
12.  % Syntax: [lognm, logns, lognsk, lognk, lognp50, lognp95, ...
13.  %     normalm, normals, normalsk, normalk, normalp50, ...
14.  %     normalp95] = distributionStatistics(n, mux, sigmax, ...
15.  %     muy, sigmay, muz, sigmaz, muw, sigmaw)
16.  % Input:
17.  %   -- n: the number of random elements for each variable
18.  %   -- mux: the mean of variable x
19.  %   -- sigmax: the standard deviation of variable x
20.  %   -- muy: the mean of variable y
21.  %   -- sigmay: the standard deviation of variable y
22.  %   -- muz: the mean of variable z
```

```
23.  %    -- sigmaz: the standard deviation of variable z
24.  %    -- muw: the mean of variable w
25.  %    -- sigmaw: the standard deviation of variable w
26.  % Output:
27.  %    -- lognm: the mean of variable r for lognormal distribution
28.  %    -- logns: the standard deviation of variable r for lognormal
29.  %       distributinon
30.  %    -- lognsk: the skewness of variable r for lognormal
31.  %       distribution
32.  %    -- lognk: the kurtosis of variable r for lognormal
33.  %       distribution
34.  %    -- lognp50: the 50th percentile of variable r for lognormal
35.  %       distribution
36.  %    -- lognp95: the 95th percentile of variable r for lognormal
37.  %       distribution
38.  %    -- normalm: the mean of variable r for ormal distribution
39.  %    -- normals: the standard deviation of variable r for normal
40.  %       distributinon
41.  %    -- normalsk: the skewness of variable r for normal
42.  %       distribution
43.  %    -- normalk: the kurtosis of variable r for normal
44.  %       distribution
45.  %    -- normalp50: the 50th percentile of variable r for normal
46.  %       distribution
47.  %    -- normalp95: the 95th percentile of variable r for normal
48.  %       distribution
49.
50.  % calculate statistics for lognormal distribution
51.  % create random input vector x, y, z, w
52.  lognx = lognrnd(mux, sigmax, n, 1);
53.  logny = lognrnd(muy, sigmay, n, 1);
54.  lognz = lognrnd(muz, sigmaz, n, 1);
55.  lognw = lognrnd(muw, sigmaw, n, 1);
56.  % calculate variable r
57.  lognr = 2 * lognx + logny + lognz - lognw;
58.  lognm = mean(lognr); % calculate mean
59.  logns = std(lognr); % calculate standard deviation
60.  lognsk = skewness(lognr); % calculate skewness
61.  lognk = kurtosis(lognr); % calculate kurtosis
62.  lognp50 = prctile(lognr, 50); % calculate 50th percentile
63.  lognp95 = prctile(lognr, 95); % calculate 95th percentile
64.  % calculate statistics for normal distribution
65.  % create random input vector x, y, z, w
66.  normalx = normrnd(mux, sigmax, n, 1);
67.  normaly = normrnd(muy, sigmay, n, 1);
68.  normalz = normrnd(muz, sigmaz, n, 1);
69.  normalw = normrnd(muw, sigmaw, n, 1);
70.  % calculate variable r
71.  normalr = 2 * normalx + normaly + normalz - normalw;
72.  normalm = mean(normalr); % calculate mean
73.  normals = std(normalr); % calculate standard deviation
74.  normalsk = skewness(normalr); % calculate skewness
```

```
75.    normalk = kurtosis(normalr); % calculate kurtosis
76.    normalp50 = prctile(normalr, 50); % calculate 50th percentile
77.    normalp95 = prctile(normalr, 95); % calculate 95th percentile
78.    end
```

Initially, we measure the execution time of this function running on the CPU by generating $10,000,000 \times 1$ random values for variables x, y, z, and w:

```
>> tic; [lognm, logns, lognsk, lognk, lognp50, lognp95, normalm, ...
      normals, normalsk, normalk, normalp50, normalp95] = ...
      distributionStatistics(10000000, 3, 0.3, 4, 0.4, 5, 0.5, 6, 0.6); toc
Elapsed time is 4.779792 seconds.
```

To execute this function on the GPU, we do not have to perform any changes to the code because all functions and operators used are GPU-enabled. The only difference is that we should pass a *gpuArray* as input to that function. We measure the execution time of this function running on the GPU using the same data and report the execution time using an NVIDIA Tesla K40 and an NVIDIA Quadro 6000:

```
>> gd = gpuDevice(1); tic; [lognm, logns, lognsk, ...
      lognk, lognp50, lognp95, normalm, normals, ...
      normalsk, normalk, normalp50, normalp95] = ...
      distributionStatistics(1000000, gpuArray(3), ...
      gpuArray(0.3), gpuArray(4), gpuArray(0.4), ...
      gpuArray(5), gpuArray(0.5), gpuArray(6), ...
      gpuArray(0.6)); wait(gd); toc
Elapsed time is 0.526764 seconds.
>> gd = gpuDevice(2); tic; [lognm, logns, lognsk, ...
      lognk, lognp50, lognp95, normalm, normals, ...
      normalsk, normalk, normalp50, normalp95] = ...
      distributionStatistics(1000000, gpuArray(3), ...
      gpuArray(0.3), gpuArray(4), gpuArray(0.4), ...
      gpuArray(5), gpuArray(0.5), gpuArray(6), ...
      gpuArray(0.6)); wait(gd); toc
Elapsed time is 0.961352 seconds.
```

The Monte Carlo function is running $\sim 9\times$ faster on the NVIDIA Tesla K40 than the CPU and $\sim 5\times$ faster on the NVIDIA Quadro 6000 than the CPU. Now, let's try to improve the execution time by utilizing both GPUs that are present on our system. Function *distributionStatistics* calculates two different sets of descriptive statistics, one for the lognormal distribution and one for the normal distribution. These tasks are completely independent. Hence, we can use one GPU to evaluate the first task and one GPU to evaluate the second task and thus, exploit task parallelism. Function *distributionStatisticsMultiGPUs* (filename: distributionStatisticsMultiGPUs.m) is equivalent to the *distributionStatistics* function but utilizes multiple GPUs (two on the specific example).

```
1.    function [lognm, logns, lognsk, lognk, lognp50, lognp95, ...
2.        normalm, normals, normalsk, normalk, normalp50, ...
3.        normalp95] = distributionStatisticsMultiGPUs(n, mux, sigmax, ...
```

```
 4.       muy, sigmay, muz, sigmaz, muw, sigmaw)
 5.    % Filename: distributionStatisticsMultiGPUs.m
 6.    % Description: This function creates four random variables
 7.    % (x, y, z, w) from the lognormal and normal distribution and
 8.    % calculates the mean, standard deviation, skewness, kurtosis,
 9.    % 50th and 95th percentiles of r = 2 * x + y .* z - w (version
10.    % running on multiple GPUs)
11.    % Authors: Ploskas, N., & Samaras, N.
12.    % Syntax: [lognm, logns, lognsk, lognk, lognp50, lognp95, ...
13.    %    normalm, normals, normalsk, normalk, normalp50, ...
14.    %    normalp95] = distributionStatisticsMultiGPUs(n, mux, sigmax, ...
15.    %    muy, sigmay, muz, sigmaz, muw, sigmaw)
16.    % Input:
17.    %    -- n: the number of random elements for each variable
18.    %    -- mux: the mean of variable x
19.    %    -- sigmax: the standard deviation of variable x
20.    %    -- muy: the mean of variable y
21.    %    -- sigmay: the standard deviation of variable y
22.    %    -- muz: the mean of variable z
23.    %    -- sigmaz: the standard deviation of variable z
24.    %    -- muw: the mean of variable w
25.    %    -- sigmaw: the standard deviation of variable w
26.    % Output:
27.    %    -- lognm: the mean of variable r for lognormal distribution
28.    %    -- logns: the standard deviation of variable r for lognormal
29.    %       distributinon
30.    %    -- lognsk: the skewness of variable r for lognormal
31.    %       distribution
32.    %    -- lognk: the kurtosis of variable r for lognormal
33.    %       distribution
34.    %    -- lognp50: the 50th percentile of variable r for lognormal
35.    %       distribution
36.    %    -- lognp95: the 95th percentile of variable r for lognormal
37.    %       distribution
38.    %    -- normalm: the mean of variable r for ormal distribution
39.    %    -- normals: the standard deviation of variable r for normal
40.    %       distributinon
41.    %    -- normalsk: the skewness of variable r for normal
42.    %       distribution
43.    %    -- normalk: the kurtosis of variable r for normal
44.    %       distribution
45.    %    -- normalp50: the 50th percentile of variable r for normal
46.    %       distribution
47.    %    -- normalp95: the 95th percentile of variable r for normal
48.    %       distribution
49.
50.    spmd(2)
51.       if labindex == 1
52.           % calculate statistics for lognormal distribution
53.           % create random input vector x, y, z, w
54.           lognx = lognrnd(mux, sigmax, n, 1);
55.           logny = lognrnd(muy, sigmay, n, 1);
56.           lognz = lognrnd(muz, sigmaz, n, 1);
57.           lognw = lognrnd(muw, sigmaw, n, 1);
58.           % calculate variable r
59.           lognr = 2 * lognx + logny + lognz - lognw;
60.           lognm = mean(lognr); % calculate mean
61.           logns = std(lognr); % calculate standard deviation
```

```
62.          lognsk = skewness(lognr); % calculate skewness
63.          lognk = kurtosis(lognr); % calculate kurtosis
64.          lognp50 = prctile(lognr, 50); % calculate 50th percentile
65.          lognp95 = prctile(lognr, 95); % calculate 95th percentile
66.     elseif labindex == 2
67.          % calculate statistics for normal distribution
68.          % create random input vector x, y, z, w
69.          normalx = normrnd(mux, sigmax, n, 1);
70.          normaly = normrnd(muy, sigmay, n, 1);
71.          normalz = normrnd(muz, sigmaz, n, 1);
72.          normalw = normrnd(muw, sigmaw, n, 1);
73.          % calculate variable r
74.          normalr = 2 * normalx + normaly + normalz - normalw;
75.          normalm = mean(normalr); % calculate mean
76.          normals = std(normalr); % calculate standard deviation
77.          normalsk = skewness(normalr); % calculate skewness
78.          normalk = kurtosis(normalr); % calculate kurtosis
79.          normalp50 = prctile(normalr, 50); % calculate 50th percentile
80.          normalp95 = prctile(normalr, 95); % calculate 95th percentile
81.     end
82. end
```

Let's measure the execution time of this function running on two GPUs using the same data:

```
>> gd1 = gpuDevice(1); gd2 = gpuDevice(2); tic; ...
    [lognm, logns, lognsk, lognk, lognp50, ...
    lognp95, normalm, normals, normalsk, ...
    normalk, normalp50, normalp95] = ...
    distributionStatisticsMultiGPUs(10000000, ...
    gpuArray(3), gpuArray(0.3), gpuArray(4), ...
    gpuArray(0.4), gpuArray(5), gpuArray(0.5), ...
    gpuArray(6), gpuArray(0.6)); wait(gd1); ...
    wait(gd2); toc
Elapsed time is 0.399595 seconds.
```

The *distributionStatisticsMultiGPUs* function runs in 0.399595 seconds and is faster $\sim 1.31\times$ than *distributionStatistics* function when executed on the NVIDIA Tesla K40. We cannot achieve a linear speedup of $2\times$ due to the communication cost and mainly due to the heterogeneous speed of the GPUs. Moreover, the *distributionStatisticsMultiGPUs* function is faster $\sim 12\times$ than the *distributionStatistics* function when executed on the CPU.

Now, let's execute again all different versions of this example using a smaller number of points. We will evaluate the functions using 1,000,000 random values for variables *x*, *y*, *z*, and *w*:

```
>> tic; [lognm, logns, lognsk, lognk, lognp50, ...
    lognp95, normalm, normals, normalsk, normalk, ...
    normalp50, normalp95] = ...
    distributionStatistics(1000000, 3, 0.3, 4, ...
    0.4, 5, 0.5, 6, 0.6); toc
Elapsed time is 0.490345 seconds.
>> gd = gpuDevice(1); tic; [lognm, logns, lognsk, ...
    lognk, lognp50, lognp95, normalm, normals, ...
```

```
          normalsk, normalk, normalp50, normalp95] = ...
          distributionStatistics(1000000, gpuArray(3), ...
          gpuArray(0.3), gpuArray(4), gpuArray(0.4), ...
          gpuArray(5), gpuArray(0.5), gpuArray(6), ...
          gpuArray(0.6)); wait(gd); toc
Elapsed time is 0.273959 seconds.
>> gd = gpuDevice(2); tic; [lognm, logns, lognsk, ...
          lognk, lognp50, lognp95, normalm, normals, ...
          normalsk, normalk, normalp50, normalp95] = ...
          distributionStatistics(1000000, gpuArray(3), ...
          gpuArray(0.3), gpuArray(4), gpuArray(0.4), ...
          gpuArray(5), gpuArray(0.5), gpuArray(6), ...
          gpuArray(0.6)); wait(gd); toc
Elapsed time is 0.342567 seconds.
>> gd1 = gpuDevice(1); gd2 = gpuDevice(2); tic; ...
          [lognm, logns, lognsk, lognk, lognp50, ...
          lognp95, normalm, normals, normalsk, ...
          normalk, normalp50, normalp95] = ...
          distributionStatisticsMultiGPUs(1000000, ...
          gpuArray(3), gpuArray(0.3), gpuArray(4), ...
          gpuArray(0.4), gpuArray(5), gpuArray(0.5), ...
          gpuArray(6), gpuArray(0.6)); wait(gd1); ...
          wait(gd2); toc
Elapsed time is 0.113732 seconds.
```

The *distributionStatistics* function running on the NVIDIA Tesla K40 is faster $\sim$1.79$\times$ than *distributionStatistics* function when executed on the CPU. The *distributionStatisticsMultiGPUs* function is faster $\sim$2.41$\times$ than *distributionStatistics* function when executed on two GPUs. We achieved a super-linear speedup. As already mentioned, a super-linear speedup can be obtained mainly due to better memory utilization. Moreover, the *distributionStatisticsMultiGPUs* function is faster $\sim$4.31$\times$ than the *distributionStatistics* function when executed on the CPU.

To conclude, we started with a code running on the CPU and explored various alternatives to improve the performance using a single GPU and multiple GPUs. The *distributionStatistics* function running on two GPUs is faster $\sim$12$\times$ than the *distributionStatistics* function when executed on the CPU using 10,000,000 random points and $\sim$4.31$\times$ than the *distributionStatistics* function when executed on the CPU using 1,000,000 random points.

Example 3: Image edge detection on multiple images
Edge detection is a common operation on images. It is a method of tracking discontinuities within the image pixels. These discontinuities may exist due to the morphology of the objects in the image, to shadows or may be abrupt changes in colors. A simple and efficient way of finding edges is image filtering. Spatial time invariant filtering is achieved by convolving the original signal (in this case the 2-D discrete image signal) with the filter kernel. The filter kernel is a matrix that assigns weights to the terms of the convolution sum.

We will extend the example presented in Section 4.3 to track image edges on multiple images. We assume that images are jpeg files and they are stored in the same folder with sequentially numbered filenames, eg, image1.jpg, image2.jpg, etc.

Function *edgeDetectionCPU* (filename: edgeDetectionCPU.m) is used to illustrate the preceding example in MATLAB.

```
1.   function edgeDetectionCPU(inputFolder, outputFolder3x3, ...
2.       outputFolder9x9)
3.   % Filename: edgeDetectionCPU.m
4.   % Description: This function detects the edges of multiple
5.   % images using the 3x3 and 9x9 Sobel kernels (version running
6.   % on CPU)
7.   % Authors: Ploskas, N., & Samaras, N.
8.   % Syntax: edgeDetectionCPU(inputFolder, outputFolder3x3, ...
9.   %     outputFolder9x9)
10.  % Input:
11.  %   -- inputFolder: the folder with the original images
12.  %   -- outputFolder3x3: the folder where the images after
13.  %       applying the 3x3 Sobel kernel will be stored
14.  %   -- outputFolder9x9: the folder where the images after
15.  %       applying the 9x9 Sobel kernel will be stored
16.  % Output: the images after applying the 3x3 and 9x9 Sobel
17.  %       kernels will be stored in outputFolder3x3 and
18.  %       outputFolder9x9 folders
19.
20.  m = 25; n = 25;    % declare the size of the blur kernel
21.  sigma = 10;    % set the sigma parameter of gaussian blur to 10
22.  % create the m x n gaussian blur kernel
23.  [h1, h2] = meshgrid(-(m - 1) / 2:(m - 1) / 2, -(n - 1) / 2:(n - 1) / 2);
24.  hg = exp(-(h1 .^ 2 + h2 .^ 2) / (2 * sigma^2));
25.  gKernel = hg ./ sum(hg(:));
26.  % create the 3x3 and 9x9 Sobel kernels
27.  sobelF3 = [-1 0 1; -2 0 2; -1 0 1];
28.  sobelF9 = [4 3 2 1 0 -1 -2 -3 -4;
29.  5 4 3 2 0 -2 -3 -4 -5;
30.  6 5 4 3 0 -3 -4 -5 -6;
31.  7 6 5 4 0 -4 -5 -6 -7;
32.  8 7 6 5 0 -5 -6 -7 -8;
33.  7 6 5 4 0 -4 -5 -6 -7;
34.  6 5 4 3 0 -3 -4 -5 -6;
35.  5 4 3 2 0 -2 -3 -4 -5;
36.  4 3 2 1 0 -1 -2 -3 -4];
37.  % the loop will perform the same operation for all images
38.  for i = 1:10
39.      % extract image filename
40.      filename = strcat(inputFolder, '\image', num2str(i), '.jpg');
41.      % read the image
42.      img = imread(filename);
43.      % convert to grayscale, double precision
44.      imgGray = im2double(rgb2gray(img));
45.      % smooth the grayscale image with the blur kernel
46.      imgBlur = conv2(imgGray, gKernel, 'same');
47.      % 3x3 Sobel kernel
48.      % calculate image derivatives
49.      imgEdgeX1 = conv2(imgBlur, sobelF3', 'same');
50.      imgEdgeY1 = conv2(imgBlur, sobelF3, 'same');
51.      % calculate the magnitude of the derivative
```

```
52.        imgEdge1 = sqrt(imgEdgeX1 .^ 2 + imgEdgeY1 .^ 2);
53.        % normalize values
54.        maxV1 = max(imgEdge1(:));
55.        minV1 = min(imgEdge1(:));
56.        range1 = maxV1 - minV1;
57.        imgEdge1 = (imgEdge1 - minV1) / range1;
58.        % suppress all values which are below a certain threshold (0.5)
59.        imgEdge1(imgEdge1 < 0.05) = 0;
60.        % store image to outputFolder3x3 folder
61.        outfilename1 = strcat(outputFolder3x3, '\image', num2str(i), '.jpg');
62.        imwrite(imgEdge1, outfilename1);
63.        % 9x9 Sobel kernel
64.        % calculate image derivatives
65.        imgEdgeX2 = conv2(imgBlur, sobelF9', 'same');
66.        imgEdgeY2 = conv2(imgBlur, sobelF9, 'same');
67.        % calculate the magnitude of the derivative
68.        imgEdge2 = sqrt(imgEdgeX2 .^ 2 + imgEdgeY2 .^ 2);
69.        % normalize values
70.        maxV2 = max(imgEdge2(:));
71.        minV2 = min(imgEdge2(:));
72.        range2 = maxV2 - minV2;
73.        imgEdge2 = (imgEdge2 - minV2) / range2;
74.        % suppress all values which are below a certain threshold (0.5)
75.        imgEdge2(imgEdge2 < 0.05) = 0;
76.        % store image to outputFolder9x9 folder
77.        outfilename2 = strcat(outputFolder9x9, '\image', num2str(i), '.jpg');
78.        imwrite(imgEdge2, outfilename2);
79.    end
80.    end
```

Initially, we measure the execution time of this function running on the CPU using 10 large images:

```
>> tic; edgeDetectionCPU('colorImages', 'colorImagesResultSobel3x3', ...
     'colorImagesResultSobel9x9'); toc
Elapsed time is 39.261040 seconds.
```

To execute this function on the GPU, we should perform some changes to the code. We should transfer some arrays and the images on the GPU using the *gpuArray* function and transfer back to the CPU the images before storing them to the disk.

Function *edgeDetectionGPU* (filename: edgeDetectionGPU.m) is used to illustrate the preceding example in MATLAB running on a single GPU.

```
1.    function edgeDetectionGPU(inputFolder, outputFolder3x3, ...
2.        outputFolder9x9)
3.    % Filename: edgeDetectionGPU.m
4.    % Description: This function detects the edges of multiple
5.    % images using the 3x3 and 9x9 Sobel kernels (version running
6.    % on a single GPU)
7.    % Authors: Ploskas, N., & Samaras, N.
8.    % Syntax: edgeDetectionGPU(inputFolder, outputFolder3x3, ...
9.    %    outputFolder9x9)
10.   % Input:
11.   %    -- inputFolder: the folder with the original images
12.   %    -- outputFolder3x3: the folder where the images after
13.   %       applying the 3x3 Sobel kernel will be stored
14.   %    -- outputFolder9x9: the folder where the images after
```

```
15.  %        applying the 9x9 Sobel kernel will be stored
16.  % Output: the images after applying the 3x3 and 9x9 Sobel
17.  %         kernels will be stored in outputFolder3x3 and
18.  %         outputFolder9x9 folders
19.
20.  m = 25; n = 25;     % declare the size of the blur kernel
21.  m = gpuArray(m);
22.  n = gpuArray(n);
23.  sigma = 10;     % set the sigma parameter of gaussian blur to 10
24.  sigma = gpuArray(sigma);
25.  % create the m x n gaussian blur kernel
26.  [h1, h2] = meshgrid(-(m - 1) / 2:(m - 1) / 2, -(n - 1) / 2:(n - 1) / 2);
27.  hg = exp(-(h1 .^ 2 + h2 .^ 2) / (2 * sigma^2));
28.  gKernel = hg ./ sum(hg(:));
29.  % create the 3x3 and 9x9 Sobel kernels
30.  sobelF3 = [-1 0 1; -2 0 2; -1 0 1];
31.  sobelF3 = gpuArray(sobelF3);
32.  sobelF9 = [4 3 2 1 0 -1 -2 -3 -4;
33.  5 4 3 2 0 -2 -3 -4 -5;
34.  6 5 4 3 0 -3 -4 -5 -6;
35.  7 6 5 4 0 -4 -5 -6 -7;
36.  8 7 6 5 0 -5 -6 -7 -8;
37.  7 6 5 4 0 -4 -5 -6 -7;
38.  6 5 4 3 0 -3 -4 -5 -6;
39.  5 4 3 2 0 -2 -3 -4 -5;
40.  4 3 2 1 0 -1 -2 -3 -4];
41.  sobelF9 = gpuArray(sobelF9);
42.  % the loop will perform the same operation for all images
43.  for i = 1:10
44.      % extract image filename
45.      filename = strcat(inputFolder, '\image', num2str(i), '.jpg');
46.      % read the image
47.      img = imread(filename);
48.      img = gpuArray(img);
49.      % convert to grayscale, double precision
50.      imgGray = im2double(rgb2gray(img));
51.      % smooth the grayscale image with the blur kernel
52.      imgBlur = conv2(imgGray, gKernel, 'same');
53.      % 3x3 Sobel kernel
54.      % calculate image derivatives
55.      imgEdgeX1 = conv2(imgBlur, sobelF3', 'same');
56.      imgEdgeY1 = conv2(imgBlur, sobelF3, 'same');
57.      % calculate the magnitude of the derivative
58.      imgEdge1 = sqrt(imgEdgeX1 .^ 2 + imgEdgeY1 .^ 2);
59.      % normalize values
60.      maxV1 = max(imgEdge1(:));
61.      minV1 = min(imgEdge1(:));
62.      range1 = maxV1 - minV1;
63.      imgEdge1 = (imgEdge1 - minV1) / range1;
64.      % suppress all values which are below a certain threshold (0.5)
65.      imgEdge1(imgEdge1 < 0.05) = 0;
66.      % store image to outputFolder3x3 folder
67.      outfilename1 = strcat(outputFolder3x3, '\image', num2str(i), '.jpg');
68.      imwrite(gather(imgEdge1), outfilename1);
69.      % 9x9 Sobel kernel
70.      % calculate image derivatives
71.      imgEdgeX2 = conv2(imgBlur, sobelF9', 'same');
72.      imgEdgeY2 = conv2(imgBlur, sobelF9, 'same');
```

```
73.      % calculate the magnitude of the derivative
74.      imgEdge2 = sqrt(imgEdgeX2 .^ 2 + imgEdgeY2 .^ 2);
75.      % normalize values
76.      maxV2 = max(imgEdge2(:));
77.      minV2 = min(imgEdge2(:));
78.      range2 = maxV2 - minV2;
79.      imgEdge2 = (imgEdge2 - minV2) / range2;
80.      % suppress all values which are below a certain threshold (0.5)
81.      imgEdge2(imgEdge2 < 0.05) = 0;
82.      % store image to outputFolder9x9 folder
83.      outfilename2 = strcat(outputFolder9x9, '\image', num2str(i), '.jpg');
84.      imwrite(gather(imgEdge2), outfilename2);
85.  end
86.  end
```

We measure the execution time of this function running on the GPU using the same data and report the execution time using an NVIDIA Tesla K40 and an NVIDIA Quadro 6000:

```
>> gd = gpuDevice(1); tic; edgeDetectionGPU('colorImages', ...
    'colorImagesResultSobel3x3', 'colorImagesResultSobel9x9'); wait(gd); toc
Elapsed time is 19.347226 seconds.
>> gd = gpuDevice(1); tic; edgeDetectionGPU('colorImages', ...
    'colorImagesResultSobel3x3', 'colorImagesResultSobel9x9'); wait(gd); toc
Elapsed time is 24.783636 seconds.
```

The *edgeDetectionGPU* function is running $\sim 2\times$ faster on the NVIDIA Tesla K40 than the CPU and $\sim 1.6\times$ faster on the NVIDIA Quadro 6000 than the CPU. Now, let's try to improve the execution time by utilizing both GPUs that are present on our system. We will distribute the images to the two GPUs. Hence, each GPU will track the edges of five images and thus, exploit data parallelism. Function *edgeDetectionMultiGPUs* (filename: edgeDetectionMultiGPUs.m) is equivalent to the *edgeDetectionGPU* function but utilizes multiple GPUs (two on the specific example).

```
1.   function edgeDetectionMultiGPUs(inputFolder, outputFolder3x3, ...
2.       outputFolder9x9)
3.   % Filename: edgeDetectionMultiGPUs.m
4.   % Description: This function detects the edges of multiple
5.   % images using the 3x3 and 9x9 Sobel kernels (version running
6.   % on multiple GPUs
7.   % Authors: Ploskas, N., & Samaras, N.
8.   % Syntax: edgeDetectionMultiGPUs(inputFolder, outputFolder3x3, ...
9.   %     outputFolder9x9)
10.  % Input:
11.  %   -- inputFolder: the folder with the original images
12.  %   -- outputFolder3x3: the folder where the images after
13.  %      applying the 3x3 Sobel kernel will be stored
14.  %   -- outputFolder9x9: the folder where the images after
15.  %      applying the 9x9 Sobel kernel will be stored
16.  % Output: the images after applying the 3x3 and 9x9 Sobel
17.  %      kernels will be stored in outputFolder3x3 and
18.  %      outputFolder9x9 folders
19.
20.  m = 25; n = 25;    % declare the size of the blur kernel
21.  m = gpuArray(m);
```

```
22.  n = gpuArray(n);
23.  sigma = 10;     % set the sigma parameter of gaussian blur to 10
24.  sigma = gpuArray(sigma);
25.  % create the m x n gaussian blur kernel
26.  [h1, h2] = meshgrid(-(m - 1) / 2:(m - 1) / 2, -(n - 1) / 2:(n - 1) / 2);
27.  hg = exp(-(h1 .^ 2 + h2 .^ 2) / (2 * sigma^2));
28.  gKernel = hg ./ sum(hg(:));
29.  % create the 3x3 and 9x9 Sobel kernels
30.  sobelF3 = [-1 0 1; -2 0 2; -1 0 1];
31.  sobelF3 = gpuArray(sobelF3);
32.  sobelF9 = [4 3 2 1 0 -1 -2 -3 -4;
33.  5 4 3 2 0 -2 -3 -4 -5;
34.  6 5 4 3 0 -3 -4 -5 -6;
35.  7 6 5 4 0 -4 -5 -6 -7;
36.  8 7 6 5 0 -5 -6 -7 -8;
37.  7 6 5 4 0 -4 -5 -6 -7;
38.  6 5 4 3 0 -3 -4 -5 -6;
39.  5 4 3 2 0 -2 -3 -4 -5;
40.  4 3 2 1 0 -1 -2 -3 -4];
41.  sobelF9 = gpuArray(sobelF9);
42.  spmd(2)
43.      if labindex == 1
44.          start = 1;
45.          stop = 5;
46.      elseif labindex == 2
47.          start = 6;
48.          stop = 10;
49.      end
50.      % the loop will perform the same operation for all images
51.      for i = start:stop
52.          % extract image filename
53.          filename = strcat(inputFolder, '\image', num2str(i), '.jpg');
54.          % read the image
55.          img = imread(filename);
56.          img = gpuArray(img);
57.          % convert to grayscale, double precision
58.          imgGray = im2double(rgb2gray(img));
59.          % smooth the grayscale image with the blur kernel
60.          imgBlur = conv2(imgGray, gKernel, 'same');
61.          % 3x3 Sobel kernel
62.          % calculate image derivatives
63.          imgEdgeX1 = conv2(imgBlur, sobelF3', 'same');
64.          imgEdgeY1 = conv2(imgBlur, sobelF3, 'same');
65.          % calculate the magnitude of the derivative
66.          imgEdge1 = sqrt(imgEdgeX1 .^ 2 + imgEdgeY1 .^ 2);
67.          % normalize values
68.          maxV1 = max(imgEdge1(:));
69.          minV1 = min(imgEdge1(:));
70.          range1 = maxV1 - minV1;
71.          imgEdge1 = (imgEdge1 - minV1) / range1;
72.          % suppress all values which are below a certain threshold (0.5)
73.          imgEdge1(imgEdge1 < 0.05) = 0;
74.          % store image to outputFolder3x3 folder
75.          outfilename1 = strcat(outputFolder3x3, '\image', num2str(i), '.jpg');
76.          imwrite(gather(imgEdge1), outfilename1);
77.          % 9x9 Sobel kernel
78.          % calculate image derivatives
79.          imgEdgeX2 = conv2(imgBlur, sobelF9', 'same');
```

```
80.            imgEdgeY2 = conv2(imgBlur, sobelF9, 'same');
81.            % calculate the magnitude of the derivative
82.            imgEdge2 = sqrt(imgEdgeX2 .^ 2 + imgEdgeY2 .^ 2);
83.            % normalize values
84.            maxV2 = max(imgEdge2(:));
85.            minV2 = min(imgEdge2(:));
86.            range2 = maxV2 - minV2;
87.            imgEdge2 = (imgEdge2 - minV2) / range2;
88.            % suppress all values which are below a certain threshold (0.5)
89.            imgEdge2(imgEdge2 < 0.05) = 0;
90.            % store image to outputFolder9x9 folder
91.            outfilename2 = strcat(outputFolder9x9, '\image', num2str(i), '.jpg');
92.            imwrite(gather(imgEdge2), outfilename2);
93.      end
94.   end
95.   end
```

Let's measure the execution time of this function running on two GPUs using the same data:

```
>> gd1 = gpuDevice(1); gd2 = gpuDevice(2); tic; ...
    edgeDetectionMultiGPUs('colorImages', 'colorImagesResultSobel3x3', ...
    'colorImagesResultSobel9x9'); wait(gd1); wait(gd2); toc
Elapsed time is 12.346593 seconds.
```

The *edgeDetectionMultiGPUs* function runs in 12.346593 seconds and is faster $\sim 1.57\times$ than *edgeDetectionGPU* function when executed on an NVIDIA Tesla K40. We cannot achieve a linear speedup of $2\times$ due to the communication cost and mainly due to the heterogeneous speed of the GPUs. Moreover, the *edgeDetectionMultiGPUs* function is faster $\sim 3.18\times$ than the *edgeDetectionCPU* function when executed on the CPU. Due to the different capabilities of our GPUs, we can try to optimize in *edgeDetectionMultiGPUs* function the number of images that each GPU tracks. If we increase the number of images that the NVIDIA Tesla K40 tracks, then the execution time will increase. The number of images is small and the task to track the edges of an image is computationally intensive. Hence, we cannot improve further the performance of our function using a different partition. Note than if we want to evaluate a larger number of images, for example, over 20, then we can further optimize our function using this strategy.

To conclude, we started with a code running on the CPU and explored various alternatives to improve the performance using a single GPU and multiple GPUs. The *edgeDetectionMultiGPUs* function running on two GPUs is faster $\sim 3.18\times$ than the *edgeDetectionCPU* function when executed on the CPU.

6.3 CHAPTER REVIEW

This chapter introduced a hot topic about utilizing multiple GPUs. In this chapter, we presented the use of multiple GPUs both on a multicore machine and on different machines. Multiple GPUs were used to improve the performance on task- or data-parallel codes and when working with data that cannot fit in the memory of a single GPU.

To sum up, you should consider utilizing multiple GPUs in the following type of applications:

(1) *Memory consuming applications*: You can execute codes when working with data that cannot fit in the memory of a single GPU.
(2) *Task-parallel applications*: You can utilize multiple GPUs to improve the performance on task-parallel codes. When an application has different tasks that should be executed, then each GPU can evaluate a portion of them.
(3) *Data-parallel applications*: You can utilize multiple GPUs to improve the performance on data-parallel codes. When an application executes the same task on different data, then each GPU can execute this task on a portion of the data.

Run CUDA or PTX code

7

CHAPTER OBJECTIVES

This Chapter explains how to create an executable kernel for a CUDA C code or PTX code and run that kernel on a GPU by calling it through MATLAB. Moreover, a brief introduction of CUDA C is presented. Furthermore, two classic examples, vector addition and matrix multiplication, are presented. After reading this Chapter, you should be able to:

- understand the basic features of a CUDA C code.
- compile kernels written in CUDA C.
- use compiled PTX codes to create *CUDAKernel* objects.
- execute kernels on a GPU by calling them through MATLAB.
- set properties on the *CUDAKernel* object to control its execution on the GPU.

7.1 A BRIEF INTRODUCTION TO CUDA C

The aim of this section is to present the basic features of CUDA C programming. Interested readers that are not familiar with CUDA C should refer to the CUDA C programming guide [2] for more information.

CUDA C extends C by allowing programmers to define C functions and kernels. A regular C function is executed once, while kernels are executed *N* times in parallel by *N* different CUDA threads. A kernel function is defined using the _ _global_ _ declaration specifier, and it is executed by defining the number of CUDA threads using a new <<< ... >>> execution configuration syntax. Each thread that evaluates a kernel has a unique thread *ID* that is accessible within the kernel through the built-in *threadIdx* variable.

For example, the following code adds a scalar number *b* to a vector *A* of size *N* and stores the result into vector *C*:

```
1.   /* kernel code */
2.   _ _global_ _ void VectorScalarAddition(float* A, float b, float* C){
```

GPU Programming in MATLAB. http://dx.doi.org/10.1016/B978-0-12-805132-0.00007-2

```
3.        int i = threadIdx.x;
4.        C[i] = A[i] + b;
5.     }
6.
7.     /* host code */
8.     int main(){
9.        ...
10.       /* invoke kernel with N threads */
11.       VectorScalarAddition<<<1, N>>>(A, b, C);
12.       ...
13.    }
```

The _ _global_ _ declaration specifier alerts the compiler that the *VectorScalarAddition* function should be compiled to run on a GPU instead of the CPU. The *main* function will be compiled by the host compiler, while the *VectorScalarAddition* function will be compiled by the compiler that handles the GPU code. Moreover, the kernel function is called by defining the number of threads that will be used for its execution. Each of the *N* threads will perform an addition.

threadIdx is a three-component vector, so that threads can be identified using a one-dimensional (using *threadIdx.x*), two-dimensional (using *threadIdx.x* and *threadIdx.y*), or three-dimensional (using *threadIdx.x*, *threadIdx.y*, and *threadIdx.z*) thread index, forming a one-dimensional (e.g., vector), two-dimensional (e.g., array), or three-dimensional (e.g., volume) block of threads, called a thread block.

The thread ID and its index relate to each other:

- For an one-dimensional block, the thread ID equals to *threadIdx.x*.
- For a two-dimensional block of size (M, N), the thread ID equals to *threadIdx.x* $+M \times$ *threadIdx.y*.
- For a three-dimensional block of size (M, N, K), the thread ID equals to *threadIdx.x* $+M \times$ *threadIdx.y* $+M \times N \times$ *threadIdx.z*.

For example, the following code adds two arrays *A* and *B* of size $N \times N$ and stores the result into array *C*:

```
1.    /* kernel code */
2.    _ _global_ _ void MatrixAddition(float A[N][N], float B[N][N], float C[N][N]){
3.       int i = threadIdx.x;
4.       int j = threadIdx.y;
5.       C[i][j] = A[i][j] + B[i][j];
6.    }
7.
8.    /* host code */
9.    int main(){
10.      ...
11.      /* invoke kernel with a block of N * N * 1 threads */
12.      int numBlocks = 1;
13.      dim3 threadsPerBlock(N, N);
14.      MatrixAddition<<<numBlocks, threadsPerBlock>>>(A, B, C);
15.      ...
16.   }
```

There is a limit to the number of threads per block because all threads of a block are expected to reside on the same processor core and must share the limited memory resources of that core. You can display the maximum number of threads per block

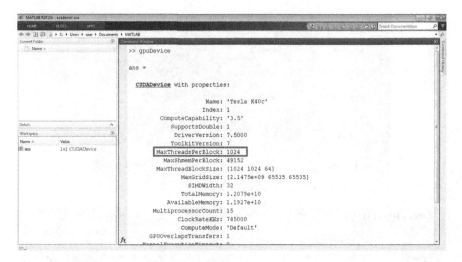

FIG. 7.1

Maximum number of thread per block.

of your GPU by typing the command *gpuDevice* on MATLAB. As of 2015, newest GPUs thread block may contain up to 1024 threads (Fig. 7.1).

However, as already mentioned in Section 1.3, a kernel can be executed by multiple thread blocks, so that the total number of threads is equal to the number of threads per block times the number of blocks (Fig. 7.2). The number of the thread blocks in a grid is usually dictated by the size of the data being processed or the number of processors in the system.

The number of threads per block and the number of blocks per grid specified in the $<<<\ldots>>>$ syntax can be of type *int* or *dim3*. Each block within the grid can be identified by a one-dimensional, two-dimensional, or three-dimensional index accessible within the kernel through the built-in *blockIdx* variable. The dimension of the thread block is accessible within the kernel through the built-in *blockDim* variable.

For example, the following code extends the matrix multiplication example by handling multiple blocks:

```
1.   /* kernel code */
2.   _ _global_ _ void MatrixAddition(float A[N][N], float B[N][N], float C[N][N]){
3.       int i = blockIdx.x * blockDim.x + threadIdx.x;
4.       int j = blockIdx.y * blockDim.y + threadIdx.y;
5.       if (i < N && j < N){
6.           C[i][j] = A[i][j] + B[i][j];
7.       }
8.   }
9.
10.  /* host code */
11.  int main(){
12.      ...
13.      /* invoke kernel */
```

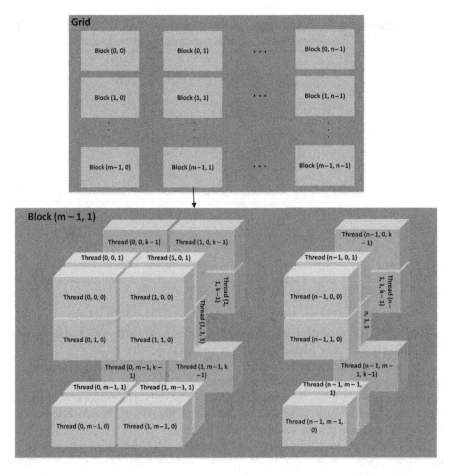

FIG. 7.2

Grid of thread blocks.

```
14.    dim3 threadsPerBlock(16, 16);
15.    dim3 numBlocks(N / threadsPerBlock.x, N / threadsPerBlock.y);
16.    MatrixAddition<<<numBlocks, threadsPerBlock>>>(A, B, C);
17.    ...
18.  }
```

In the previous example, the grid is created with enough blocks to have one thread per matrix element as before. For simplicity, this example assumes that the number of threads per grid in each dimension is evenly divisible by the number of threads per block in that dimension.

The CUDA programming model assumes a system composed of a host and a device, each with their own separate memory. Kernels operate out of device memory, so the runtime provides functions to allocate, deallocate, and copy device memory, as well as transfer data between host memory and device memory. Device memory can be allocated either as linear memory or as CUDA arrays. In a simple case, linear memory is typically allocated using *cudaMalloc* and freed using *cudaFree* and data transfers between host memory and device memory are typically done using *cudaMemcpy*. For example, the following code adds a scalar number *b* to a vector *A* of size *N* and stores the result into vector *C*:

```
1.   /* kernel code */
2.   _ _global_ _ void VectorScalarAddition(float* A, float b, float* C, int N){
3.       int i = blockDim.x * blockIdx.x + threadIdx.x;
4.       if (i < N){
5.           C[i] = A[i] + b;
6.       }
7.   }
8.
9.   /* host code */
10.  int main(){
11.      int N = ...;
12.      float b = ...;
13.      size_t size = N * sizeof(float);
14.      /* allocate input vector h_A in host memory */
15.      float* h_A = (float *)malloc(size);
16.      /* initialize input vector h_A */
17.      ...
18.      /* allocate vectors in device memory */
19.      float* d_A;
20.      cudaMalloc(&d_A, size);
21.      float* d_C;
22.      cudaMalloc(&d_C, size);
23.      /* copy input vector from host memory to device memory */
24.      cudaMemcpy(d_A, h_A, size, cudaMemcpyHostToDevice);
25.      /* invoke kernel */
26.      int threadsPerBlock = 256;
27.      int blocksPerGrid = (N + threadsPerBlock - 1) / threadsPerBlock;
28.      VectorScalarAddition<<<blocksPerGrid, threadsPerBlock>>>(d_A, b, d_C, N);
29.      /* copy result from device memory to host memory */
30.      cudaMemcpy(h_C, d_C, size, cudaMemcpyDeviceToHost);
31.      /* free device memory */
32.      cudaFree(d_A);
33.      cudaFree(d_C);
34.      /* free host memory */
35.      ...
36.  }
```

7.2 STEPS TO RUN CUDA OR PTX CODE ON A GPU THROUGH MATLAB

The steps to create an executable kernel from CU or PTX (Parallel Thread Execution) files, and run that kernel on a GPU from MATLAB are the following:

(1) Write your CU file and compile it to create a PTX file. One way to do this is with the *nvcc* compiler that is installed with the NVIDIA CUDA Toolkit (see Chapter 2). For example, if your CU file is called *myFun.cu*, you can create a compiled PTX file with the shell command: *nvcc -ptx myFun.cu* (if your system does not recognize *nvcc* as a command, make sure that *nvcc* is in your *PATH*

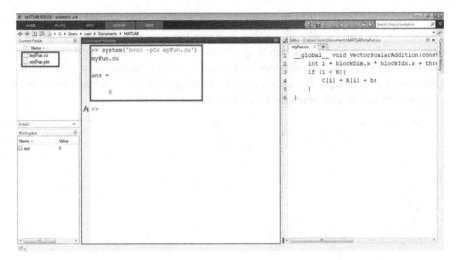

FIG. 7.3

Create PTX file from MATLAB.

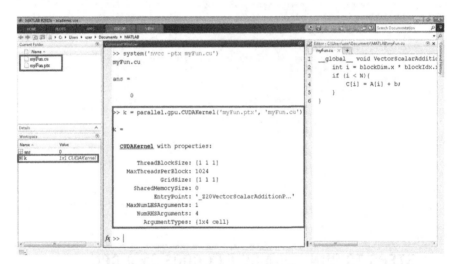

FIG. 7.4

Create a *CUDAKernel* object from a CU and a PTX file.

variable). This generates the file named *myFun.ptx*. Moreover, you can create the PTX file from MATLAB with the command *system('nvcc -ptx myFun.cu')* (Fig. 7.3).

(2) Create a *CUDAKernel* object, which can operate on MATLAB arrays or *gpuArray* variables. With a *.cu* file and a *.ptx* file, you can create a *CUDAKernel* object in MATLAB with the following command (Fig. 7.4):

```
>> k = parallel.gpu.CUDAKernel('myFun.ptx', 'myFun.cu')
```

The following properties are displayed for a *CUDAKernel* object [12]:

- *ThreadBlockSize*: Size of the block of threads on the kernel. As mentioned in the previous section, this can be an integer vector of length 1 (one-dimensional thread blocks), 2 (two-dimensional thread blocks), or 3 (three-dimensional thread blocks) because the thread blocks can be up to three-dimensional. The product of the elements of *ThreadBlockSize* must not exceed the *MaxThreadsPerBlock* for this kernel, and no element of *ThreadBlockSize* can exceed the corresponding element of the GPU property *MaxThreadBlockSize* (Fig. 7.1).
- *MaxThreadsPerBlock*: Maximum number of threads permissible in a single block. The product of the elements of *ThreadBlockSize* must not exceed this value.
- *GridSize*: Size of grid (effectively the number of thread blocks that will be launched independently by the GPU). This is an integer vector of length 3. None of the elements of this vector can exceed the corresponding element in the vector of the *MaxGridSize* property of the GPU property *MaxGridSize* (Fig. 7.1).
- *SharedMemorySize*: The amount of dynamic shared memory (in bytes) that each thread block can use. Each thread block has an available shared memory region. As of 2015, the size of this region is limited in high-end cards to 48Kb, and is shared with registers on the multiprocessors. As with all memory, this needs to be allocated before the kernel is launched. It is also common for the size of this shared memory region to be tied to the size of the thread block. Setting this value on the kernel ensures that each thread in a block can access this available shared memory region.
- *EntryPoint*: A string containing the actual entry point name in the PTX code that this kernel is going to call. An example might look like '*_Z20VectorScalarAdditionPffS_i*'. This property is read-only.
- *MaxNumLHSArguments*: The maximum number of left-hand side arguments that this kernel supports. It cannot be greater than the number of right-hand side arguments, and if any inputs are constant or scalar it will be less. This property is read-only.
- *NumRHSArguments*: The required number of right-hand side arguments needed to call this kernel. All inputs need to define either the scalar value of an input, the elements for a vector input/output, or the size of an output argument. This option is read-only.
- *ArgumentTypes*: Cell array of strings, the same length as *NumRHSArguments*. Each of the strings indicates what the expected MATLAB type for that input is (a numeric type such as *uint8*, *single*, or *double* followed by the word scalar or vector to indicate if we are passing by reference or value). In addition, if that argument is only an input to the kernel, it is prefixed by *in*; and if it is an input/output, it is prefixed by *inout*. This allows you to decide how to efficiently call the kernel with both MATLAB arrays and *gpuArray*

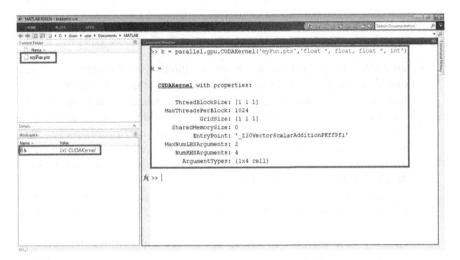

FIG. 7.5

Create a *CUDAKernel* object from a PTX file.

variables, and to see which of the kernel inputs are being treated as outputs. This property is read-only.

If you do not have the CU file corresponding to the PTX file, for example, someone gave you only the PTX file, you can specify the C prototype for your C kernel instead of the CU file. For example (Fig. 7.5):

```
>> k = parallel.gpu.CUDAKernel('myFun.ptx','float *, float, float *, int');
```

Another use for C prototype input is when your source code uses an unrecognized renaming of a supported data type. For example, suppose your kernel comprises of the following code:

```
1.   typedef float ArgType;
2.   _ _global_ _ void VectorScalarAddition(ArgType* A, ArgType b,
3.       ArgType* C, int N){
4.       int i = blockDim.x * blockIdx.x + threadIdx.x;
5.       if (i < N){
6.           C[i] = A[i] + b;
7.       }
8.   }
```

ArgType itself is not recognized as a supported data type, so the CU file cannot be directly used as input when creating the *CUDAKernel* object in MATLAB. However, the supported input types to the *VectorScalarAddition* kernel can be specified as C prototype input to the *CUDAKernel* constructor. For example (Fig. 7.6):

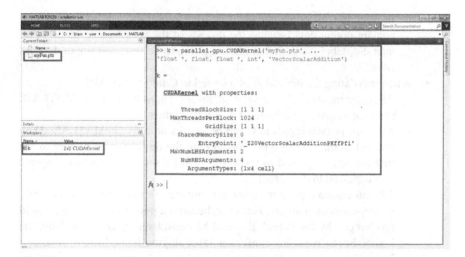

FIG. 7.6

Create a *CUDAKernel* object from a PTX file that includes an unrecognized renaming of a supported data type.

```
>> k = parallel.gpu.CUDAKernel('myFun.ptx', ...
    'float *, float, float *, int', 'VectorScalarAddition');
```

The supported C/C++ standard data types are the following:

- **Float types**: *float, float2, double, double2.*
- **Integer Types**: *short, unsigned short, short2, ushort2, int, unsigned int, int2, uint2, long, unsigned long, long2, ulong2, long long, unsigned long long, longlong2, ulonglong2, ptrdiff_t, size_t.*
- **Boolean Types**: *bool.*
- **Character Types**: *char, unsigned char, char2, uchar2.*

Moreover, the following integer types are supported when you include the *tmwtypes.h* header file (*matlabroot/extern/include/tmwtypes.h*) in your program (*#include "tmwtypes.h"*): *int8_T, int16_T, int32_T, int64_T, uint8_T, uint16_T, uint32_T, uint64_T.*

Some other arguments restrictions [5]:

- All inputs can be scalars or pointers and can be labeled as *const.*
- The C declaration of a kernel is always of the form *__global__ void aKernel(inputs...)* and the following restrictions apply:
  - The kernel must return nothing, and operate only on its input arguments (scalars or pointers).
  - A kernel is unable to allocate any form of memory, so all outputs must be preallocated before the kernel is executed. Therefore, the sizes of all outputs must be known before you run the kernel.

- In principle, all pointers passed into the kernel that are not *const* could contain output data because the threads of the kernel could modify that data. So, label the data that are not going to be modified (input data) as *const*.
- When translating the definition of a kernel in C into MATLAB:
  - All scalar inputs in C (*double, float, int*, etc.) must be scalars in MATLAB, or scalar *gpuArray* variables (i.e., single-element).
  - All *const* pointer inputs in C can be scalars or arrays in MATLAB. They are cast to the correct type, copied onto the device, and a pointer to the first element is passed to the kernel. No information about the original size is passed to the kernel.
  - All non-constant pointer inputs in C are transferred to the kernel exactly as non-constant pointers. However, because a non-constant pointer could be changed by the kernel, this will be considered as an output from the kernel. So, to avoid any confusion, label all your input data as *const*.
  - Inputs from MATLAB workspace, scalars and arrays, are cast into the requested type and then passed to the kernel. However, *gpuArray* inputs are not automatically cast, so their type and complexity must exactly match those expected.
- Every output from a kernel must necessarily also be an input to the kernel because the input allows the user to define the size of the output (which follows from being unable to allocate memory on the GPU).

If your PTX file contains multiple entry points, you can identify the particular kernel that you want the kernel object to refer to. For example, assume that your PTX file consists of two kernels, *VectorScalarAddition* and *VectorVectorAddition*. If you want to use the *VectorScalarAddition* kernel, then you should create the *CUDAKernel* with the following command (Fig. 7.7):

```
>> k = parallel.gpu.CUDAKernel('myFun.ptx', 'myFun.cu', ...
    'VectorScalarAddition');
```

Note that the *CUDAKernel* function searches for your entry name in the PTX file and matches on any substring occurrences. Therefore, you should not name any of your entries as substrings of any others.

(3) Set properties on the *CUDAKernel* object to control its execution on the GPU. You can specify the number of computational threads for your *CUDAKernel* by setting two of its object properties: *GridSize* and *ThreadBlockSize*. The default value for both of these properties is [1, 1, 1]. For example, if you want to execute the *VectorScalarAddition* without changing the default properties, then you will get the correct solution only on the first element of vector *C* because only one thread will evaluate the kernel. Hence, if vector *A* has 100 elements, then you should use at least 100 threads and 1 grid or at least 50 threads and 2 grids:

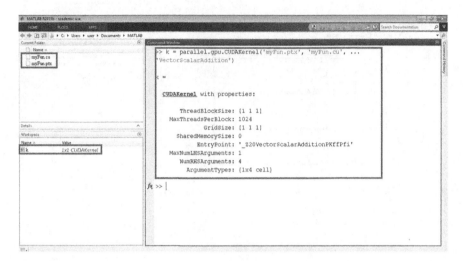

FIG. 7.7

Create a *CUDAKernel* object from a PTX file that includes multiple entry points.

```
>> k = parallel.gpu.CUDAKernel('myFun.ptx', 'myFun.cu');
>> k.ThreadBlockSize = [100, 1, 1];
```

or:

```
>> k = parallel.gpu.CUDAKernel('myFun.ptx', 'myFun.cu');
>> k.ThreadBlockSize = [50, 1, 1];
>> k.GridSize = [5, 1, 1];
```

Generally, you set the grid and thread block sizes based on the sizes of your inputs. For information on thread hierarchy, and multiple-dimension grids and blocks, see the NVIDIA CUDA C Programming Guide [2].

(4) Call *feval* on the *CUDAKernel* with the required inputs and outputs to execute the kernel on the GPU. You can execute a kernel using MATLAB workspace and/or *gpuArray* variables. However, the outputs will be always *gpuArray* variables. For example, suppose your kernel comprises the following code:

```
1.    _ _global_ _ void VectorScalarAddition(float* A, float b,
2.        float* C, int N){
3.        int i = blockDim.x * blockIdx.x + threadIdx.x;
4.        if (i < N){
5.            C[i] = A[i] + b;
6.        }
7.    }
```

Because we are interested in calculating vector *C*, it is better to label all input data as *const*. Hence, the following is the revised kernel:

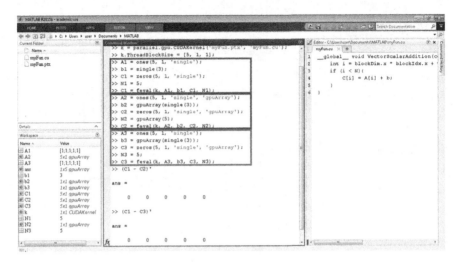

FIG. 7.8

Executing a *CUDAKernel* object using MATLAB arrays and *gpuArray* variables.

```
1.   _ _global_ _ void VectorScalarAddition(const float* A,
2.      const float b, float* C, const int N){
3.      int i = blockDim.x * blockIdx.x + threadIdx.x;
4.      if (i < N){
5.          C[i] = A[i] + b;
6.      }
7.   }
```

The following code executes the kernel using: (i) only MATLAB arrays, (ii) only *gpuArray* variables, and (iii) a mix of MATLAB arrays and *gpuArray* variables (Fig. 7.8):

```
>> system('nvcc -ptx myFun.cu');
>> k = parallel.gpu.CUDAKernel('myFun.ptx', 'myFun.cu');
>> k.ThreadBlockSize = [5, 1, 1];
>> A1 = ones(5, 1, 'single');
>> b1 = single(3);
>> C1 = zeros(5, 1, 'single');
>> N1 = 5;
>> C1 = feval(k, A1, b1, C1, N1);
>> A2 = ones(5, 1, 'single', 'gpuArray');
>> b2 = gpuArray(single(3));
>> C2 = zeros(5, 1, 'single', 'gpuArray');
>> N2 = gpuArray(5);
>> C2 = feval(k, A2, b2, C2, N2);
>> A3 = ones(5, 1, 'single');
>> b3 = gpuArray(single(3));
```

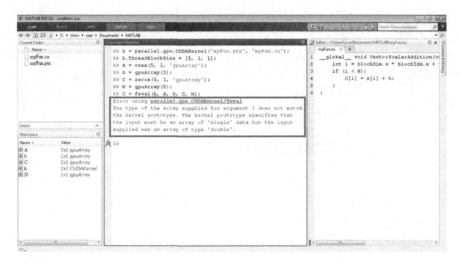

FIG. 7.9

Error while executing a *CUDAKernel* object using *gpuArray* variables that are not casted into the requested data type.

```
>> C3 = zeros(5, 1, 'single', 'gpuArray');
>> N3 = 5;
>> C3 = feval(k, A3, b3, C3, N3);
>> (C1 - C2)'
>> (C1 - C3)'
```

Note that the first three input arguments of the kernel are *float*. As already mentioned, inputs from MATLAB workspace, scalars and arrays, are cast into the requested type and then passed to the kernel. However, *gpuArray* inputs are not automatically cast, so their type and complexity must exactly match those expected. Hence, we need to convert a *double* to *float* using the *single* function or option. Otherwise, MATLAB generates an error (Fig. 7.9).

Note that it is always preferable to use *gpuArray* variables when executing a *CUDAKernel* object because it will lead to better execution times (Fig. 7.10).

The main reasons that you should use CU or PTX files in your applications are the following:

- Further optimize the performance of your application.
- Implement GPU-based functions that are not GPU-enabled in MATLAB, that is, cannot be executed using a *gpuArray* object.
- Implement a function that is already GPU-enabled in MATLAB but you want to optimize its performance or implement a different algorithm.

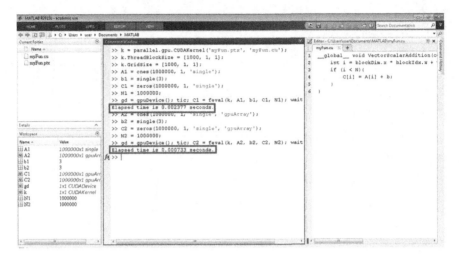

FIG. 7.10

Measure execution time while executing a *CUDAKernel* object using MATLAB arrays and *gpuArray* variables.

7.3 EXAMPLE: VECTOR ADDITION

This example summarizes the steps to run a kernel code on a GPU through MATLAB. It is a classic example that implements element by element vector addition. The following code is the kernel code (filename: vectorAddition.cu):

```
1.   /*==========================================================
2.    * Filename: vectorAddition.cu
3.    * Description: This function is a vector addition kernel
4.    * Authors: Ploskas, N., & Samaras, N.
5.    * Syntax: C = vectorAddition(A, B, C, N)
6.    * Input:
7.    *    -- A: a double-precision, floating point vector of size
8.    *       N
9.    *    -- B: a double-precision, floating point vector of size
10.   *       N
11.   *    -- C: a double-precision, floating point vector of size
12.   *       N
13.   *    -- numElements: the size of vectors A and B
14.   * Output:
15.   *    -- C: a double-precision, floating point vector of size
16.   *       N
17.   *==========================================================*/
18.
19.  _ _global_ _ void vectorAddition(const double *A, const double *B,
         double *C, const int numElements){
```

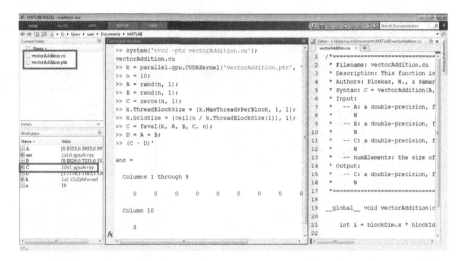

FIG. 7.11

Executing the kernel of the vector addition.

```
20.
21.     int i = blockDim.x * blockIdx.x + threadIdx.x;
22.
23.     if (i < numElements){
24.         C[i] = A[i] + B[i];
25     }
26.  }
```

The following MATLAB code compiles the CU file; creates a *CUDAKernel* object; creates the appropriate input and output data as MATLAB arrays and scalars; sets the properties for the threads, blocks, and grids that will evaluate the code; and executes the kernel (Fig. 7.11).

```
>> system('nvcc -ptx vectorAddition.cu');
>> k = parallel.gpu.CUDAKernel('vectorAddition.ptx', 'vectorAddition.cu');
>> n = 10;
>> A = rand(n, 1);
>> B = rand(n, 1);
>> C = zeros(n, 1);
>> k.ThreadBlockSize = [k.MaxThreadsPerBlock, 1, 1];
>> k.GridSize = [ceil(n / k.ThreadBlockSize(1)), 1];
>> C = feval(k, A, B, C, n);
>> D = A + B;
>> (C - D)'
```

As already mentioned, it is better to pass *gpuArray* variables to the kernel because it will reduce the execution time (Fig. 7.12).

FIG. 7.12

Executing the kernel of the vector addition using MATLAB arrays and GPU arrays.

```
>> k = parallel.gpu.CUDAKernel('vectorAddition.ptx', 'vectorAddition.cu');
>> n = 10000000;
>> k.ThreadBlockSize = [k.MaxThreadsPerBlock, 1, 1];
>> k.GridSize = [ceil(n / k.ThreadBlockSize(1)), 1];
>> A = rand(n, 1);
>> B = rand(n, 1);
>> C = zeros(n, 1);
>> gd = gpuDevice(); tic; C = feval(k, A, B, C, n); wait(gd); toc
>> gpuA = gpuArray(A);
>> gpuB = gpuArray(B);
>> C = zeros(n, 1, 'gpuArray');
>> gd = gpuDevice(); tic; C = feval(k, gpuA, gpuB, C, n); wait(gd); toc
```

Finally, let's measure the execution time of the vector addition on the CPU with MATLAB and on the GPU with the kernel file using *gpuArray* variables (Fig. 7.13).

```
>> k = parallel.gpu.CUDAKernel('vectorAddition.ptx', 'vectorAddition.cu');
>> n = 10000000;
>> k.ThreadBlockSize = [k.MaxThreadsPerBlock, 1, 1];
>> k.GridSize = [ceil(n / k.ThreadBlockSize(1)), 1];
>> A = rand(n, 1);
>> B = rand(n, 1);
>> tic; C = A + B; toc
>> gpuA = gpuArray(A);
>> gpuB = gpuArray(B);
>> C = zeros(n, 1, 'gpuArray');
>> gd = gpuDevice(); tic; C = feval(k, gpuA, gpuB, C, n); wait(gd); toc
```

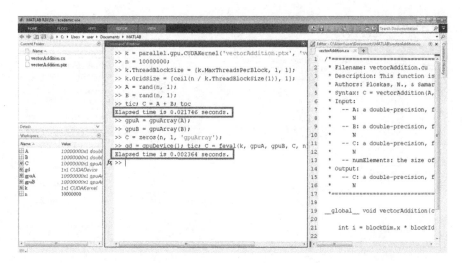

FIG. 7.13

Comparison of CPU and GPU implementations of the vector addition.

7.4 EXAMPLE: MATRIX MULTIPLICATION

This example summarizes the steps to run a kernel code on a GPU through MATLAB. It is a classic example that implements a matrix multiplication. The following code is the kernel code (filename: matrixMutliplication.cu):

```
1.   /*=========================================================
2.    * Filename: matrixMultiplication.cu
3.    * Description: This function is a matrix multiplication
4.    * kernel
5.    * Authors: Ploskas, N., & Samaras, N.
6.    * Syntax: C = matrixMultiplication(A, B, C, N)
7.    * Input:
8.    *    -- A: a double-precision, floating point NxN array
9.    *    -- B: a double-precision, floating point NxN array
10.   *    -- C: a double-precision, floating point NxN array
11.   *    -- N: the size of arrays A and B
12.   * Output:
13.   *    -- C: a double-precision, floating point NxN array
14.   *=========================================================*/
15.
16.   _ _global_ _ void matrixMultiplication(const double *A,
         const double *B, double *C, int N){
17.
18.      int i = blockDim.y * blockIdx.y + threadIdx.y;
19.      int j = blockDim.x * blockIdx.x + threadIdx.x;
```

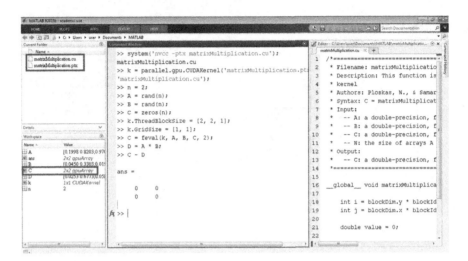

FIG. 7.14

Executing the kernel of the matrix multiplication.

```
20.
21.    double value = 0;
22.
23.    for(int k = 0; k < N; k++){
24.        value += A[k * N + j] * B[i * N + k];
25.    }
26.
27.    C[i * N + j] = value;
28.  }
```

The following MATLAB code compiles the CU file; creates a *CUDAKernel* object; creates the appropriate input and output data as MATLAB arrays and scalars; sets the properties for the threads, blocks, and grids that will evaluate the code; and executes the kernel (Fig. 7.14).

```
>> system('nvcc -ptx matrixMultiplication.cu');
>> k = parallel.gpu.CUDAKernel('matrixMultiplication.ptx', ...
      'matrixMultiplication.cu');
>> n = 2;
>> A = rand(n);
>> B = rand(n);
>> C = zeros(n);
>> k.ThreadBlockSize = [2, 2, 1];
>> k.GridSize = [1, 1];
>> C = feval(k, A, B, C, 2);
>> D = A * B;
>> C - D
```

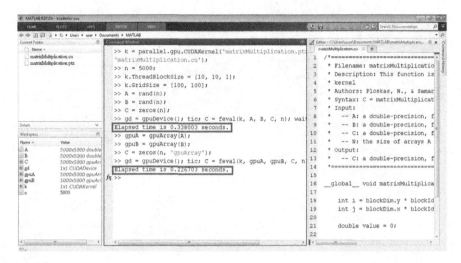

FIG. 7.15

Executing the kernel of the matrix multiplication using MATLAB arrays and GPU arrays.

As already mentioned, it is better to pass *gpuArray* variables to the kernel because it will reduce the execution time (Fig. 7.15).

```
>> k = parallel.gpu.CUDAKernel('matrixMultiplication.ptx', ...
     'matrixMultiplication.cu');
>> n = 5000;
>> k.ThreadBlockSize = [10, 10, 1];
>> k.GridSize = [100, 100];
>> A = rand(n);
>> B = rand(n);
>> C = zeros(n);
>> gd = gpuDevice(); tic; C = feval(k, A, B, C, n); wait(gd); toc
>> gpuA = gpuArray(A);
>> gpuB = gpuArray(B);
>> C = zeros(n, 'gpuArray');
>> gd = gpuDevice(); tic; C = feval(k, gpuA, gpuB, C, n); wait(gd); toc
```

Finally, let's measure the execution time of the matrix multiplication on the CPU with MATLAB and on the GPU with the kernel file using *gpuArray* variables (Fig. 7.16).

```
>> k = parallel.gpu.CUDAKernel('matrixMultiplication.ptx', ...
     'matrixMultiplication.cu');
>> n = 5000;
>> k.ThreadBlockSize = [10, 10, 1];
>> k.GridSize = [100, 100];
>> A = rand(n);
>> B = rand(n);
>> tic; C = A * B; toc
>> gpuA = gpuArray(A);
```

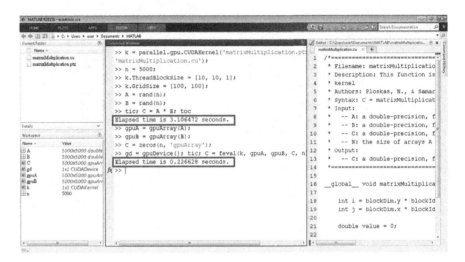

FIG. 7.16

Comparison of CPU and GPU implementations of the matrix multiplication.

```
>> gpuB = gpuArray(B);
>> C = zeros(n, 'gpuArray');
>> gd = gpuDevice(); tic; C = feval(k, gpuA, gpuB, C, n); wait(gd); toc
```

7.5 CHAPTER REVIEW

This chapter described how to create an executable kernel for a CUDA C code or PTX code and run that kernel on a GPU by calling it through MATLAB. Moreover, a brief introduction of CUDA C was presented. Furthermore, two classic examples, vector addition and matrix multiplication, were presented.

To sum up, you should consider utilizing CU or PTX files in your applications in order to:

- Further optimize the performance of your application.
- Implement GPU-based functions that are not GPU-enabled in MATLAB, that is, cannot be executed using a *gpuArray* object.
- Implement a function that is already GPU-enabled in MATLAB but you want to optimize its performance or implement a different algorithm.

MATLAB MEX functions containing CUDA code

8

CHAPTER OBJECTIVES

This Chapter explains how to create a MATLAB MEX file that contains CUDA code and run it on a GPU by calling it through MATLAB. Furthermore, two classic examples, vector addition and matrix multiplication, are presented. After reading this Chapter, you should be able to:

- understand the basic features of a MEX file.
- compile MEX files that contain CUDA code.
- execute MEX files that contain CUDA code by calling them through MATLAB.
- understand the difference of a MEX file that contains CUDA code and a *CUDAKernel* object.
- use host-side libraries in your MEX files.

8.1 A BRIEF INTRODUCTION TO MATLAB MEX FILES

The aim of this section is to present the basic features of a MATLAB MEX file. Interested readers that are not familiar with MATLAB MEX files should refer to the MATLAB's external interfaces user's guide [17] for more information.

A MEX file contains C, C++, or Fortran source code. Compiling a MEX file using the command *mex*, MATLAB creates a binary MEX file, which is a dynamically linked subroutine that the MATLAB interpreter can execute. A MEX file contains only one function or subroutine, and its name is the MEX file name. To call a MEX file, use the name of the file, without the file extension.

You cannot use a binary MEX file on a platform if you compiled it on a different platform because MATLAB identifies MEX files by platform-specific extensions:

- Microsoft Windows 32-bit: *mexw32*
- Microsoft Windows 64-bit: *mexw64*
- Linux 64-bit: *mexa64*
- Apple MAC 64-bit: *mexmaci64*

Recompile the source code on the platform for which you want to use the MEX file.

While MATLAB works with a single object type, the MATLAB array, the MATLAB array in C/C++ is declared to be of type *mxArray*. The *mxArray* structure contains the following information about the array:

- Its type
- Its dimensions
- Its data
- If numeric, whether the variable is real or complex
- If sparse, its indices and nonzero maximum elements
- If a structure or object, the number of fields and field names

To access the *mxArray* structure, there are a number of Matrix Library functions that allow programmers to create, read, and query information about the MATLAB data in the MEX files. Matrix Library functions use the *mwSize* type to avoid portability issues and allow MEX source files to be compiled correctly on all systems.

The gateway routine is the entry point to the MEX file. It is through this routine that MATLAB accesses the rest of the routines in your MEX files. The name of the gateway routine is *mexFunction*. It takes the place of the main function in your source code.

The signature of the *mexfunction* is

```
void mexFunction(int nlhs, mxArray *plhs[], int nrhs, const mxArray *
    prhs[])
```

where:

- *prhs*: array of right-hand side input arguments.
- *plhs*: array of left-hand side output arguments.
- *nrhs*: number of right-hand side arguments.
- *nlhs*: number of left-hand side arguments.

prhs and *plhs* are of type *mxArray ***, which means they point to MATLAB arrays. They are vectors that contain pointers to the arguments of the MEX file. The keyword *const*, which modifies *prhs*, means that your MEX file does not modify the input arguments. Place *mexFunction* function after your computational routine and any other functions in your source file.

For example, the following code adds a scalar number *b* to a vector *A* of size *N* and stores the result into vector *C*:

```
1.   #include "mex.h"
2.
3.   /* the computational routine */
4.   void VectorScalarAddition(double* A, double b, double* C, mwSize N){
5.       mwSize i;
6.       for(i = 0; i < N; i++){
7.           C[i] = A[i] + b;
8.       }
9.   }
10.
11.  /* The gateway function */
12.  void mexFunction(int nlhs, mxArray *plhs[], int nrhs,
     const mxArray *prhs[]){
13.      ...
14.      /* call the computational routine */
15.      VectorScalarAddition(...);
16.      ...
17.  }
```

In the previous example, we declared variable *N* as *mwSize* instead of *int* in order to write a compiler-independent MEX file.

The following data types are available for use in a MEX file:

- *mxArray*: Type for MATLAB array.
- *mwSize*: Type of size values.
- *mwIndex*: Type for index values.
- *mwSignedIndex*: Signed integer type for size values.
- *mxChar*: Type for string array.
- *mxLogical*: Type for logical array.
- *mxClassID*: Enumerated value identifying class of array.
- *mxComplexity*: Flag specifying whether the array has imaginary components.

Matrix Library offers various functions to create arrays in C/C++ files. The most common of them are:

- *mxCreateDoubleMatrix*: Create two-dimensional, double-precision, floating-point array.
- *mxCreateDoubleScalar*: Create scalar, double-precision array initialized to specified value.
- *mxCreateNumericMatrix*: Create two-dimensional numeric matrix.
- *mxCreateNumericArray*: Create *N*-dimensional numeric array.
- *mxCreateSparse*: Create two-dimensional sparse array.
- *mxMalloc*: Allocate uninitialized dynamic memory.
- *mxCalloc*: Allocate dynamic memory for array, initialized to 0.
- *mxRealloc*: Reallocate dynamic memory.
- *mxFree*: Free dynamic memory allocated by *mxMalloc*, *mxCalloc*, *mxRealloc*, etc.

Matrix Library also offers various functions for validating data. The most common functions used to determine the type or characteristic of an array data are:

- *mxIsDouble*: Determine whether mxArray represents data as double-precision, floating-point numbers.
- *mxIsSingle*: Determine whether array represents data as single-precision, floating-point numbers.
- *mxIsComplex*: Determine whether data is complex.
- *mxIsNumeric*: Determine whether array is numeric.
- *mxIsSparse*: Determine whether input is sparse array.
- *mxIsEmpty*: Determine whether array is empty.

Finally, Matrix Library offers various functions to access data. The most common of them are:

- *mxGetNumberOfDimensions*: Number of dimensions in array.
- *mxGetDimensions*: Pointer to dimensions array.
- *mxSetDimensions*: Modify number of dimensions and size of each dimension.
- *mxGetNumberOfElements*: Number of elements in array.
- *mxGetM*: Number of rows in array.
- *mxSetM*: Set number of rows in array.
- *mxGetN*: Number of columns in array.
- *mxSetN*: Set number of columns in array.
- *mxGetScalar*: Real component of first data element in array.
- *mxGetPr*: Real data elements in array of type *double*.
- *mxSetPr*: Set new real data elements in array of type *double*.
- *mxGetPi*: Imaginary data elements in array of type *double*.
- *mxSetPi*: Set new imaginary data elements in array of type *double*.
- *mxGetData*: Pointer to real numeric data elements in array.
- *mxSetData*: Set pointer to real numeric data elements in array.
- *mxGetImagData*: Pointer to imaginary data elements in array.
- *mxSetImagData*: Set pointer to imaginary data elements in array.

For example, the following code adds a scalar number b to a vector A of size N and stores the result into vector C (filename: VectorScalarAddition.cpp):

```
1.   /*=============================================================
2.    * Filename: VectorScalarAddition.cpp
3.    * Description: This function adds a scalar number b to a
4.    * vector A of size N and stores the result into vector
5.    * C
6.    * Authors: Ploskas, N., & Samaras, N.
7.    * Syntax: C = VectorScalarAddition(A, b)
8.    * Input:
9.    *    -- A: a double-precision, floating point array of size N
```

```
10.    *    -- b: a double-precision, floating point scalar
11.    * Output:
12.    *    -- C: a double-precision, floating point array of size N
13.    *================================================================*/
14.
15.   #include "mex.h"
16.
17.   /*
18.    * The computational routine
19.    */
20.   void VectorScalarAddition(double* A, double b, double* C, mwSize N){
21.
22.      mwSize i;
23.
24.      for(i = 0; i < N; i++){
25.         C[i] = A[i] + b;
26.      }
27.   }
28.
29.   /*
30.    * The gateway function
31.    */
32.   void mexFunction(int nlhs, mxArray *plhs[], int nrhs,
         const mxArray *prhs[]){
33.
34.      /* declare all variables */
35.      double *A;
36.      double b;
37.      double *C;
38.      size_t N;
39.
40.      /* define error messages */
41.      char const * const errId =
            "parallel:gpu:VectorScalarAddition:InvalidInput";
42.      char const * const errMsg = "Invalid input to MEX file.";
43.
44.      /* check input data */
45.      if(nrhs != 2 || !mxIsDouble(prhs[0]) || mxIsComplex(prhs[0]) ||
            !mxIsDouble(prhs[1]) || mxIsComplex(prhs[1]) ||
            mxGetNumberOfElements(prhs[1]) !=1 ){
46.         mexErrMsgIdAndTxt(errId, errMsg);
47.      }
48.
49.      /* get input arrays */
50.      A = mxGetPr(prhs[0]);
51.      b = mxGetScalar(prhs[1]);
52.
53.      /* find array dimensions */
54.      N = mxGetN(prhs[0]);
55.
56.      /* initialize output array */
57.      plhs[0] = mxCreateDoubleMatrix(1, (mwSize)N, mxREAL);
58.      C = mxGetPr(plhs[0]);
59.
60.      /* call the computational routine */
61.      VectorScalarAddition(A, b, C, (mwSize)N);
62.   }
```

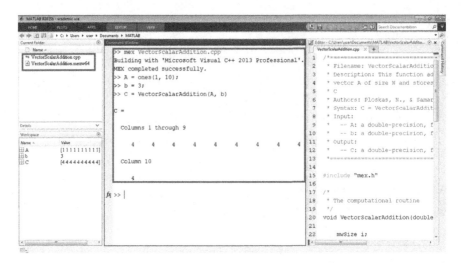

FIG. 8.1

Compile and execute MEX file through MATLAB.

We can compile and execute this MEX file through MATLAB using the following code (Fig. 8.1):

```
>> mex VectorScalarAddition.cpp
>> A = ones(1, 10);
>> b = 3;
>> C = VectorScalarAddition(A, b)
```

Note that a supported compiler should be installed to compile the MEX file. MathWorks publishes the supported compilers for each operating system. You can find the supported compilers for MATLAB R2015b here: http://www.mathworks.com/support/compilers/R2015b/index.html.

8.2 STEPS TO RUN MATLAB MEX FUNCTIONS ON GPU

There are two options that you can use to execute MATLAB MEX functions on GPU:

- Create a CU MEX file that contains CUDA code, compile it with the *mexcuda* command, and execute it passing as argument MATLAB arrays. For example, we will extend the *VectorScalarAddition* example to add the vector and the scalar on the GPU. The arguments of this MEX function are MATLAB arrays (Fig. 8.2):

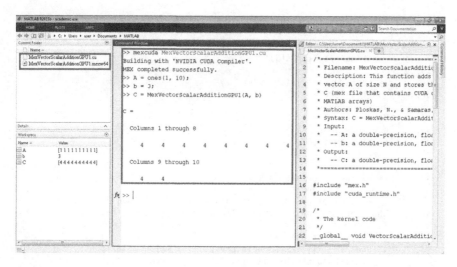

FIG. 8.2

Compile and execute MEX file that contains CUDA code (arguments as MATLAB arrays).

```
1.    /*===========================================================
2.    * Filename: MexVectorScalarAdditionGPU1.cu
3.    * Description: This function adds a scalar number b to a
4.    * vector A of size N and stores the result into vector
5.    * C (mex file that contains CUDA code and takes as inputs
6.    * MATLAB arrays)
7.    * Authors: Ploskas, N., & Samaras, N.
8.    * Syntax: C = MexVectorScalarAdditionGPU1(A, b)
9.    * Input:
10.   *   -- A: a double-precision, floating point array of size N
11.   *   -- b: a double-precision, floating point scalar
12.   * Output:
13.   *   -- C: a double-precision, floating point array of size N
14.   *===========================================================*/
15.
16.   #include "mex.h"
17.   #include "cuda_runtime.h"
18.
19.   /*
20.    * The kernel code
21.    */
22.   _ _global_ _ void VectorScalarAddition(const double* A,
         const double b, double* C, const int N){
23.
24.      int i = blockDim.x * blockIdx.x + threadIdx.x;
25.
26.      if(i < N){
27.          C[i] = A[i] + b;
28.      }
29.   }
30.
31.   /*
```

```
32.    * The gateway function
33.    */
34.  void mexFunction(int nlhs, mxArray *plhs[], int nrhs,
         const mxArray *prhs[]){
35.
36.      /* declare all variables */
37.      const double *A;
38.      double *deviceA;
39.      double b;
40.      double *C;
41.      double *deviceC;
42.      size_t N;
43.
44.      /* define error messages */
45.      char const * const errId =
             "parallel:gpu:MexVectorScalarAdditionGPU1:InvalidInput";
46.      char const * const errMsg = "Invalid input to MEX file.";
47.
48.      /* check input data */
49.      if(nrhs != 2 || !mxIsDouble(prhs[0]) || mxIsComplex(prhs[0]) ||
             !mxIsDouble(prhs[1]) || mxIsComplex(prhs[1]) ||
             mxGetNumberOfElements(prhs[1]) !=1 ){
50.          mexErrMsgIdAndTxt(errId, errMsg);
51.      }
52.
53.      /* get input arrays */
54.      A = mxGetPr(prhs[0]);
55.      b = mxGetScalar(prhs[1]);
56.
57.      /* find array dimensions */
58.      N = mxGetN(prhs[0]);
59.
60.      /* initialize output array */
61.      plhs[0] = mxCreateDoubleMatrix(1, (mwSize)N, mxREAL);
62.      C = mxGetPr(plhs[0]);
63.
64.      /* allocate memory */
65.      cudaMalloc(&deviceA, sizeof(double) * (int)N);
66.      cudaMalloc(&deviceC, sizeof(double) * (int)N);
67.
68.      /* copy input vector from host memory to device memory */
69.      cudaMemcpy(deviceA, A, (int)N * sizeof(double),
             cudaMemcpyHostToDevice);
70.
71.      /* invoke kernel */
72.      int threadsPerBlock = 256;
73.      int blocksPerGrid = (N + threadsPerBlock - 1) / threadsPerBlock;
74.      VectorScalarAddition<<<blocksPerGrid, threadsPerBlock>>>
             (deviceA, b, deviceC, (int)N);
75.
76.      /* copy result from device memory to host memory */
77.      cudaMemcpy(C, deviceC, (int)N * sizeof(double),
             cudaMemcpyDeviceToHost);
78.
79.      /* destroy the arrays on the device */
80.      cudaFree(deviceA);
81.      cudaFree(deviceC);
82.  }
```

- Create a CU MEX file that contains CUDA code, compile it with the *mexcuda* command, and execute it passing as arguments *gpuArray* variables. The previous example uses MEX and CUDA functions to implement the operation on the GPU. However, the inputs need to be transferred from the host to the device and the outputs from the device to the host. So, it is only appropriate to use this method when you have a function that you want to optimize its execution time but your data in MATLAB are stored on the main memory and not the device memory. On the other hand, if your MATLAB application uses *gpuArray* variables, then you expect to be able to pass them as arguments to a MEX function without the need to convert them to MATLAB arrays. MATLAB extended the MEX interface to be able to handle *gpuArray* variables. As with regular MEX files, those containing CUDA code have a single entry point, known as *mexFunction*. The *mexFunction* contains the host code that interacts with *gpuArray* objects from MATLAB and launches the CUDA code. The CUDA code in the MEX file must conform to the CUDA runtime API. Initially, you should call the *mxInitGPU* function at the entry to your MEX file. This ensures that the GPU device is properly initialized and known to MATLAB. The interface you use to write a MEX file for *gpuArray* objects is different from the MEX interface for standard MATLAB arrays. Using the *mxGPU API*, you can perform calculations on a *gpuArray* and return *gpuArray* results to MATLAB. You can perform calculations by passing the pointers to CUDA functions that you write or that are available in external libraries. MATLAB offers the following functions that handle *gpuArray* variables inside a MEX file [5]:

  (1) *mxGPUArray*: *mxGPUArray* is an opaque C language type that allows a MEX function access to the elements in a MATLAB *gpuArray*. All MEX functions receive inputs and pass outputs as *mxArrays*. A *gpuArray* in MATLAB is a special kind of *mxArray* that represents an array stored on the GPU. In your MEX function, you use *mxGPUArray* objects to access an array stored on the GPU.

  (2) *mxGPUCopyFromMxArray*: *mxGPUCopyFromMxArray* produces a new *mxGPUArray* object with the same characteristics as the input *mxArray*. If the input *mxArray* contains a *gpuArray*, the output is a new copy of the data on the GPU. If the input *mxArray* contains numeric or logical CPU data, the output is copied to the GPU.

  (3) *mxGPUCopyGPUArray*: *mxGPUCopyGPUArray* produces a new array on the GPU and copies the data, and then returns a new *mxGPUArray* that refers to the copy.

  (4) *mxGPUCopyImag*: *mxGPUCopyImag* copies the imaginary part of GPU data and returns a new *mxGPUArray* object that refers to the copy. The returned array is real, with element values equal to the imaginary values of the input, similar to how the MATLAB *imag* function behaves. If the input is real rather than complex, the function returns an array of zeros.

  (5) *mxGPUCopyReal*: *mxGPUCopyReal* copies the real part of GPU data and returns a new *mxGPUArray* object that refers to the copy. If the input is real rather than complex, the function returns a copy of the input.

(6) *mxGPUCreateComplexGPUArray*: *mxGPUCreateComplexGPUArray* creates a new complex *mxGPUArray* from two real *mxGPUArray* objects. The function allocates memory on the GPU and copies the data. The inputs must both be real and have matching sizes and classes.

(7) *mxGPUCreateFromMxArray*: *mxGPUCreateFromMxArray* produces a read-only *mxGPUArray* object from an *mxArray*. If the input *mxArray* contains a *gpuArray*, this function extracts a reference to the GPU data from an *mxArray* passed as an input to the function. If the input *mxArray* contains CPU data, the data is copied to the GPU, but the returned object is still read-only.

(8) *mxGPUCreateGPUArray*: *mxGPUCreateGPUArray* creates a new *mxGPUArray* object with the specified size, type, and complexity. It also allocates the required memory on the GPU, and initializes the memory if requested.

(9) *mxGPUCreateMxArrayOnCPU*: *mxGPUCreateMxArrayOnCPU* copies the GPU data from the specified *mxGPUArray* into an *mxArray* on the CPU for return to MATLAB. This is similar to the *gather* function.

(10) *mxGPUCreateMxArrayOnGPU*: *mxGPUCreateMxArrayOnGPU* puts the *mxGPUArray* into an *mxArray* for return to MATLAB. The data remains on the GPU and the returned class in MATLAB is *gpuArray*.

(11) *mxGPUDestroyGPUArray*: *mxGPUDestroyGPUArray* deletes an *mxGPUArray* object on the CPU.

(12) *mxGPUGetClassID*: *mxGPUGetClassID* returns an *mxClassID* type indicating the underlying class of the input data.

(13) *mxGPUGetComplexity*: *mxGPUGetComplexity* returns an *mxComplexity* type indicating the complexity of the GPU data.

(14) *mxGPUGetData*: *mxGPUGetData* returns a raw pointer to the underlying data.

(15) *mxGPUGetDataReadOnly*: *mxGPUGetDataReadOnly* returns a read-only raw pointer to the underlying data.

(16) *mxGPUGetDimensions*: *mxGPUGetDimensions* returns a pointer to an array of *mwSize* indicating the dimensions of the input argument.

(17) *mxGPUGetNumberOfDimensions*: *mxGPUGetNumberOfDimensions* returns the size of the dimension array for the *mxGPUArray* input argument, indicating the number of its dimensions.

(18) *mxGPUGetNumberOfElements*: *mxGPUGetNumberOfElements* returns the total number of elements on the GPU for this array.

(19) *mxGPUIsSame*: *mxGPUIsSame* returns an integer indicating if two *mxGPUArray* pointers refer to the same GPU data. A value of 1 (true) indicates that the inputs refer to the same data, while a value of 0 (false) indicates that the inputs do not refer to the same data.

(20) *mxGPUIsSparse*: *mxGPUIsSparse* returns an integer indicating if an *mxGPUArray* is sparse or not. A value of 1 (true) indicates the input is a sparse *gpuArray*, while a value of 0 (false) indicates the input is not a sparse *gpuArray*.

(21) *mxGPUIsValidGPUData*: *mxGPUIsValidGPUData* returns an integer indicating if an *mxArray* is a pointer to valid GPU data. A value of 1 (true) indicates that the *mxArray* is a pointer to valid GPU data, while a value of 1 (false) indicates that the *mxGPUArray* is not a pointer to valid GPU data.

(22) *mxInitGPU*: Before using any CUDA code in your MEX file, initialize the MATLAB GPU library if you intend to use any *mxGPUArray* functionality in MEX or any GPU calls in MATLAB.

(23) *mxIsGPUArray*: *mxIsGPUArray* returns an integer indicating if an *mxArray* is a *gpuArray* or not. A value of 1 indicates that the *mxArray* is a *gpuArray*, while a value of 0 indicates that the *mxArray* is not a gpuArray.

The basic structure of a GPU MEX function is

(1) Call *mxInitGPU* function to initialize MathWorks GPU library.

(2) Determine which *mxArray* inputs contain GPU data.

(3) Create *mxGPUArray* objects from the input *mxArray* arguments, and get pointers to the input elements on the device.

(4) Create *mxGPUArray* objects to hold the outputs, and get the pointers to the output elements on the device.

(5) Set properties, for example, number of blocks and number of threads per block, to control its execution on the GPU.

(6) Call a CUDA function, passing to it the device pointers.

(7) Wrap the output *mxGPUArray* as an *mxArray* for return to MATLAB.

(8) Destroy the *mxGPUArray* objects you created.

The header file that contains this type is *mxGPUArray.h*.

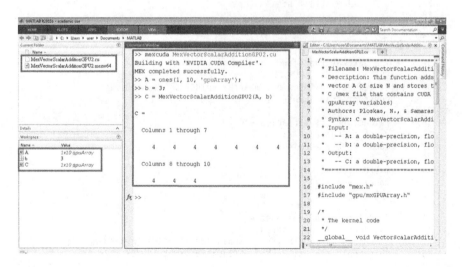

FIG. 8.3

Compile and execute MEX file that contains CUDA code (arguments as *gpuArray* objects).

For example, we will extend the *VectorScalarAddition* example of the previous section to add the vector and the scalar on the GPU using the MathWorks GPU library (Fig. 8.3):

```
1.    /*===============================================================
2.     * Filename: MexVectorScalarAdditionGPU2.cu
3.     * Description: This function adds a scalar number b to a
4.     * vector A of size N and stores the result into vector
5.     * C (mex file that contains CUDA code and takes as inputs
6.     * gpuArray variables)
7.     * Authors: Ploskas, N., & Samaras, N.
8.     * Syntax: C = MexVectorScalarAdditionGPU2(A, b)
9.     * Input:
10.    *    -- A: a double-precision, floating point GPU array of size N
11.    *    -- b: a double-precision, floating point scalar
12.    * Output:
13.    *    -- C: a double-precision, floating point GPU array of size N
14.    *===============================================================*/
15.
16.   #include "mex.h"
17.   #include "gpu/mxGPUArray.h"
18.
19.   /*
20.    * The kernel code
21.    */
22.   _ _global_ _ void VectorScalarAddition(const double* A,
          const double b, double* C, const int N){
23.
24.       int i = blockDim.x * blockIdx.x + threadIdx.x;
25.
26.       if(i < N){
27.           C[i] = A[i] + b;
28.       }
29.   }
30.
31.   /*
32.    * The gateway function
33.    */
34.   void mexFunction(int nlhs, mxArray *plhs[], int nrhs,
          const mxArray *prhs[]){
35.
36.       /* declare all variables */
37.       const mxGPUArray *A;
38.       const double *deviceA;
39.       double b;
40.       mxGPUArray *C;
41.       double *deviceC;
42.       int N;
43.
44.       /* define error messages */
45.       char const * const errId =
              "parallel:gpu:MexVectorScalarAdditionGPU2:InvalidInput";
46.       char const * const errMsg = "Invalid input to MEX file.";
47.
48.       /* initialize the MathWorks GPU API */
```

```
49.    mxInitGPU();
50.
51.    /* check input data */
52.    if((nrhs != 2) || !(mxIsGPUArray(prhs[0]))) {
53.        mexErrMsgIdAndTxt(errId, errMsg);
54.    }
55.
56.    /* get input arrays */
57.    A = mxGPUCreateFromMxArray(prhs[0]);
58.    b = mxGetScalar(prhs[1]);
59.
60.    /* verify that A is double array before extracting the pointer */
61.    if (mxGPUGetClassID(A) != mxDOUBLE_CLASS){
62.        mexErrMsgIdAndTxt(errId, errMsg);
63.    }
64.
65.    /* extract a pointer to the input data on the device */
66.    deviceA = (double const *)(mxGPUGetDataReadOnly(A));
67.
68.    /* create a GPUArray to hold the result and get its
           underlying pointer. */
69.    C = mxGPUCreateGPUArray(mxGPUGetNumberOfDimensions(A),
70.                            mxGPUGetDimensions(A),
71.                            mxGPUGetClassID(A),
72.                            mxGPUGetComplexity(A),
73.                            MX_GPU_DO_NOT_INITIALIZE);
74.    deviceC = (double *)(mxGPUGetData(C));
75.
76.     /* invoke kernel */
77.    N = (int)(mxGPUGetNumberOfElements(A));
78.    int const threadsPerBlock = 256;
79.    int blocksPerGrid = (N + threadsPerBlock - 1) / threadsPerBlock;
80.    VectorScalarAddition<<<blocksPerGrid, threadsPerBlock>>>
           (deviceA, b, deviceC, N);
81.
82.    /* wrap the result up as a MATLAB gpuArray for return */
83.    plhs[0] = mxGPUCreateMxArrayOnGPU(C);
84.
85.    /*
86.     * the mxGPUArray pointers are host-side structures that refer to
87.     * device data. These must be destroyed before leaving the MEX
88.     * function.
89.     */
90.    mxGPUDestroyGPUArray(A);
91.    mxGPUDestroyGPUArray(C);
92.  }
```

If we compare the execution time of the examples of the preceding options, the second option, where the GPU MEX file is used, is faster because the input data are already on the GPU, and there is no need for transfer between the CPU and the GPU (Fig. 8.4).

Comparing with the use of *CUDAKernel* objects (see Chapter 7), it is preferable to use GPU MEX files for the following reasons [5]:

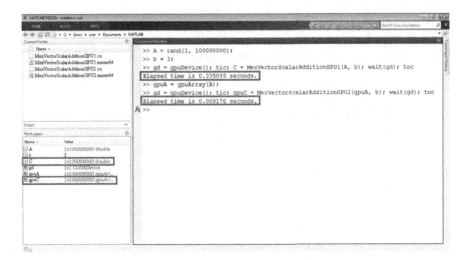

FIG. 8.4

Compare the execution time of the two examples.

- GPU MEX files can interact with host-side libraries, such as *cuBLAS* or *cuFFT* libraries and can also contain calls from the host to functions in the CUDA runtime library.
- GPU MEX files can analyze the size of the input and allocate memory of a different size, or launch grids of a different size, from C or C++ code. In comparison, MATLAB code that calls *CUDAKernel* objects must pre-allocate output memory and determine the grid size.
- GPU MEX files can utilize multiple GPUs.

On the contrary, the use of *CUDAKernel* is easier because you only need to write the kernel code.

The main reasons that you should use GPU MEX files in your applications are the following:

- Further optimize the performance of your application.
- Implement GPU-based functions that are not GPU-enabled in MATLAB, that is, cannot be executed using a *gpuArray* object.
- Implement a function that is already GPU-enabled in MATLAB but you want to optimize its performance or implement a different algorithm.
- Access host-side libraries, such as *cuBLAS* or *cuFFT* libraries, or call from the host functions in the CUDA runtime library.
- Allocate memory of a different size or launch grids of a different size.
- Utilize multiple GPUs.

8.3 **EXAMPLE: VECTOR ADDITION**

This example summarizes the steps to create a MATLAB MEX file that contains CUDA code and run it on a GPU by calling it through MATLAB. It is a classic example that implements element by element vector addition. The following code is the GPU MEX file that contains CUDA code and takes as inputs *gpuArray* variables (filename: mexVectorAddition.cu):

```
1.   /*==================================================================
2.    * Filename: mexVectorAddition.cu
3.    * Description: This function implements element by element
4.    * vector addition (GPU mex file that contains CUDA code and
5.    * takes as inputs gpuArray variables)
6.    * Authors: Ploskas, N., & Samaras, N.
7.    * Syntax: C = mexVectorAddition(A, b)
8.    * Input:
9.    *    -- A: a double-precision, floating point GPU array of size N
10.   *    -- B: a double-precision, floating point GPU array of size N
11.   * Output:
12.   *    -- C: a double-precision, floating point GPU array of size N
13.   *==================================================================*/
14.
15.  #include "mex.h"
16.  #include "gpu/mxGPUArray.h"
17.
18.  /*
19.   * The kernel code
20.   */
21.  _ _global_ _ void vectorAddition(const double *A,const double *B,
         double *C, const int N){
22.
23.      int i = blockDim.x * blockIdx.x + threadIdx.x;
24.
25.      if(i < N){
26.          C[i] = A[i] + B[i];
27.      }
28.  }
29.
30.  /*
31.   * The gateway function
32.   */
33.  void mexFunction(int nlhs, mxArray *plhs[], int nrhs, mxArray
         const *prhs[]){
34.
35.      /* declare all variables */
36.      mxGPUArray const *A;
37.      mxGPUArray const *B;
38.      mxGPUArray *C;
39.      double const *d_A;
40.      double const *d_B;
41.      double *d_C;
42.      int N;
43.
44.      /* define error messages */
45.      char const * const errId =
             "parallel:gpu:mexVectorAddition:InvalidInput";
46.      char const * const errMsg = "Invalid input to MEX file.";
47.
48.      /* initialize the MathWorks GPU API */
49.      mxInitGPU();
50.
51.      /* check input data */
52.      if((nrhs != 2) || !(mxIsGPUArray(prhs[0])) || !(mxIsGPUArray(prhs[1]))) {
```

```
53.          mexErrMsgIdAndTxt(errId, errMsg);
54.      }
55.
56.      /* get input arrays */
57.      A = mxGPUCreateFromMxArray(prhs[0]);
58.      B = mxGPUCreateFromMxArray(prhs[1]);
59.
60.      /* verify that A and B are double arrays before extracting
             the pointer */
61.      if (mxGPUGetClassID(A) != mxDOUBLE_CLASS ||
             mxGPUGetClassID(B) != mxDOUBLE_CLASS){
62.          mexErrMsgIdAndTxt(errId, errMsg);
63.      }
64.
65.      /* extract a pointer to the input data on the device */
66.      d_A = (double const *)(mxGPUGetDataReadOnly(A));
67.      d_B = (double const *)(mxGPUGetDataReadOnly(B));
68.
69.      /* create a GPUArray to hold the result and get its
             underlying pointer. */
70.      C = mxGPUCreateGPUArray(mxGPUGetNumberOfDimensions(A),
71.                              mxGPUGetDimensions(A),
72.                              mxGPUGetClassID(A),
73.                              mxGPUGetComplexity(A),
74.                              MX_GPU_DO_NOT_INITIALIZE);
75.      d_C = (double *)(mxGPUGetData(C));
76.
77.      /* invoke kernel */
78.      N = (int)(mxGPUGetNumberOfElements(A));
79.      int const threadsPerBlock = 256;
80.      int blocksPerGrid = (N + threadsPerBlock - 1) / threadsPerBlock;
81.      vectorAddition<<<blocksPerGrid, threadsPerBlock>>>(d_A, d_B, d_C, N);
82.
83.      /* wrap the result up as a MATLAB gpuArray for return */
84.      plhs[0] = mxGPUCreateMxArrayOnGPU(C);
85.
86.      /*
87.       * the mxGPUArray pointers are host-side structures that refer to
88.       * device data. These must be destroyed before leaving the MEX
89.       * function.
90.       */
91.      mxGPUDestroyGPUArray(A);
92.      mxGPUDestroyGPUArray(B);
93.      mxGPUDestroyGPUArray(C);
94.  }
```

The following MATLAB code compiles the CU file, creates a binary MEX file, creates the appropriate input and output data as *gpuArray* variables, and executes the kernel (Fig. 8.5).

```
>> mexcuda mexVectorAddition.cu
>> n = 10;
>> A = rand(n, 1, 'gpuArray');
>> B = rand(n, 1, 'gpuArray');
>> C = mexVectorAddition(A, B);
>> D = A + B;
>> (C - D)'
```

The following code compares the execution of the vector addition on the CPU using MATLAB built-in commands and using the GPU MEX file running on the GPU (Fig. 8.6):

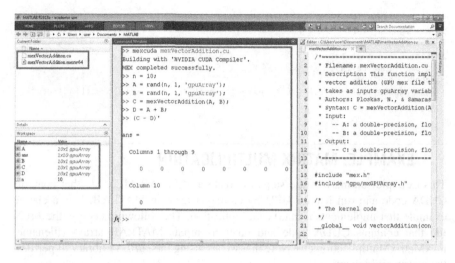

FIG. 8.5

Invoking the MEX function of the vector addition.

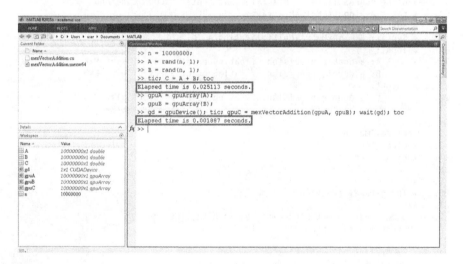

FIG. 8.6

Comparison of CPU and GPU implementation of the vector addition.

```
>> n = 10000000;
>> A = rand(n, 1);
>> B = rand(n, 1);
>> tic; C = A + B; toc
>> gpuA = gpuArray(A);
>> gpuB = gpuArray(B);
>> gd = gpuDevice(); tic; gpuC = mexVectorAddition(gpuA, gpuB); wait(gd); toc
```

8.4 EXAMPLE: MATRIX MULTIPLICATION

This example summarizes the steps to create a MATLAB MEX file that contains CUDA code and run it on a GPU by calling it through MATLAB. It is a classic example that implements a matrix multiplication. The following code is the MEX file that contains CUDA code and takes as inputs MATLAB arrays (filename: mexMatrixMultiplication.cu). Note that we are using the *cuBLAS* library to perform the matrix multiplication.

```
1.   /*=========================================================
2.    * Filename: mexMatrixMultiplication.cu
3.    * Description: This function implements a matrix multiplication
4.    * using cuBLAS library (MEX file that contains CUDA code and
5.    * takes as inputs MATLAB arrays)
6.    * Authors: Ploskas, N., & Samaras, N.
7.    * Syntax: C = mexMatrixMultiplication(A, b)
8.    * Input:
9.    *    -- A: a double-precision, floating point array of size MxK
10.   *    -- B: a double-precision, floating point array of size KxN
11.   * Output:
12.   *    -- C: a double-precision, floating point array of size MxN
13.   *=========================================================*/
14.
15.  #include "mex.h"
16.  #include "cuda_runtime.h"
17.  #include "cublas_v2.h"
18.
19.  /*
20.   * The gateway function
21.   */
22.  void mexFunction(int nlhs, mxArray *plhs[], int nrhs,
         const mxArray *prhs[]){
23.
24.      /* declare all variables */
25.      double *deviceA, *deviceB, *deviceC;
26.      const double *A, *B;
27.      double *C;
28.      int numARows, numACols;
29.      int numBRows, numBCols;
30.      int numCRows, numCCols;
31.
32.      /* define error messages */
33.      char const * const errId =
             "parallel:gpu:mexMatrixMultiplication:InvalidInput";
34.      char const * const errMsg = "Invalid input to MEX file.";
```

```
35.
36.      /* check input data */
37.      if(nrhs != 2){
38.          mexErrMsgIdAndTxt(errId, errMsg);
39.      }
40.
41.      /* get input arrays */
42.      A = (double *)mxGetData(prhs[0]);
43.      B = (double *)mxGetData(prhs[1]);
44.
45.      /* find arrays dimensions */
46.      numARows = (int)mxGetM(prhs[0]);
47.      numACols = (int)mxGetN(prhs[0]);
48.      numBRows = (int)mxGetM(prhs[1]);
49.      numBCols = (int)mxGetN(prhs[1]);
50.      numCRows = numARows;
51.      numCCols = numBCols;
52.
53.      /* initialize output array */
54.      plhs[0] = mxCreateNumericMatrix(numCRows, numCCols,
                 mxDOUBLE_CLASS, mxREAL);
55.      C = (double *)mxGetData(plhs[0]);
56.
57.      /* allocate memory on the GPU */
58.      cudaMalloc(&deviceA, sizeof(double) * numARows * numACols);
59.      cudaMalloc(&deviceB, sizeof(double) * numBRows * numBCols);
60.      cudaMalloc(&deviceC, sizeof(double) * numCRows * numCCols);
61.
62.      /* set arrays and perform the matrix multiplication using CUBLAS */
63.      cublasHandle_t handle;
64.      cublasCreate(&handle);
65.      cublasSetMatrix(numARows,
66.                      numACols,
67.                      sizeof(double),
68.                      A,
69.                      numARows,
70.                      deviceA,
71.                      numARows);
72.      cublasSetMatrix(numBRows,
73.                      numBCols,
74.                      sizeof(double),
75.                      B,
76.                      numBRows,
77.                      deviceB,
78.                      numBRows);
79.      double alpha = 1.0;
80.      double beta = 0.0;
81.      cublasDgemm(handle,
82.                  CUBLAS_OP_N,
83.                  CUBLAS_OP_N,
84.                  numARows,
85.                  numBCols,
86.                  numACols,
87.                  &alpha,
88.                  deviceA,
89.                  numARows,
90.                  deviceB,
91.                  numBRows,
```

```
92.              &beta,
93.              deviceC,
94.              numCRows);
95.
96.      /* retrieve result */
97.      cublasGetMatrix(numCRows,
98.                  numCCols,
99.                  sizeof(double),
100.                 deviceC,
101.                 numCRows,
102.                 C,
103.                 numCRows);
104.
105.     /* destroy the handle and the arrays on the device */
106.     cublasDestroy(handle);
107.     cudaFree(deviceA);
108.     cudaFree(deviceB);
109.     cudaFree(deviceC);
110. }
```

The following MATLAB code compiles the CU file, creates a binary MEX file, creates the appropriate input and output data as MATLAB arrays, and executes the kernel (Fig. 8.7).

Note that when compiling the MEX file with the *mexcuda* command, we need to specify that we are using the *cuBLAS* library (-*lcublas*) and the directory where the header files for CUDA and *cuBLAS* are located (-I"C:\ProgramFiles\ NVIDIAGPUComputingToolkit\CUDA\v7.0\include"). You need to change that directory according to your operating system and the version of the CUDA Toolkit.

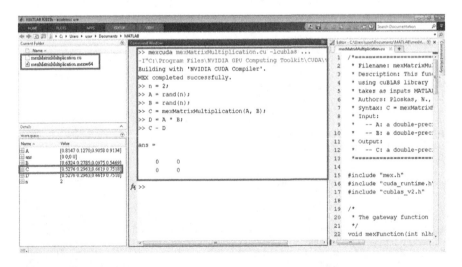

FIG. 8.7

Invoking the MEX function of the matrix multiplication.

```
>> mexcuda mexMatrixMultiplication.cu -lcublas ...
    -I"C:\Program Files\NVIDIA GPU Computing Toolkit\CUDA\v7.0\include"
>> n = 2;
>> A = rand(n);
>> B = rand(n);
>> C = mexMatrixMultiplication(A, B);
>> D = A * B;
>> C - D
```

The following code compares the execution time of the matrix multiplication on the CPU using MATLAB built-in commands and using the MEX file running on the GPU (Fig. 8.8):

```
>> n = 5000;
>> A = rand(n);
>> B = rand(n);
>> tic; C = A * B; toc
>> gd = gpuDevice(); tic; D = mexMatrixMultiplication(A, B); wait(gd); toc
```

8.5 CHAPTER REVIEW

This chapter described how to create a MATLAB MEX file that contains CUDA code and run it on a GPU by calling it through MATLAB. Furthermore, two classic examples, vector addition and matrix multiplication, were presented.

To sum up, you should consider utilizing GPU MEX files in your applications in order to:

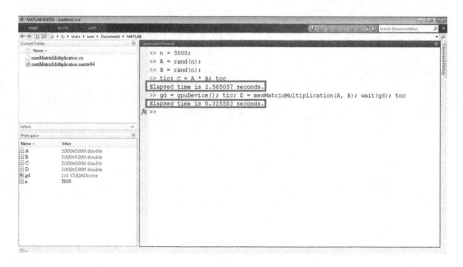

FIG. 8.8

Comparison of CPU and GPU implementation of the matrix multiplication.

- Further optimize the performance of your application.
- Implement GPU-based functions that are not GPU-enabled in MATLAB, that is, cannot be executed using a *gpuArray* object.
- Implement a function that is already GPU-enabled in MATLAB but you want to optimize its performance or implement a different algorithm.
- Access host-side libraries, such as *cuBLAS* or *cuFFT* libraries, or call from the host functions in the CUDA runtime library.
- Allocate memory of a different size or launch grids of a different size.
- Utilize multiple GPUs.

CUDA-accelerated libraries

9

CHAPTER OBJECTIVES

This chapter presents the CUDA-accelerated libraries, like *cuBLAS*, *cuFFT*, *cuRAND*, *cuSOLVER*, *cuSPARSE*, *NPP* and *Thrust*, that are incorporated into CUDA Toolkit. These libraries provide highly-optimized algorithms that can be incorporated into MATLAB applications through MEX files. Examples are presented for each library. After reading this Chapter, you should be able to use:

- CUDA Basic Linear Algebra Subroutines (cuBLAS) library to accelerate BLAS operations.
- CUDA Fast Fourier Transform (cuFFT) library to accelerate FFTs.
- CUDA Random Number Generation (cuRAND) library to create high-quality random numbers on the GPU.
- NVIDIA cuSOLVER library to perform sparse and dense factorizations and use direct solvers on the GPU.
- CUDA Sparse Matrix (cuSPARSE) library to accelerate sparse BLAS operations.
- NVIDIA Performance Primitives (NPP) library to accelerate image, video and signal processing algorithms.
- Thrust to accelerate sort, scan, transform and reduction operations on the GPU.

9.1 INTRODUCTION

CUDA-accelerated libraries provide highly optimized algorithms that can be incorporated into MATLAB applications through MEX files. As already presented in Chapter 8, you can write a MEX file that contains CUDA code. Instead of writing your own kernels, you can use CUDA-accelerated libraries that are optimized. Many of these libraries support drop-in compatibility to replace industry standard CPU-only libraries such as MKL, IPP, FFTW, and other widely used libraries. Some also feature automatic multi-GPU performance scaling.

GPU Programming in MATLAB. http://dx.doi.org/10.1016/B978-0-12-805132-0.00009-6

NVIDIA maintains a list with most widely used CUDA-accelerated libraries [18]. However, only a subset of the list's libraries are included into CUDA toolkit and are ready-to-use:

- CUDA Basic Linear Algebra Subroutines (*cuBLAS*) library.
- CUDA Fast Fourier Transform (*cuFFT*) library.
- CUDA Random Number Generation (*cuRAND*) library.
- NVIDIA *cuSOLVER* library.
- CUDA Sparse Matrix (*cuSPARSE*) library.
- NVIDIA Performance Primitives (*NPP*) library.
- *Thrust* template library.

Other CUDA-accelerated libraries are also available, and you can use them in a similar way. However, you need to download (and purchase a license for some of them) and install them before using the libraries on your applications.

The following sections briefly introduce the previously mentioned libraries and present an example on how to use them on your MATLAB applications. All examples are MEX files that take as input MATLAB arrays and return as output MATLAB arrays. We kept these examples as simple as possible to highlight the ease of use of these libraries without taking into account optimizations that can be made to reduce the execution time. Finally, each example is also presented using MATLAB, and we compare the execution of the codes using MATLAB on the CPU and the codes using the CUDA-accelerated libraries on the GPU.

9.2 cuBLAS

CUDA Basic Linear Algebra Subroutines (*cuBLAS*) [19] library is an implementation of BLAS (Basic Linear Algebra Subprograms) on top of the NVIDIA CUDA runtime. It allows the user to access the computational resources of an NVIDIA GPU. To use the *cuBLAS* API, the application must allocate the required matrices and vectors in the GPU memory space, fill them with data, call the sequence of desired *cuBLAS* functions, and then upload the results from the GPU memory space back to the host. The *cuBLAS* API also provides helper functions for writing and retrieving data from the GPU.

As of CUDA Toolkit 7.5, the key features of *cuBLAS* are [19]:

- Complete support for all 152 standard BLAS routines
- Single, double, complex, and double complex data types
- Support for CUDA streams
- Fortran bindings
- Support for multiple GPUs and concurrent kernels
- Batched GEMM API
- Device API that can be called from CUDA kernels
- Batched LU factorization API

- Batched matrix inverse API
- A new TRSV (triangular solve) function

The following MEX file (filename: cuBLASDemo.cu) implements a matrix multiplication using *cuBLAS* library. It takes as input two double-precision, floating point arrays of size $M \times K$ and $K \times N$, respectively, and returns a double-precision, floating point array of size $M \times N$.

```
1.  /*=============================================================
2.   * Filename: cuBLASDemo.cu
3.   * Description: This function implements a matrix
       multiplication
4.   * using cuBLAS library (MEX file that contains CUDA code and
5.   * takes as inputs MATLAB arrays)
6.   * Authors: Ploskas, N., & Samaras, N.
7.   * Syntax: C = cuBLASDemo(A, B)
8.   * Input:
9.   *   -- A: a double-precision, floating point array of size MxK
10.  *   -- B: a double-precision, floating point array of size KxN
11.  * Output:
12.  *   -- C: a double-precision, floating point array of size MxN
13.   *=============================================================*/
14.
15.  #include "mex.h"
16.  #include "cuda_runtime.h"
17.  #include "cublas_v2.h"
18.
19.  /*
20.   * The gateway function
21.   */
22.  void mexFunction(int nlhs, mxArray *plhs[], int nrhs,
       const mxArray *prhs[]){
23.
24.      /* declare all variables */
25.      double *deviceA, *deviceB, *deviceC;
26.      const double *A, *B;
27.      double *C;
28.      int numARows, numACols;
29.      int numBRows, numBCols;
30.      int numCRows, numCCols;
31.
32.      /* define error messages */
33.      char const * const errId = "parallel:gpu:cuBLASDemo:InvalidInput";
34.      char const * const errMsg = "Invalid input to MEX file.";
35.
36.      /* check input data */
37.      if(nrhs != 2 || !mxIsDouble(prhs[0]) || !mxIsDouble(prhs[0]) ||
           mxGetN(prhs[0]) != mxGetM(prhs[1])){
38.          mexErrMsgIdAndTxt(errId, errMsg);
39.      }
40.
41.      /* get input arrays */
42.      A = (double *)mxGetData(prhs[0]);
43.      B = (double *)mxGetData(prhs[1]);
44.
45.      /* find arrays dimensions */
```

```
46.     numARows = (int)mxGetM(prhs[0]);
47.     numACols = (int)mxGetN(prhs[0]);
48.     numBRows = (int)mxGetM(prhs[1]);
49.     numBCols = (int)mxGetN(prhs[1]);
50.     numCRows = numARows;
51.     numCCols = numBCols;
52.
53.     /* initialize output array */
54.     plhs[0] = mxCreateNumericMatrix(numCRows, numCCols,
                mxDOUBLE_CLASS, mxREAL);
55.     C = (double *)mxGetData(plhs[0]);
56.
57.     /* allocate memory on the GPU */
58.     cudaMalloc(&deviceA, sizeof(double) * numARows * numACols);
59.     cudaMalloc(&deviceB, sizeof(double) * numBRows * numBCols);
60.     cudaMalloc(&deviceC, sizeof(double) * numCRows * numCCols);
61.
62.     /* create handle, set arrays and perform the matrix
                multiplication using cuBLAS */
63.     cublasHandle_t handle;
64.     cublasCreate(&handle);
65.     cublasSetMatrix(numARows,
66.                     numACols,
67.                     sizeof(double),
68.                     A,
69.                     numARows,
70.                     deviceA,
71.                     numARows);
72.     cublasSetMatrix(numBRows,
73.                     numBCols,
74.                     sizeof(double),
75.                     B,
76.                     numBRows,
77.                     deviceB,
78.                     numBRows);
79.     double alpha = 1.0;
80.     double beta = 0.0;
81.     cublasDgemm(handle,
82.                 CUBLAS_OP_N,
83.                 CUBLAS_OP_N,
84.                 numARows,
85.                 numBCols,
86.                 numACols,
87.                 &alpha,
88.                 deviceA,
89.                 numARows,
90.                 deviceB,
91.                 numBRows,
92.                 &beta,
93.                 deviceC,
94.                 numCRows);
95.
96.     /* retrieve result */
97.     cublasGetMatrix(numCRows,
98.                     numCCols,
99.                     sizeof(double),
100.                    deviceC,
101.                    numCRows,
```

```
102.                    C,
103.                    numCRows);
104.
105.    /* destroy the handle and the arrays on the device */
106.    cublasDestroy(handle);
107.    cudaFree(deviceA);
108.    cudaFree(deviceB);
109.    cudaFree(deviceC);
110. }
```

Function *RuncuBLASDemo* (filename: RuncuBLASDemo.m) compiles the file cuBLASDemo.cu and compares the execution time of a matrix multiplication of two $5,000 \times 5,000$ arrays using MATLAB on the CPU and using *cuBLAS* on the GPU through the MEX file (Fig. 9.1).

Note that when compiling the MEX file with the *mexcuda* command, we need to specify that we are using the *cuBLAS* library (-*lcublas*) and the directory where the header files for CUDA and *cuBLAS* are located (-I"C:\ProgramFiles\ NVIDIAGPUComputingToolkit\CUDA\v7.0\include"). You need to change that directory according to your operating system and the version of the CUDA Toolkit.

```
1.    function RuncuBLASDemo
2.    % Filename: RuncuBLASDemo.m
3.    % Description: This function compiles the file cuBLASDemo.cu
4.    % and compares the execution time of a matrix multiplication
5.    % of two 5,000x5,000 arrays using MATLAB on the CPU and using
6.    % cuBLAS on the GPU through the MEX file
7.    % Authors: Ploskas, N., & Samaras, N.
8.    % Syntax: RuncuBLASDemo
9.    % Input: no inputs
```

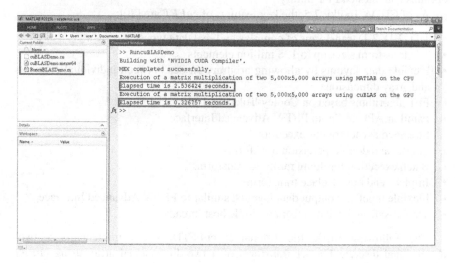

FIG. 9.1

Compile and execute MEX file using *cuBLAS* through MATLAB.

```
10.  % Output: the execution time of a matrix multiplication of
11.  % two 5,000x5,000 arrays using MATLAB on the CPU and using
12.  % cuBLAS on the GPU through the MEX file
13.
14.  mexcuda cublasDemo.cu -lcublas ...
15.       -I"C:\Program Files\NVIDIA GPU Computing Toolkit\CUDA\v7.0\include"
16.  A = rand(5000);
17.  B = rand(5000);
18.  disp(['Execution of a matrix multiplication of two ' ...
19.     '5,000x5,000 arrays using MATLAB on the CPU']);
20.  tic; C1 = A * B; toc
21.  disp(['Execution of a matrix multiplication of two ' ...
22.     '5,000x5,000 arrays using cuBLAS on the GPU']);
23.  gd = gpuDevice(); tic; C2 = cuBLASDemo(A, B); wait(gd); toc
```

9.3 cuFFT

CUDA Fast Fourier Transform (*cuFFT*) [20] library provides a simple interface for computing FFTs. By using hundreds of processor cores inside NVIDIA GPUs, *cuFFT* delivers the floating-point performance of a GPU without having to develop your own custom GPU FFT implementation. The FFT is a divide-and-conquer algorithm for efficiently computing discrete Fourier transforms of complex or real-valued data sets. It is one of the most important and widely used numerical algorithms in computational physics and general signal processing. The *cuFFT* library provides a simple interface for computing FFTs on an NVIDIA GPU, which allows users to quickly leverage the floating-point power and parallelism of the GPU in a highly optimized and tested FFT library.

As of CUDA Toolkit 7.5, the key features of *cuFFT* are [20]:

- 1-D, 2-D, 3-D transforms of complex and real data types
- 1-D transform sizes up to 128 million elements
- Flexible data layouts by allowing arbitrary strides between individual elements and array dimensions
- FFT algorithms based on Cooley-Tukey and Bluestein
- Familiar API similar to FFTW Advanced Interface
- Streamed asynchronous execution
- Single- and double-precision transforms
- Batch execution for doing multiple transforms
- In-place and out-of-place transforms
- Flexible input and output data layouts, similar to FFTW Advanced Interface
- Thread-safe and callable from multiple host threads

The following MEX file (filename: cuFFTDemo.cu) implements a two-dimensional discrete Fourier transform of a two-dimensional array using *cuFFT* library. It takes as input a double-precision, floating point array of size $M \times N$ and returns a double-precision, floating point array of size $(M/2 + 1) \times N$.

```
1.   /*=========================================================
2.    * Filename: cuFFTDemo.cu
3.    * Description: This function implements a two-dimensional
4.    * discrete Fourier transform of a two-dimensional array
5.    * using cuFFT library (MEX file that contains CUDA code and
6.    * takes as inputs MATLAB arrays)
7.    * Authors: Ploskas, N., & Samaras, N.
8.    * Syntax: B = cuFFTDemo(A)
9.    * Input:
10.   *   -- A: a double-precision, floating point array of size MxN
11.   * Output:
12.   *   -- C: a double-precision, floating point array of size
13.   *       (M / 2 + 1)xN
14.   *=========================================================*/
15.
16.  #include "mex.h"
17.  #include <cuda_runtime.h>
18.  #include <cufft.h>
19.
20.  /*
21.   * The gateway function
22.   */
23.  void mexFunction(int nlhs, mxArray *plhs[], int nrhs,
         const mxArray *prhs[]){
24.
25.      /* declare all variables */
26.      double *deviceA;
27.      cufftDoubleComplex *deviceB;
28.      double *A, *B;
29.      int numARows, numACols;
30.      int numBRows, numBCols;
31.
32.      /* define error messages */
33.      char const * const errId = "parallel:gpu:cuFFTDemo:InvalidInput";
34.      char const * const errMsg = "Invalid input to MEX file.";
35.
36.      /* check input data */
37.      if(nrhs != 1 || !mxIsDouble(prhs[0])){
38.          mexErrMsgIdAndTxt(errId, errMsg);
39.      }
40.
41.      /* get input array */
42.      A = (double *)mxGetData(prhs[0]);
43.
44.      /* find array dimensions */
45.      numARows = mxGetM(prhs[0]);
46.      numACols = mxGetN(prhs[0]);
47.
48.      /* initialize output array */
49.      numBRows = numARows / 2 + 1;
50.      numBCols = numACols;
51.      plhs[0] = mxCreateNumericMatrix(numBRows, numBCols,
             mxDOUBLE_CLASS, mxCOMPLEX);
52.      B = (double *)mxMalloc(sizeof(cufftDoubleComplex) *
             numBRows * numBCols);
53.
54.      /* allocate memory on the GPU */
55.      cudaMalloc(&deviceA, sizeof(double) * numARows * numACols);
```

```
56.     cudaMalloc(&deviceB, sizeof(cufftDoubleComplex) *
            numBRows * numBCols);
57.     cudaMemcpy(deviceA, A, numARows * numACols *
            sizeof(double), cudaMemcpyHostToDevice);
58.     cudaMemcpy(B, deviceB, numBRows * numBCols *
            sizeof(cufftDoubleComplex), cudaMemcpyDeviceToHost);
59.
60.     /* create handle and perform the two-dimensional discrete
61.        Fourier transform using cuFFT */
62.     cufftHandle plan;
63.     cufftPlan2d(&plan, numACols, numARows, CUFFT_D2Z);
64.     cufftExecD2Z(plan, deviceA, deviceB);
65.
66.     /* retrieve result */
67.     double* real = (double *)mxGetPr(plhs[0]);
68.     double* imag = (double *)mxGetPi(plhs[0]);
69.     double* complex = B;
70.     for(int i = 0; i < numBCols; ++i){
71.         for(int j = 0; j < numBRows; ++j){
72.             *real++ = *complex++;
73.             *imag++ = *complex++;
74.         }
75.     }
76.
77.     /* destroy the handle and the arrays on the device */
78.     cufftDestroy(plan);
79.     cudaFree(deviceA);
80.     cudaFree(deviceB);
81.  }
```

Function *RuncuFFTDemo* (filename: RuncuFFTDemo.m) compiles the file cuFFTDemo.cu and compares the execution time of a two-dimensional discrete Fourier transform of a 5,000 × 5,000 array using MATLAB on the CPU and using *cuFFT* on the GPU through the MEX file (Fig. 9.2).

Note that when compiling the MEX file with the *mexcuda* command, we need to specify that we are using the *cuFFT* library (*-lcufft*) and the directory where the header files for CUDA and *cuFFT* are located (-I"C:\ProgramFiles\ NVIDIAGPUComputingToolkit\CUDA\v7.0\include"). You need to change that directory according to your operating system and the version of the CUDA Toolkit.

```
1.   function RuncuFFTDemo
2.   % Filename: RuncuFFTDemo.m
3.   % Description: This function compiles the file cuFFTDemo.cu
4.   % and compares the execution time of a two-dimensional
5.   % discrete Fourier transform of a 5,000x5,000 array using
6.   % MATLAB on the CPU and using cuFFT on the GPU through
7.   % the MEX file
8.   % Authors: Ploskas, N., & Samaras, N.
9.   % Syntax: RuncuFFTDemo
10.  % Input: no inputs
11.  % Output: the execution time of a two-dimensional discrete
12.  % Fourier transform of a 5,000x5,000 array using MATLAB on
13.  % the CPU and using cuBLAS on the GPU through the MEX file
14.
15.  mexcuda cuFFTDemo.cu -lcufft ...
16.      -I"C:\Program Files\NVIDIA GPU Computing Toolkit\CUDA\v7.0\include"
```

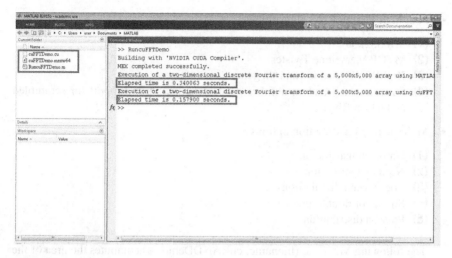

FIG. 9.2

Compile and execute MEX file using *cuFFT* through MATLAB.

```
17.   A = rand(5000);
18.   disp(['Execution of a two-dimensional discrete ' ...
19.      'Fourier transform of a 5,000x5,000 array ' ...
20.      'using MATLAB on the CPU']);
21.   tic; B1 = fft2(A); toc
22.   disp(['Execution of a two-dimensional discrete ' ...
23.      'Fourier transform of a 5,000x5,000 array ' ...
24.      'using cuFFT on the GPU']);
25.   gd = gpuDevice(); tic; B2 = cuFFTDemo(A); wait(gd); toc
```

9.4 cuRAND

The CUDA Random Number Generation (*cuRAND*) [21] library delivers high-performance GPU-accelerated random number generation (RNG). *cuRAND* also provides two flexible interfaces, allowing you to generate random numbers in bulk from host code running on the CPU or from within your CUDA functions/kernels running on the GPU. A variety of RNG algorithms and distribution options from which you can select the best solution for your needs.

As of CUDA Toolkit 7.5, the key features of *cuRAND* are [21]:

- Flexible usage model

    (1) Host API for generating random numbers in bulk on the GPU
    (2) Inline implementation allows use inside GPU functions/kernels, or in your host code

- Four high-quality RNG algorithms

  (1) MRG32k3a
  (2) MTGP Merseinne Twister
  (3) XORWOW pseudo-random generation
  (4) Sobol's quasi-random number generators, including support for scrambled and 64-bit RNG

- Multiple RNG distribution options

  (1) Uniform distribution
  (2) Normal distribution
  (3) Log-normal distribution
  (4) Single- or double-precision
  (5) Poisson distribution

The following MEX file (filename: cuRANDDemo.cu) computes the area of the definite integral $\int_0^2 x(x-2)^6 dx$ using *cuRAND* library. It returns the area of the integral as a double value.

```
1.    /*================================================================
2.     * Filename: cuRANDDemo.cu
3.     * Description: This function computes the area of the
4.     * definite integral int(x * (x - 2) ^ 6, x = 0..2) (MEX file
5.     * that contains CUDA code and takes as inputs MATLAB arrays)
6.     * Authors: Ploskas, N., & Samaras, N.
7.     * Syntax: area = cuRANDDemo()
8.     * Input: no inputs
9.     * Output:
10.    *   -- area: the area of the definite integral
11.    *================================================================*/
12.
13.   #include "mex.h"
14.   #include <cuda_runtime.h>
15.   #include <curand.h>
16.
17.   /*
18.    * The kernel code
19.    */
20.   _ _global_ _ void kernel(int* d_count, double* randomNums){
21.
22.       /* declare all variables */
23.       int i, tid, xidx, yidx;
24.       double x, y, z;
25.
26.       /* Find the overall ID of the thread */
27.       tid = blockDim.x * blockIdx.x + threadIdx.x;
28.       i = tid;
29.
30.       /* Implement the Monte Carlo method */
31.       xidx = i + i;
32.       yidx = xidx + 1;
33.
```

```
34.     /*get the random x, y points */
35.     x = 2 * randomNums[xidx];
36.     y = 8 * randomNums[yidx];
37.
38.     /* calculate the value for the selected x point */
39.     z = x * pow((x - 2), 6);
40.
41.     /* compare the two values and update the counter */
42.     if(y <= z){
43.         d_count[tid] = 1;
44.     }
45.     else{
46.         d_count[tid] = 0;
47.     }
48. }
49.
50. /*
51.  * The gateway function
52.  */
53. void mexFunction(int nlhs, mxArray *plhs[], int nrhs,
        const mxArray *prhs[]){
54.
55.     /* declare all variables */
56.     double *B;
57.     int niter = 1000000;
58.     double *randomNums;
59.     double area;
60.     int threads, blocks;
61.     int *count, *d_count;
62.     unsigned int reducedcount = 0;
63.
64.     /* initialize output array */
65.     plhs[0] = mxCreateNumericMatrix(1, 1, mxDOUBLE_CLASS, mxREAL);
66.     B = (double *)mxGetData(plhs[0]);
67.
68.     /* allocate the array for the random numbers */
69.     cudaMalloc((void**)&randomNums, (2 * niter) * sizeof(double));
70.
71.     /* use CuRand to generate an array of random
72.        numbers on the device */
73.     curandGenerator_t gen;
74.     curandCreateGenerator(&gen, CURAND_RNG_PSEUDO_MRG32K3A);
75.     curandSetPseudoRandomGeneratorSeed(gen, 4294967296ULL^time (NULL));
76.     curandGenerateUniformDouble(gen, randomNums, 2 * niter);
77.     curandDestroyGenerator(gen);
78.
79.     /* set the number of thread blocks and the number
80.        of threads per thread block to be launched */
81.     threads = 1000;
82.     blocks = 1000;
83.
84.     /* initialize the array that stores the count values */
85.     count = (int *)malloc(blocks * threads * sizeof(int));
86.
87.     /* allocate the array to hold a value (1, 0) whether
88.        the point is inside the area (1) or not (0) */
89.     cudaMalloc((void**)&d_count, blocks * threads * sizeof(int));
90.
```

```
91.    /* launch the kernel */
92.    kernel<<<blocks, threads>>> (d_count, randomNums);
93.
94.    /* synchronize the device */
95.    cudaDeviceSynchronize();
96.
97.    /* copy the resulting array back */
98.    cudaMemcpy(count, d_count, blocks * threads * sizeof(int),
           cudaMemcpyDeviceToHost);
99.
100.   /* Reduce the array into int */
101.   for(int i = 0; i < niter; i++){
102.       reducedcount += count[i];
103.   }
104.
105.   /* Calculate the area */
106.   area = ((double)reducedcount / niter) * 2.0 * 8.0;
107.
108.   /* Write area to output */
109.   *B = area;
110.
111.   /* destroy the arrays on the device and the host */
112.   cudaFree(randomNums);
113.   cudaFree(count);
114.   free(count);
115. }
```

Function *RuncuRANDDemo* (filename: RuncuRANDDemo.m) compiles the file cuRANDDemo.cu and compares the execution time of the computation of the area of the definite integral $\int_0^2 x(x-2)^6 dx$ using MATLAB on the CPU and using *cuRAND* on the GPU through the MEX file (Fig. 9.3).

Note that when compiling the MEX file with the *mexcuda* command, we need to specify that we are using the *cuRAND* library (*-lcurand*) and the directory where the header files for CUDA and *cuRAND* are located (-I"C:\ProgramFiles\ NVIDIAGPUComputingToolkit\CUDA\v7.0\include"). You need to change that directory according to your operating system and the version of the CUDA Toolkit.

```
1.    function RuncuRANDDemo
2.    % Filename: RuncuRANDDemo.m
3.    % Description: This function compiles the file cuRANDDemo.cu
4.    % and compares the execution time of the computation of the area
5.    % of the definite integral int(x * (x - 2) ^ 6, x = 0..2) using
6.    % MATLAB on the CPU and using cuRAND on the GPU through the MEX
7.    % file
8.    % Authors: Ploskas, N., & Samaras, N.
9.    % Syntax: RuncuRANDDemo
10.   % Input: no inputs
11.   % Output: the execution time of the computation of the area of
12.   % the definite integral int(x * (x - 2) ^ 6, x = 0..2) using
13.   % MATLAB on the CPU and using cuRAND on the GPU through the MEX
14.   % file
15.
16.   mexcuda cuRandDemo.cu -lcurand ...
17.       -I"C:\Program Files\NVIDIA GPU Computing Toolkit\CUDA\v7.0\include"
18.   disp(['Execution of the computation of the area of the ' ...
19.       'the definite integral int(x * (x - 2) ^ 6, x = 0..2) ' ...
20.       'using MATLAB on the CPU']);
```

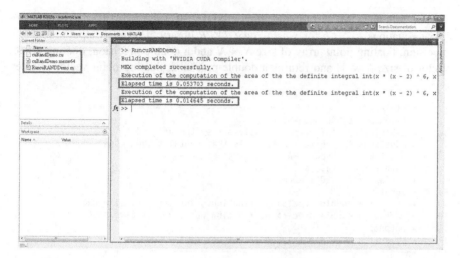

FIG. 9.3

Compile and execute MEX file using *cuRAND* through MATLAB.

```
21.   tic;
22.   n = 1000000;
23.   x = 2 * rand(n, 1);
24.   y = 8 * rand(n, 1);
25.   counter = sum(y < (x .* (x - 2) .^ 6));
26.   area = counter / n * 2 * 8;
27.   toc
28.   disp(['Execution of the computation of the area of the ' ...
29.       'the definite integral int(x * (x - 2) ^ 6, x = 0..2) ' ...
30.       'using cuRAND on the GPU']);
31.   gd = gpuDevice(); tic; area = cuRandDemo(); wait(gd); toc
```

9.5 cuSOLVER

NVIDIA *cuSOLVER* [22] library provides a collection of dense and sparse direct solvers, which deliver significant acceleration for Computer Vision, CFD, Computational Chemistry, and Linear Optimization applications. The intent of *cuSolver* is to provide useful LAPACK-like features, such as common matrix factorization and triangular solve routines for dense matrices, a sparse least-squares solver, and an eigenvalue solver.

It combines three separate libraries under a single umbrella, each of which can be used independently or in concert with other toolkit libraries [22]:

- *cusolverDN*: Key LAPACK dense solvers: Cholesky, LU, SVD, and QR
- *cusolverSP*: Sparse direct solvers and Eigensolvers
- *cusolverRF*: Sparse refactorization solver

The following MEX file (filename: cuSOLVERDemo.cu) solves a system of linear equations $Ax = b$ for x using *cuSOLVER* library. It takes as input a double-precision, floating point array of size $N \times N$ and a double-precision, floating point vector of size $N \times 1$, and returns a double-precision, floating point vector of size $N \times 1$.

```
1.   /*=============================================================
2.    * Filename: cuSOLVERDemo.cu
3.    * Description: This function solves a system of linear
4.    * equations Ax = b for x (MEX file that contains CUDA code
5.    * and takes as inputs MATLAB arrays)
6.    * Authors: Ploskas, N., & Samaras, N.
7.    * Syntax: x = cuSOLVERDemo(A, b)
8.    * Input:
9.    *   -- A: a double-precision, floating point array of size NxN
10.   *   -- b: a double-precision, floating point vector of size Nx1
11.   * Output:
12.   *   -- x: a double-precision, floating point vector of size Nx1
13.   *=============================================================*/
14.
15.  #include "mex.h"
16.  #include <cuda_runtime.h>
17.  #include <cublas_v2.h>
18.  #include <cusolverDn.h>
19.
20.  /*
21.   * The gateway function
22.   */
23.  void mexFunction(int nlhs, mxArray *plhs[], int nrhs,
         const mxArray *prhs[]){
24.
25.      /* declare all variables */
26.      double *deviceA, *deviceB, *deviceX;
27.      double *A, *b, *x;
28.      int N;
29.      int lwork = 0;
30.      double *d_work = NULL;
31.      int *devInfo = NULL;
32.      const double one = 1;
33.
34.      /* define error messages */
35.      char const * const errId = "parallel:gpu:cuSOLVERDemo:InvalidInput";
36.      char const * const errMsg = "Invalid input to MEX file.";
37.
38.      /* check input data */
39.      if(nrhs != 2 || !mxIsDouble(prhs[0]) || !mxIsDouble(prhs[0]) ||
            mxGetM(prhs[0]) != mxGetN(prhs[0]) ||
            mxGetM(prhs[0]) != mxGetM(prhs[1])){
40.          mexErrMsgIdAndTxt(errId, errMsg);
41.      }
42.
43.      /* get input arrays */
44.      A = (double *)mxGetData(prhs[0]);
45.      b = (double *)mxGetData(prhs[1]);
46.
47.      /* find arrays dimensions */
48.      N = (int)mxGetN(prhs[0]);
49.
```

```
50.     /* initialize output array */
51.     plhs[0] = mxCreateNumericMatrix(N, 1, mxDOUBLE_CLASS, mxREAL);
52.     x = (double *)mxGetData(plhs[0]);
53.
54.     /* allocate memory on the GPU */
55.     cudaMalloc(&deviceA, sizeof(double) * N * N);
56.     cudaMalloc(&deviceB, sizeof(double) * N);
57.     cudaMalloc(&deviceX, sizeof(double) * N);
58.     cudaMemcpy(deviceA, A, sizeof(double) * N * N,
            cudaMemcpyHostToDevice);
59.     cudaMemcpy(deviceB, b, sizeof(double) * N, cudaMemcpyHostToDevice);
60.
61.     /* create handle */
62.     cusolverDnHandle_t cudenseH = NULL;
63.     cusolverDnCreate(&cudenseH);
64.
65.     /* query working space of geqrf */
66.     cusolverDnDgeqrf_bufferSize(cudenseH, N, N, deviceA, N, &lwork);
67.     cudaMalloc((void**)&d_work, sizeof(double) * lwork);
68.     cudaMalloc((void **)&devInfo, sizeof(int));
69.
70.     /* compute QR factorization */
71.     cusolverDnDgeqrf(cudenseH, N, N, deviceA, N, deviceX, d_work,
            lwork, devInfo);
72.
73.     /* synchronize the device */
74.     cudaDeviceSynchronize();
75.
76.     /* compute Q^T*b */
77.     cusolverDnDormqr(cudenseH, CUBLAS_SIDE_LEFT, CUBLAS_OP_T, N, 1, N,
            deviceA, N, deviceX, deviceB, N, d_work, lwork, devInfo);
78.
79.     /* synchronize the device */
80.     cudaDeviceSynchronize();
81.
82.     /* create handle */
83.     cublasHandle_t cublasH = NULL;
84.     cublasCreate(&cublasH);
85.
86.     /* compute x = R \ Q^T*b */
87.     cublasDtrsm(cublasH, CUBLAS_SIDE_LEFT, CUBLAS_FILL_MODE_UPPER,
            CUBLAS_OP_N, CUBLAS_DIAG_NON_UNIT, N, 1, &one, deviceA, N,
            deviceB, N);
88.
89.     /* synchronize the device */
90.     cudaDeviceSynchronize();
91.
92.     /* copy the result */
93.     cudaMemcpy(x, deviceB, sizeof(double) * N,
            cudaMemcpyDeviceToHost);
94.
95.     /* destroy the handles and the arrays on the device */
96.     cublasDestroy(cublasH);
97.     cusolverDnDestroy(cudenseH);
98.     cudaFree(deviceA);
99.     cudaFree(deviceB);
100.    cudaFree(deviceX);
101. }
```

Function *RuncuSOLVERDemo* (filename: RuncuSOLVERDemo.m) compiles the file cuSOLVERDemo.cu and compares the execution time of the solution of a system of linear equations $Ax = b$ for x using MATLAB on the CPU and using *cuSOLVER* on the GPU through the MEX file (Fig. 9.4).

Note that when compiling the MEX file with the *mexcuda* command, we need to specify that we are using the *cuSOLVER* library (*-lcusolver*), the *cuBLAS* library (*-lcublas*), and the directory where the header files for CUDA, *cuSOLVER*, and *cuBLAS* are located (-I"C:\ProgramFiles\NVIDIAGPUComputingToolkit\CUDA\ v7.0\include"). You need to change that directory according to your operating system and the version of the CUDA Toolkit.

```
1.    function RuncuSOLVERDemo
2.    % Filename: RuncuSOLVERDemo.m
3.    % Description: This function compiles the file cuSOLVERDemo.cu
4.    % and compares the execution time of the solution of a system of
5.    % linear equations Ax = b for x using MATLAB on the CPU and using
6.    % cuSOLVER and cuBLAS on the GPU through the MEX file
7.    % Authors: Ploskas, N., & Samaras, N.
8.    % Syntax: RuncuSOLVERDemo
9.    % Input: no inputs
10.   % Output: the execution time of the computation of the solution of
11.   % a system of linear equations Ax = b for x using MATLAB on the CPU
12.   % and using cuSOLVER and cuBLAS on the GPU through the MEX file
13.
14.   mexcuda cuSOLVERDemo.cu -lcublas -lcusolver ...
15.     -I"C:\Program Files\NVIDIA GPU Computing Toolkit\CUDA\v7.0\include"
16.   disp(['Execution of the computation of the solution of a ' ...
17.     'system of linear equations Ax = b for x using MATLAB ' ...
```

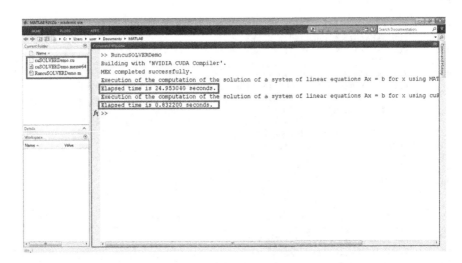

FIG. 9.4

Compile and execute MEX file using *cuSOLVER* through MATLAB.

```
18.      'on the CPU']);
19.   A = rand(5000, 5000);
20.   b = rand(5000, 1);
21.   tic;
22.   [~, n] = size(A);
23.   [Q, R, P] = qr(A);
24.   c = Q' * b;
25.   y = R(1:n, 1:n) \ c(1:n);
26.   x1 = P * y;
27.   toc
28.   disp(['Execution of the computation of the solution of a ' ...
29.      'system of linear equations Ax = b for x using cuSOLVER ' ...
30.      'and cuBLAS on the GPU']);
31.   gd = gpuDevice(); tic; x2 = cuSOLVERDemo(A, b); wait(gd); toc
```

9.6 cuSPARSE

CUDA Sparse Matrix (*cuSPARSE*) [23] library contains a set of basic linear algebra subroutines used for handling sparse matrices. It is implemented on top of the CUDA runtime, which is part of the CUDA Toolkit and is designed to be called from C and C++. The library routines can be classified into four categories:

- *Level 1*: operations between a vector in sparse format and a vector in dense format.
- *Level 2*: operations between a matrix in sparse format and a vector in dense format.
- *Level 3*: operations between a matrix in sparse format and a set of vectors in dense format (which can also usually be viewed as a dense tall matrix).
- *Conversion*: operations that allow conversion between different matrix storage formats.

As of CUDA Toolkit 7.5, the key features of *cuSPARSE* are [23]:

- Supports dense, COO, CSR, CSC, ELL/HYB, and Blocked CSR sparse matrix formats.
- Level 1 routines for sparse vector by dense vector operations.
- Level 2 routines for sparse matrix by dense vector operations.
- Level 3 routines for sparse matrix by multiple dense vectors (tall matrix).
- Routines for sparse matrix by sparse matrix addition and multiplication.
- Conversion routines that allow conversion between different matrix formats.
- Sparse Triangular Solve.
- Tri-diagonal solver.
- Incomplete factorization preconditioners *ilu0* and *ic0*

The following MEX file (filename: cuSPARSEDemo.cu) implements a sparse matrix-vector multiplication using *cuSPARSE* library. It takes as input a double-precision, floating point array of size $N \times N$ and a double-precision, floating point vector of size $N \times 1$, and returns a double-precision, floating point vector of size $N \times 1$.

Note that the input array is a sparse array using the *CSC* sparse format, so when calling the *cusparseDcsrmv* function, we need to specify to compute the transpose (*CUSPARSE_OPERATION_TRANSPOSE* option) to transform the array to the *CSR* sparse format.

```
1.   /*==========================================================
2.    * Filename: cuSPARSEDemo.cu
3.    * Description: This function implements a sparse matrix-vector
4.    * multiplication (MEX file that contains CUDA code and takes
5.    * as inputs MATLAB arrays)
6.    * Authors: Ploskas, N., & Samaras, N.
7.    * Syntax: x = cuSPARSEDemo(A, b)
8.    * Input:
9.    *    -- A: a sparse double-precision, floating point array of size NxN
10.   *    -- b: a double-precision, floating point vector of size Nx1
11.   * Output:
12.   *    -- x: a double-precision, floating point vector of size Nx1
13.   *==========================================================*/
14.
15.  #include "mex.h"
16.  #include <cuda_runtime.h>
17.  #include <cusparse.h>
18.
19.  /*
20.   * The gateway function
21.   */
22.  void mexFunction(int nlhs, mxArray *plhs[], int nrhs,
         const mxArray *prhs[]){
23.
24.      /* declare all variables */
25.      double *s, *b, *x;
26.      double *d_s, *d_b, *d_x;
27.      mwSize *iir, *jjc;
28.      int *ir, *jc;
29.      int *d_ir, *d_jc;
30.      int N, nz;
31.
32.      /* define error messages */
33.      char const * const errId = "parallel:gpu:cuSPARSEDemo:InvalidInput";
34.      char const * const errMsg = "Invalid input to MEX file.";
35.
36.      /* check input data */
37.      if(nrhs != 2 || !mxIsSparse(prhs[0]) || !mxIsDouble(prhs[0]) ||
         !mxIsDouble(prhs[0]) || mxGetM(prhs[0]) != mxGetN(prhs[0]) ||
         mxGetN(prhs[0]) != mxGetM(prhs[1])){
38.          mexErrMsgIdAndTxt(errId, errMsg);
39.      }
40.
41.      /* initialize output array */
42.      plhs[0] = mxCreateDoubleMatrix(mxGetM(prhs[0]), 1, mxREAL);
43.
44.      /* get input arrays */
45.      iir = mxGetIr(prhs[0]); /* Row indexing */
46.      jjc = mxGetJc(prhs[0]); /* Column count */
47.      s   = mxGetPr(prhs[0]); /* Nonzero elements */
48.      b   = mxGetPr(prhs[1]); /* Rhs vector */
49.      x   = mxGetPr(plhs[0]); /* Output vector */
```

```
50.
51.     /* find arrays dimensions */
52.     N = mxGetN(prhs[0]);
53.
54.     /* find the number of nonzero elements */
55.     nz = (int) mxGetNzmax(prhs[0]);
56.
57.     /* convert row indexing and column count from mwsize
58.        to int */
59.     ir = new int[nz];
60.     jc = new int[N + 1];
61.     for(int i = 0; i < nz; i++){
62.         ir[i] = (int)(iir[i]);
63.     }
64.     for(int i = 0; i <= N; i++){
65.         jc[i] = (int)(jjc[i]);
66.     }
67.
68.     /* allocate memory on the GPU */
69.     cudaMalloc((void **)&d_ir, nz * sizeof(int));
70.     cudaMalloc((void **)&d_jc, (N + 1) * sizeof(int));
71.     cudaMalloc((void **)&d_s, nz * sizeof(double));
72.     cudaMalloc((void **)&d_x, N * sizeof(double));
73.     cudaMalloc((void **)&d_b, N * sizeof(double));
74.     cudaMemcpy(d_ir, ir, nz * sizeof(int), cudaMemcpyHostToDevice);
75.     cudaMemcpy(d_jc, jc, (N + 1) * sizeof(int), cudaMemcpyHostToDevice);
76.     cudaMemcpy(d_s, s, nz * sizeof(double), cudaMemcpyHostToDevice);
77.     cudaMemcpy(d_b, b, N * sizeof(double), cudaMemcpyHostToDevice);
78.
79.     /* create handle */
80.     cusparseHandle_t cusparseHandle = 0;
81.     cusparseCreate(&cusparseHandle);
82.
83.     /* create and set matrix description and matrix
84.        index base */
85.     cusparseMatDescr_t descr = 0;
86.     cusparseCreateMatDescr(&descr);
87.     cusparseSetMatType(descr, CUSPARSE_MATRIX_TYPE_GENERAL);
88.     cusparseSetMatIndexBase(descr, CUSPARSE_INDEX_BASE_ZERO);
89.
90.     /* perform the sparse matrix-vector multiplication
91.        using cuSPARSE */
92.     double alpha = 1.0;
93.     double beta = 0.0;
94.     cusparseDcsrmv(cusparseHandle, CUSPARSE_OPERATION_TRANSPOSE, N, N,
95.         nz, &alpha, descr, d_s, d_jc, d_ir, d_b, &beta, d_x);
95.
96.     /* copy result */
97.     cudaMemcpy(x, d_x, N * sizeof(double), cudaMemcpyDeviceToHost);
98.
99.     /* destroy the handle and the arrays on the device */
100.    cusparseDestroy(cusparseHandle);
101.    cudaFree(d_s);
102.    cudaFree(d_ir);
103.    cudaFree(d_jc);
104.    cudaFree(d_b);
105.    cudaFree(d_x);
106. }
```

Function *RuncuSPARSEDemo* (filename: RuncuSPARSEDemo.m) compiles the file cuSPARSEDemo.cu and compares the execution time of a sparse matrix-vector multiplication of a 5,000 × 5,000 array and a 5,000 × 1 vector using MATLAB on the CPU and using *cuSPARSE* on the GPU through the MEX file (Fig. 9.5).

Note that when compiling the MEX file with the *mexcuda* command, we need to specify that we are using the *cuSPARSE* library (*-lcusparse*) and the directory where the header files for CUDA and *cuSPARSE* are located (-I"C:\ProgramFiles\ NVIDIAGPUComputingToolkit\CUDA\v7.0\include"). You need to change that directory according to your operating system and the version of the CUDA Toolkit.

```
1.    function RuncuSPARSEDemo
2.    % Filename: RuncuSPARSEDemo.m
3.    % Description: This function compiles the file cuSPARSEDemo.cu
4.    % and compares the execution time of a sparse matrix-vector
5.    % multiplication of a 5,000x5,000 array and a 5,000x1 vector
6.    % using MATLAB on the CPU and using cuSPARSE on the GPU
7.    % through the mex file
8.    % Authors: Ploskas, N., & Samaras, N.
9.    % Syntax: RuncuSPARSEDemo
10.   % Input: no inputs
11.   % Output: the execution time of a sparse matrix-vector
12.   % multiplication of a 5,000x5,000 array and a 5,000x1 vector
13.   % using MATLAB on the CPU and using cuSPARSE on the GPU
14.   % through the mex file
15.
16.   mexcuda cuSparseDemo.cu -lcusparse ...
17.      -I"C:\Program Files\NVIDIA GPU Computing Toolkit\CUDA\v7.0\include"
18.   A = sprand(5000, 5000, 0.1);
19.   b = rand(5000, 1);
```

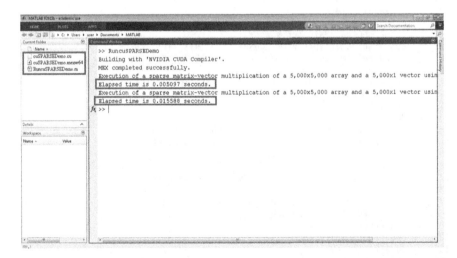

FIG. 9.5

Compile and execute MEX file using *cuSPARSE* through MATLAB.

```
20.  disp(['Execution of a sparse matrix-vector ' ...
21.      'multiplication of a 5,000x5,000 array and a ' ...
22.      '5,000x1 vector using MATLAB on the CPU']);
23.  tic; x1 = A * b; toc
24.  disp(['Execution of a sparse matrix-vector ' ...
25.      'multiplication of a 5,000x5,000 array and a ' ...
26.      '5,000x1 vector using cuSPARSE on the GPU']);
27.  gd = gpuDevice(); tic; x2 = cuSPARSEDemo(A, b); wait(gd); toc
```

9.7 NPP

NVIDIA *NPP* [24] is a library of functions for performing CUDA-accelerated processing. The initial set of functionality in the library focuses on imaging and video processing and is widely applicable for developers in these areas. The *NPP* library is written to maximize flexibility, while maintaining high performance. NPP can be used in one of two ways:

- As stand-alone library for adding GPU acceleration to an application with minimal effort. This route allows developers to add GPU acceleration to their applications in a matter of hours.
- As cooperative library for interoperating with a developer's GPU code efficiently.

    As of CUDA Toolkit 7.5, the key features of *NPP* are [24]:

- Eliminates unnecessary copying of data to/from CPU memory
- Data exchange and initialization
- Arithmetic and logical operations
- Color conversion
- Filter functions
- Geometry transforms
- Statistics functions

    The following MEX file (filename: NPPDemo.cu) implements a two-dimensional box filtering of a pgm image using *NPP* library. It takes as input a string to the path of the pgm image.

```
1.   /*=======================================================
2.    * Filename: NPPDemo.cu
3.    * Description: This function implements a 2-D box filtering
4.    * of a pgm image using NPP library (MEX file that contains
5.    * CUDA code and takes as inputs MATLAB arrays)
6.    * Authors: Ploskas, N., & Samaras, N.
7.    * Syntax: NPPDemo(filename)
8.    * Input:
9.    *   -- filename: the path to a pgm image
10.   * Output: a new pgm image is stored at the same location
11.   * with the original image with a name name_boxFilter.pgm,
12.   * where name is the name of the original image
13.   *=======================================================*/
14.
```

```
15.  #include "mex.h"
16.  #include <cuda_runtime.h>
17.  #include <npp.h>
18.  #include <string.h>
19.  #include <fstream>
20.  #include <iostream>
21.  #include <ImagesCPU.h>
22.  #include <ImagesNPP.h>
23.  #include <ImageIO.h>
24.  #include <Exceptions.h>
25.  #include <helper_string.h>
26.  #include <helper_cuda.h>
27.
28.  /*
29.   * The gateway function
30.   */
31.  void mexFunction(int nlhs, mxArray *plhs[], int nrhs,
         const mxArray *prhs[]){
32.
33.      /* declare all variables */
34.      char *filename;
35.      std::string name, sResultFilename;
36.
37.      /* define error messages */
38.      char const * const errId = "parallel:gpu:NPPDemo:InvalidInput";
39.      char const * const errMsg1 = "Invalid input to MEX file.";
40.      char const * const errMsg2 = "An exception occurred.";
41.
42.      /* check input data */
43.      if(nrhs != 1){
44.          mexErrMsgIdAndTxt(errId, errMsg1);
45.      }
46.
47.      /* copy the image filename from prhs[0] into filename */
48.      filename = mxArrayToString(prhs[0]);
49.      name = filename;
50.
51.      try{
52.          /* try to open the image */
53.          std::ifstream infile(name.data(), std::ifstream::in);
54.          if (!infile.good()){
55.              infile.close();
56.              mexErrMsgIdAndTxt(errId, errMsg1);
57.          }
58.
59.          /* create the name of the final image */
60.          sResultFilename = name;
61.          std::string::size_type dot = sResultFilename.rfind('.');
62.          if (dot != std::string::npos){
63.              sResultFilename = sResultFilename.substr(0, dot);
64.          }
65.          sResultFilename += "_boxFilterNPP.pgm";
66.
67.          /* declare a host image object for an 8-bit grayscale
68.             image */
69.          npp::ImageCPU_8u_C1 oHostSrc;
70.
71.          /* load the image from disk */
```

```
72.          npp::loadImage(name, oHostSrc);
73.
74.          /* declare a device image and copy construct from the
75.             host image */
76.          npp::ImageNPP_8u_C1 oDeviceSrc(oHostSrc);
77.
78.          /* create struct with box-filter mask size */
79.          NppiSize oMaskSize = {11, 11};
80.          NppiSize oSrcSize = {(int)oDeviceSrc.width(),
                  (int)oDeviceSrc.height()};
81.          NppiPoint oSrcOffset = {0, 0};
82.
83.          /* create struct with ROI size */
84.          NppiSize oSizeROI = {(int)oDeviceSrc.width(),
                  (int)oDeviceSrc.height()};
85.
86.          /* allocate device image of appropriately reduced size */
87.          npp::ImageNPP_8u_C1 oDeviceDst(oSizeROI.width, oSizeROI.height);
88.
89.          /* set anchor point inside the mask to (oMaskSize.width / 2,
90.          oMaskSize.height / 2). It should round down when odd */
91.          NppiPoint oAnchor = {oMaskSize.width / 2, oMaskSize.height / 2};
92.
93.          /* perform the box filter */
94.          NPP_CHECK_NPP(nppiFilterBoxBorder_8u_C1R(oDeviceSrc.data(),
95.                          oDeviceSrc.pitch(),
96.                          oSrcSize,
97.                          oSrcOffset,
98.                          oDeviceDst.data(),
99.                          oDeviceDst.pitch(),
100.                         oSizeROI,
101.                         oMaskSize,
102.                         oAnchor,
103.                         NPP_BORDER_REPLICATE) );
104.
105.         /* declare a host image for the result and copy the
106.            device result data into it*/
107.         npp::ImageCPU_8u_C1 oHostDst(oDeviceDst.size());
108.         oDeviceDst.copyTo(oHostDst.data(), oHostDst.pitch());
109.         npp::saveImage(sResultFilename, oHostDst);
110.
111.         /* destroy the data on the device */
112.         nppiFree(oDeviceSrc.data());
113.         nppiFree(oDeviceDst.data());
114.     }
115.     catch (npp::Exception &rException){
116.         mexErrMsgIdAndTxt(errId, errMsg2);
117.     }
118.     catch (...){
119.         mexErrMsgIdAndTxt(errId, errMsg2);
120.     }
121. }
```

Function *RunNPPDemo* (filename: RunNPPDemo.m) compiles the file NPPDemo.cu and compares the execution time of a two-dimensional box filtering on a 3,867 × 5,789 pgm image using MATLAB on the CPU and using *NPP* on the GPU through the MEX file (Fig. 9.6).

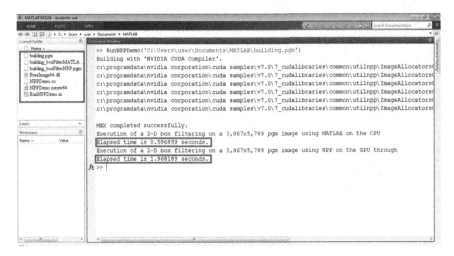

FIG. 9.6

Compile and execute MEX file using *NPP* through MATLAB.

Note that when compiling the MEX file with the *mexcuda* command, we need to specify:

- that we are using the *NPP* library (-*lnppi*).
- the directory where the *FreeImage* library is located (-L"C:\ProgramData\ NVIDIACorporation\CUDASamples\v7.0\7_CUDALibraries\common\FreeImage \lib\x64") (*FreeImage* is a library that *NPP* uses and is located on the directory with the CUDA Samples).
- the directory with the header files of some common utilities that *NPP* uses (-I"C:\ProgramData\NVIDIACorporation\CUDASamples\v7.0\common\inc").
- the directory with the header files of some utilities that *NPP* uses (I"C: \ProgramData\NVIDIACorporation\CUDASamples\v7.0\7_CUDALibraries\ common\UtilNPP").
- the directory where the header files for CUDA and *NPP* are located (-I"C: \ProgramFiles\NVIDIAGPUComputingToolkit\CUDA\v7.0\include").

You need to change that directory according to your operating system and the version of the CUDA Toolkit. Moreover, when running this code, you need either to add to your path the folder that *FreeImage* library is located (it is located inside the CUDA Samples directory) or copy the *FreeImage* library file to the directory of the *RunNPPDemo* function.

```
1.  function RunNPPDemo(filename)
2.  % Filename: RunNPPDemo.m
3.  % Description: This function compiles the file NPPDemo.cu
4.  % and compares the execution time of a 2-D box filtering
```

```
5.    % on a 3,867x5,789 pgm image using MATLAB on the CPU and
6.    % using NPP on the GPU through the MEX file
7.    % Authors: Ploskas, N., & Samaras, N.
8.    % Syntax: RunNPPDemo
9.    % Input:
10.   %  -- filename: the full path a pgm image
11.   % Output: the execution time of a 2-D box filtering on a
12.   % 3,867x5,789 pgm image using MATLAB on the CPU and
13.   % using NPP on the GPU through the MEX file
14.
15.   mexcuda NPPDemo.cu -lnppi -lFreeImage64 ...
16.       -L"C:\ProgramData\NVIDIA Corporation\CUDA Samples\v7.0\
              7_CUDALibraries\common\FreeImage\lib\x64" ...
17.       -I"C:\Program Files\NVIDIA GPU Computing Toolkit\CUDA\v7.0\include" ...
18.       -I"C:\ProgramData\NVIDIA Corporation\CUDA Samples\v7.0\common\inc" ...
19.       -I"C:\ProgramData\NVIDIA Corporation\CUDA Samples\v7.0\
              7_CUDALibraries\common\UtilNPP" ...
20.       -I"C:\ProgramData\NVIDIA Corporation\CUDA Samples\v7.0\
              7_CUDALibraries\common\FreeImage\include"
21.   disp(['Execution of a 2-D box filtering on a ' ...
22.       '3,867x5,789 pgm image using MATLAB on the CPU']);
23.   tic;
24.   A = imread(filename);
25.   B = imboxfilt(A, 11, 'padding', 'replicate');
26.   [pathstr, name, ext] = fileparts(filename);
27.   newFilename = strcat(pathstr, '\', name, '_boxFilterMATLAB', ext);
28.   imwrite(B, newFilename);
29.   toc
30.   disp(['Execution of a 2-D box filtering on a ' ...
31.       '3,867x5,789 pgm image using NPP on the GPU through']);
32.   gd = gpuDevice(); tic; NPPDemo(filename); wait(gd); toc
```

9.8 THRUST

Thrust [25] is a C++ template library for CUDA based on the Standard Template Library (STL). Thrust allows you to implement high-performance parallel applications with minimal programming effort through a high-level interface that is fully interoperable with CUDA C. Using Thrust, C++ developers can write just a few lines of code to perform GPU-accelerated sort, scan, transform, and reduction operations orders of magnitude faster than the latest multicore CPUs. Thrust provides STL-like templated interfaces to several algorithms and data structures designed for high performance heterogeneous parallel computing.

The following MEX file (filename: ThrustDemo.cu) calculates the sum of vector elements using *Thrust* library. It takes as input a double-precision, floating point vector of size $N \times 1$ or $1 \times N$ and returns the sum of the vector elements as a double value.

```
1.    /*===============================================================
2.     * Filename: ThrustDemo.cu
3.     * Description: This function calculates the sum of vector
4.     * elements using Thrust (MEX file that contains CUDA code
```

```
5.    * and takes as inputs MATLAB arrays)
6.    * Authors: Ploskas, N., & Samaras, N.
7.    * Syntax: b = ThrustDemo(A)
8.    * Input:
9.    *   -- A: a double-precision, floating point vector of size
10.   *      Nx1 or 1xN
11.   * Output:
12.   *   -- b: the sum of the vector elements
13.   *=========================================================*/
14.
15.   #include "mex.h"
16.   #include <thrust/reduce.h>
17.   #include <thrust/device_vector.h>
18.
19.   /*
20.    * The gateway function
21.    */
22.   void mexFunction(int nlhs, mxArray *plhs[], int nrhs,
          const mxArray *prhs[]){
23.
24.       /* declare all variables */
25.       double *A, *B;
26.       int numARows, numACols;
27.       int N;
28.
29.       /* define error messages */
30.       char const * const errId = "parallel:gpu:ThrustDemo:InvalidInput";
31.       char const * const errMsg = "Invalid input to MEX file.";
32.
33.       /* check input data */
34.       if(nrhs != 1 || !mxIsDouble(prhs[0])){
35.           mexErrMsgIdAndTxt(errId, errMsg);
36.       }
37.
38.       /* get input array */
39.       A = (double *)mxGetData(prhs[0]);
40.
41.       /* find array dimensions */
42.       numARows = mxGetM(prhs[0]);
43.       numACols = mxGetN(prhs[0]);
44.       N = (numARows > numACols) ? numARows : numACols;
45.
46.       /* initialize output array */
47.       plhs[0] = mxCreateNumericMatrix(1, 1, mxDOUBLE_CLASS, mxREAL);
48.       B = (double *)mxGetData(plhs[0]);
49.
50.       /* calculate the sum of the vector using Thurst */
51.       thrust::device_vector<double> deviceA(A, A + N);
52.       *B = thrust::reduce(deviceA.begin(), deviceA.end(), 0.0,
              thrust::plus<double>());
53.   }
```

Function *RunThrustDemo* (filename: RunThrustDemo.m) compiles the file ThrustDemo.cu and compares the execution time of the calculation of the sum of a $100,000,000 \times 1$ vector elements using MATLAB on the CPU and using *Thrust* on the GPU through the MEX file (Fig. 9.7).

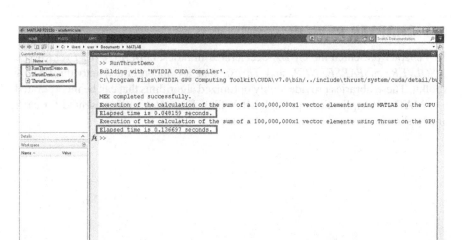

FIG. 9.7

Compile and execute MEX file using *Thrust* through MATLAB.

```
1.    function RunThrustDemo
2.    % Filename: RunThrustDemo.m
3.    % Description: This function compiles the file ThrustDemo.cu
4.    % and compares the execution time of the calculation of
5.    % the sum of a 100,000,000x1 vector elements using MATLAB
6.    % on the CPU and using Thrust on the GPU through the MEX
7.    % file
8.    % Authors: Ploskas, N., & Samaras, N.
9.    % Syntax: RunThrustDemo
10.   % Input: no inputs
11.   % Output: the execution time of the calculation of the
12.   % sum of a 100,000,000x1 vector elements using MATLAB
13.   % on the CPU and using Thrust on the GPU through the MEX
14.   % file
15.
16.   mexcuda ThrustDemo.cu
17.   A = rand(100000000, 1);
18.   disp(['Execution of the calculation of the sum of ' ...
19.       'a 100,000,000x1 vector elements using MATLAB ' ...
20.       'on the CPU']);
21.   tic; b1 = sum(A); toc
22.   disp(['Execution of the calculation of the sum of ' ...
23.       'a 100,000,000x1 vector elements using Thrust ' ...
24.       'on the GPU']);
25.   gd = gpuDevice(); tic; b2 = ThrustDemo(A); wait(gd); toc
```

9.9 **CHAPTER REVIEW**

This chapter presented the CUDA-accelerated libraries, *cuBLAS*, *cuFFT*, *cuRAND*, *cuSOLVER*, *cuSPARSE*, *NPP*, and *Thrust*, that are incorporated into the CUDA Toolkit. These libraries provide highly optimized algorithms that can be incorporated into MATLAB applications through MEX files. Examples were presented for each library showing great speedups on most cases.

Profiling code and improving GPU performance

10

CHAPTER OBJECTIVES

This chapter presents two advanced topics for better utilization of GPUs on computationally intensive applications: (i) profiling a code running on GPUs, and (ii) improving GPU performance. Didactical examples are given in this chapter in order for the reader to understand these topics. Moreover, best practices that you should follow to improve GPU performance are discussed in detail. After reading this Chapter, you should be able to:

- Utilize the MATLAB profiler to find the bottlenecks in files running on the CPU.
- Utilize the MATLAB profiler to profile files running on the GPU.
- Use the NVIDIA Visual Profiler to profile CUDA codes.
- Understand best strategies to improve GPU performance.

10.1 MATLAB PROFILING

Until now, we have used *tic* and *toc*, and *gputimeit* functions to measure the execution time of our applications. We can use several *tic* and *toc* commands in a code to measure the execution time of several parts. However, that is almost impossible and time consuming on large codes. Instead, we can utilize MATLAB profiling utilities to accomplish this task easier. Profiling is a way to measure the execution time of the different parts of a code and identify the time-consuming tasks and possible bottlenecks. After you identify which parts are consuming the most time, you can evaluate them for possible performance improvements.

MATLAB includes two different profile utilities. The *profile* command is used to profile codes that are not using several MATLAB workers, while the *mpiprofile* command is used to profile codes that are utilizing multiple MATLAB workers. Because we are interested mainly on profiling GPU codes, we will use the *profile* command. The general guidelines that you should follow to profile your applications are the following [26]:

(1) Run the *profiler* on your code.
(2) In the Profile Summary report, look for functions that use a significant amount of time or that are called most frequently.
(3) View the Profile Detail report for those functions, and look for the lines of code that take the most time or are called most often.
(4) Consider keeping a copy of your first detail report as a basis for comparison. After you change your code, you can run the Profiler again and compare the reports.
(5) Determine whether there are changes you can make to those lines of code to improve performance.
(6) Implement the potential performance improvements in your code. Save the files, and run clear all. Run the Profiler again and compare the results to the original report.
(7) If you profile the identical code twice, you can get slightly different results each time due to inherent time fluctuations that are not dependent on your code.
(8) To continue improving the performance of your code, repeat these steps.

Note that the profiler runs each line of code independently, so it cannot account for overlapping (asynchronous) execution such as might occur during normal operation. Also, the profiler might not yield correct results for user-defined MEX functions if they run asynchronously. Hence, when you want to measure the execution time of whole codes, you should use *tic* and *toc*, or *gputimeit*.

To understand the basic capabilities of the MATLAB *profiler*, we will use the fast convolution example that was presented in Section 4.4. Function *fastConvolution* (filename: fastConvolution.m) is used to illustrate the preceding example in MATLAB.

```
1.    function filteredData = fastConvolution(data, filter)
2.    % Filename: fastConvolution.m
3.    % Description: This function performs fast convolution on
4.    % the columns of a signal (array data) using a filter
5.    % (vector filter) (version running on the CPU)
6.    % Authors: Ploskas, N., & Samaras, N.
7.    % Syntax: filteredData = fastConvolution(data, filter)
8.    % Input:
9.    %    -- data: the signal (array)
10.   %    -- filter: the filter (vector)
11.   % Output:
12.   %    -- filteredData: the filtered signal (array)
13.
14.   [m, n] = size(data); % get the size of the signal
15.   % pad filter with zeros and calculate its DFT
16.   filterf = fft(filter, m);
```

```
17.   % initialize output variable filteredData
18.   filteredData = zeros(m, n, 'like', data);
19.   % transform each column of the signal
20.   for i = 1:n
21.       dataf = fft(data(:, i));
22.       filteredData(:, i) = ifft(dataf .* filterf);
23.   end
24. end
```

Initially, load the *fastConvolutionData.mat* file that contains the signal and filter data (the inputs to our code) and run the command *profile viewer* to open the MATLAB profiler (Fig. 10.1).

Call the *fastConvolution* function in the "Run this code" field. The MATLAB *profiler* displays the function names, number of calls to each function, total execution time, and self execution time for each function (Fig. 10.2).

If you click on the *fastConvolution* function, you get more specific information about this function. The MATLAB *profiler* displays the lines, number of calls, execution time and the time percentage for each line of code (Figs. 10.3 and 10.4).

Figs. 10.3 and 10.4 show that 99.1% of the total execution time is spent in the *fft* and *ifft* functions. More specifically, MATLAB performs 10,336 calls to each of these functions. Hence, we should focus on reducing the execution time of these two functions. MATLAB provides GPU enabled *fft* and *ifft* commands. So, we will try to implement this function utilizing the GPU. Function *fastConvolutionGPU* (filename: fastConvolutionGPU.m) is used to illustrate the preceding example in MATLAB using the GPU.

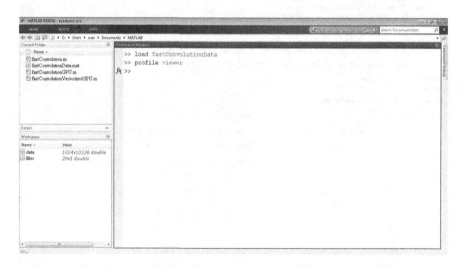

FIG. 10.1

Load data and open the MATLAB profiler.

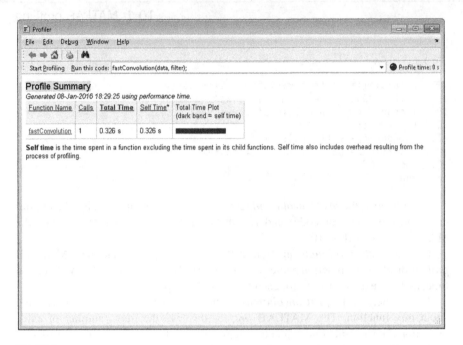

FIG. 10.2

Profile summary for the *fastConvolution* function.

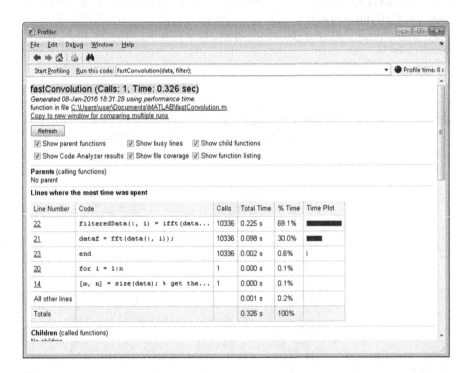

FIG. 10.3

Profile results for the *fastConvolution* function.

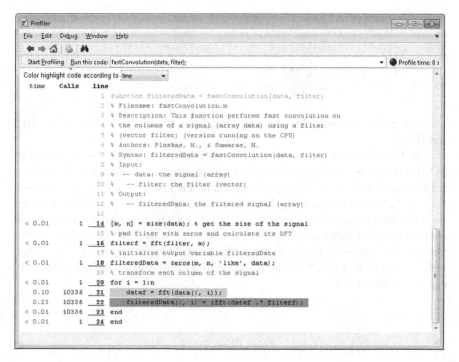

FIG. 10.4

Profile results for the *fastConvolution* function.

```
1.    function filteredData = fastConvolutionGPU(data, filter)
2.    % Filename: fastConvolutionGPU.m
3.    % Description: This function performs fast convolution on
4.    % the columns of a signal (array data) using a filter
5.    % (vector filter) (version running on the GPU)
6.    % Authors: Ploskas, N., & Samaras, N.
7.    % Syntax: filteredData = fastConvolutionGPU(data, filter)
8.    % Input:
9.    %    -- data: the signal (array)
10.   %    -- filter: the filter (vector)
11.   % Output:
12.   %    -- filteredData: the filtered signal (array)
13.
14.   % transfer data to the GPU
15.   gpuData = gpuArray(data);
16.   gpuFilter = gpuArray(filter);
17.   [m, n] = size(gpuData); % get the size of the signal
18.   % pad filter with zeros and calculate its DFT
19.   filterf = fft(gpuFilter, m);
20.   % initialize output variable filteredData
21.   gpuFilteredData = zeros(m, n, 'like', gpuData);
22.   % transform each column of the signal
```

```
23.  for i = 1:n
24.      dataf = fft(gpuData(:, i));
25.      gpuFilteredData(:, i) = ifft(dataf .* filterf);
26.  end
27.  % transfer data to the CPU
28.  filteredData = gather(gpuFilteredData);
29.  end
```

Let's profile the preceding function using the MATLAB *profiler* (Figs. 10.5 and 10.6).

The fast convolution function is running faster on the CPU. We also see that MATLAB performs 10,336 calls to *fft* and *ifft* functions because the code structure is the same as before. As already mentioned in this book, the *for-loops* slow down the GPU because it is executing the FFT, multiplication, and inverse FFT operations on individual columns. So, the number of calls to each of these two functions should warn us to find a better solution. We can optimize our function by vectorizing the *for-loop* with the use of *bsxfun*. Function *fastConvolutionVectorizedGPU* (filename: fastConvolutionVectorizedGPU.m) is used to illustrate the use of *bsxfun* on the above example in MATLAB.

```
1.   function filteredData = fastConvolutionVectorizedGPU(data, filter)
2.   % Filename: fastConvolutionVectorizedGPU.m
3.   % Description: This function performs fast convolution on
4.   % the columns of a signal (array data) using a filter
5.   % (vector filter) (vectorized version using bsxfun running on the GPU)
6.   % Authors: Ploskas, N., & Samaras, N.
7.   % Syntax: filteredData = fastConvolutionVectorizedGPU(data, filter)
8.   % Input:
9.   %    -- data: the signal (array)
10.  %    -- filter: the filter (vector)
11.  % Output:
12.  %    -- filteredData: the filtered signal (array)
13.
14.  % transfer data to the GPU
15.  gpuData = gpuArray(data);
16.  gpuFilter = gpuArray(filter);
17.  [m, ~] = size(data); % get the size of the signal
18.  % pad filter with zeros and calculate its DFT
19.  filterf = fft(gpuFilter, m);
20.  % transform each column of the signal
21.  dataf = fft(gpuData);
22.  % multiply each column of the signal by the filter and
23.  % compute the inverse transform
24.  gpuFilteredData = ifft(bsxfun(@times, dataf, filterf));
25.  % transfer data to the CPU
26.  filteredData = gather(gpuFilteredData);
27.  end
```

Let's profile the preceding function using the MATLAB *profiler* (Figs. 10.7 and 10.8).

Using the *bsxfun* function, we achieved reduction of the execution time of the code (note that the total execution time of the function is not accurate in the *profiler*. Use *tic* and *toc*, or *gputimeit* to measure the total execution time of the function). The main reason that we reduced the execution time is that MATLAB performs only

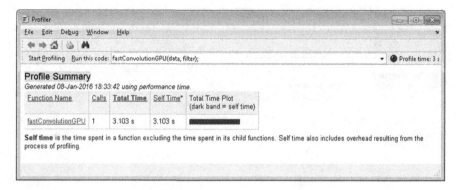

FIG. 10.5

Profile summary for the *fastConvolutionGPU* function.

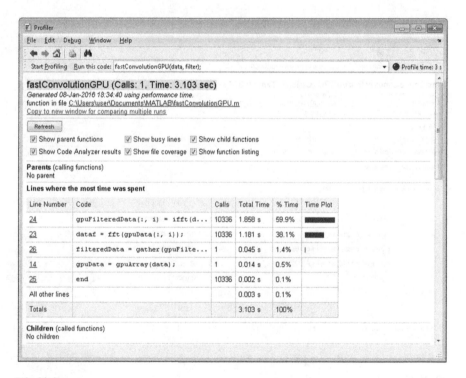

FIG. 10.6

Profile results for the *fastConvolutionGPU* function.

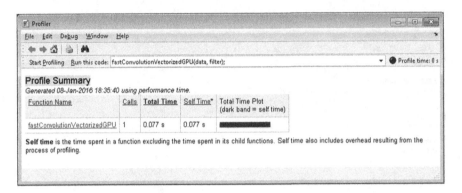

FIG. 10.7

Profile summary for the *fastConvolutionVectorizedGPU* function.

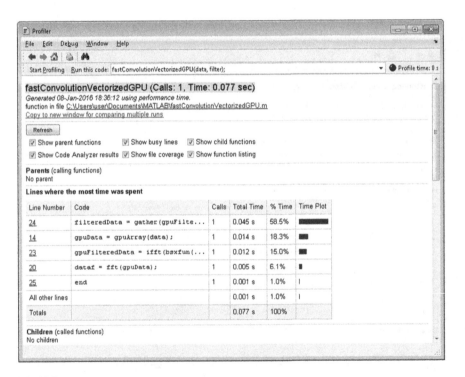

FIG. 10.8

Profile results for the *fastConvolutionVectorizedGPU* function.

one call to *fft* and *ifft* commands. Moreover, we can observe that the more time-consuming functions in this code are the *gpuArray* and *gather* commands that are used to transfer the data between the CPU and the GPU. We cannot reduce the execution time of these functions, and we need to call them to transfer our data. Hence, the only possible improvement that we can make is to implement the *fft* and *ifft* functions using a kernel or a GPU MEX file. For this example, there is no need to do that because the execution time of these two functions is very small and we will not benefit too much from further reductions to their execution time.

We can also use the MATLAB *profiler* to profile kernels and MEX files. However, the MATLAB *profiler* displays only limited information about these files. For example, we will use the matrix multiplication kernel and MEX file that we presented in Sections 7.4 and 8.4, respectively. The *matrixMultiplication* kernel (filename: matrixMultiplication.cu) is a matrix multiplication kernel.

```
1.   /*==========================================================
2.    * Filename: matrixMultiplication.cu
3.    * Description: This function is a matrix multiplication
4.    * kernel
5.    * Authors: Ploskas, N., & Samaras, N.
6.    * Syntax: C = matrixMultiplication(A, B, C, N)
7.    * Input:
8.    *    -- A: a double-precision, floating point NxN array
9.    *    -- B: a double-precision, floating point NxN array
10.   *    -- C: a double-precision, floating point NxN array
11.   *    -- N: the size of arrays A and B
12.   * Output:
13.   *    -- C: a double-precision, floating point NxN array
14.   *==========================================================*/
15.
16.   _ _global_ _ void matrixMultiplication(const double *A,
         const double *B, double *C, int N){
17.
18.       int i = blockDim.y * blockIdx.y + threadIdx.y;
19.       int j = blockDim.x * blockIdx.x + threadIdx.x;
20.
21.       double value = 0;
22.
23.       for(int k = 0; k < N; k++){
24.           value += A[k * N + j] * B[i * N + k];
25.       }
26.
27.       C[i * N + j] = value;
28.   }
```

We will also use the *RunMatrixMultiplicationKernel* function (filename: RunMatrixMultiplicationKernel.m) to prepare the data and invoke the kernel (you need to create a PTX file from the kernel before executing this function).

```
1.   function C = RunMatrixMultiplicationKernel(A, B)
2.   % Filename: RunMatrixMultiplicationKernel.m
3.   % Description: This function creates a CUDAKernel object
4.   % and executes matrixMultiplication kernel to perform a
5.   % a matrix multiplication on two gpuArray variables
```

```
6.    % Authors: Ploskas, N., & Samaras, N.
7.    % Syntax: C = RunMatrixMultiplicationKernel(A, B)
8.    % Input:
9.    %    -- A: a double-precision, floating point NxN array
10.   %    -- B: a double-precision, floating point NxN array
11.   % Output:
12.   %    -- C: a double-precision, floating point NxN array
13.
14.   [~, n] = size(A);
15.   k = parallel.gpu.CUDAKernel('matrixMultiplication.ptx', ...
          'matrixMultiplication.cu');
16.   k.ThreadBlockSize = [10, 10, 1];
17.   k.GridSize = [100, 100];
18.   gpuA = gpuArray(A);
19.   gpuB = gpuArray(B);
20.   gpuC = zeros(n, 'gpuArray');
21.   gpuC = feval(k, gpuA, gpuB, gpuC, n);
22.   C = gather(gpuC);
23.   end
```

Let's profile the preceding function using the MATLAB *profiler* (Figs. 10.9 and 10.10).

We can observe that the most time-consuming part of this code is the execution of the matrix multiplication but we cannot get more information about that. In the next section, we will use CUDA profiling tools to accomplish that.

We will repeat the profiling for the matrix multiplication MEX file. The *mexMatrixMultiplication* MEX file (filename: mexMatrixMultiplication.cu) implements a matrix multiplication using the *cuBLAS* library.

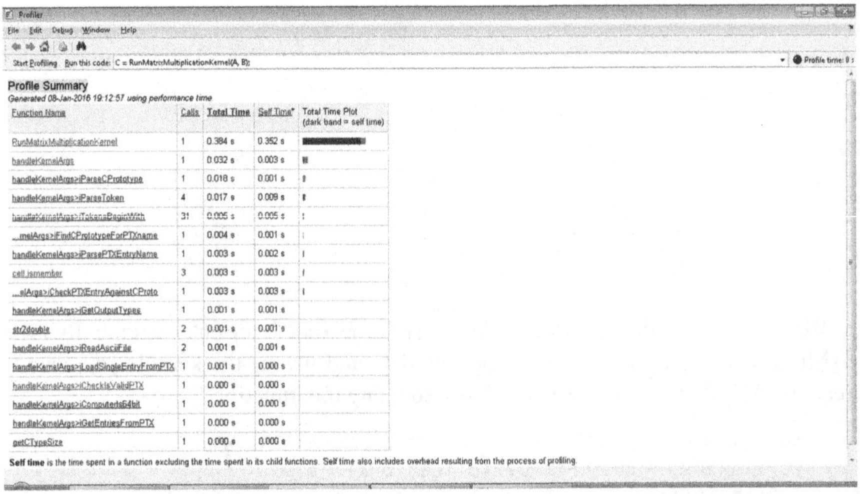

FIG. 10.9

Profile summary for the *RunMatrixMultiplicationKernel* function.

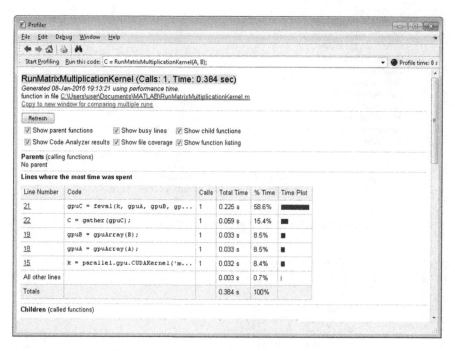

FIG. 10.10

Profile results for the *RunMatrixMultiplicationKernel* function.

```
1.    /*==========================================================
2.     * Filename: mexMatrixMultiplication.m
3.     * Description: This function implements a matrix multiplication
4.     * using cuBLAS library (MEX file that contains CUDA code and
5.     * takes as inputs MATLAB arrays)
6.     * Authors: Ploskas, N., & Samaras, N.
7.     * Syntax: C = mexMatrixMultiplication(A, b)
8.     * Input:
9.     *    -- A: a double-precision, floating point array of size MxK
10.    *    -- B: a double-precision, floating point array of size KxN
11.    * Output:
12.    *    -- C: a double-precision, floating point array of size MxN
13.    *==========================================================*/
14.
15.    #include "mex.h"
16.    #include "cuda_runtime.h"
17.    #include "cublas_v2.h"
18.
19.    /*
20.     * The gateway function
21.     */
22.    void mexFunction(int nlhs, mxArray *plhs[], int nrhs,
           const mxArray *prhs[]){
23.
24.       /* declare all variables */
25.       double *deviceA;
```

```
26.     double *deviceB;
27.     double *deviceC;
28.     const double *A;
29.     const double *B;
30.     double * C;
31.     int numARows;
32.     int numACols;
33.     int numBRows;
34.     int numBCols;
35.     int numCRows;
36.     int numCCols;
37.
38.     char const * const errId =
            "parallel:gpu:mexMatrixMultiplication:InvalidInput";
39.     char const * const errMsg = "Invalid input to MEX file.";
40.
41.     if(nrhs != 2){
42.         mexErrMsgIdAndTxt(errId, errMsg);
43.     }
44.
45.     /* get input arrays */
46.     A = (double *)mxGetData(prhs[0]);
47.     B = (double *)mxGetData(prhs[1]);
48.
49.     /* find arrays dimensions */
50.     numARows = (int)mxGetM(prhs[0]);
51.     numACols = (int)mxGetN(prhs[0]);
52.     numBRows = (int)mxGetM(prhs[1]);
53.     numBCols = (int)mxGetN(prhs[1]);
54.     numCRows = numARows;
55.     numCCols = numBCols;
56.
57.     /* initialize output array */
58.     plhs[0] = mxCreateNumericMatrix(numCRows,
            numCCols, mxDOUBLE_CLASS, mxREAL);
59.     C = (double *)mxGetData(plhs[0]);
60.
61.     /* allocate memory on the GPU */
62.     cudaMalloc(&deviceA, sizeof(double) * numARows * numACols);
63.     cudaMalloc(&deviceB, sizeof(double) * numBRows * numBCols);
64.     cudaMalloc(&deviceC, sizeof(double) * numCRows * numCCols);
65.
66.     /* set arrays and perform the matrix multiplication using CUBLAS */
67.     cublasHandle_t handle;
68.     cublasCreate(&handle);
69.     cublasSetMatrix(numARows,
70.                     numACols,
71.                     sizeof(double),
72.                     A,
73.                     numARows,
74.                     deviceA,
75.                     numARows);
76.     cublasSetMatrix(numBRows,
77.                     numBCols,
78.                     sizeof(double),
79.                     B,
80.                     numBRows,
81.                     deviceB,
```

```
82.                    numBRows);
83.    double alpha = 1.0;
84.    double beta = 0.0;
85.    cublasDgemm(handle,
86.                CUBLAS_OP_N,
87.                CUBLAS_OP_N,
88.                numARows,
89.                numBCols,
90.                numACols,
91.                &alpha,
92.                deviceA,
93.                numARows,
94.                deviceB,
95.                numBRows,
96.                &beta,
97.                deviceC,
98.                numCRows);
99.
100.   /* retrieve result */
101.   cublasGetMatrix(numCRows,
102.                   numCCols,
103.                   sizeof(double),
104.                   deviceC,
105.                   numCRows,
106.                   C,
107.                   numCRows);
108.
109.   /* destroy the handle and the arrays on the device */
110.   cublasDestroy(handle);
111.   cudaFree(deviceA);
112.   cudaFree(deviceB);
113.   cudaFree(deviceC);
114. }
```

We will also use the *RunMatrixMultiplicationMEX* function (filename: RunMatrixMultiplicationMEX.m) to prepare the data and invoke the MEX file (you need to compile the MEX file before executing this function).

```
1.    function C = RunMatrixMultiplicationMEX(A, B)
2.    % Filename: RunMatrixMultiplicationMEX.m
3.    % Description: This function executes the
4.    % mexMatrixMultiplication MEX file to perform a
5.    % a matrix multiplication on two MATLAB arrays
6.    % Authors: Ploskas, N., & Samaras, N.
7.    % Syntax: C = RunMatrixMultiplicationMEX(A, B)
8.    % Input:
9.    %   -- A: a double-precision, floating point NxN array
10.   %   -- B: a double-precision, floating point NxN array
11.   % Output:
12.   %   -- C: a double-precision, floating point NxN array
13.
14.   C = mexMatrixMultiplication(A, B);
15.   end
```

Let's profile the preceding function using the MATLAB *profiler* (Figs. 10.11 and 10.12).

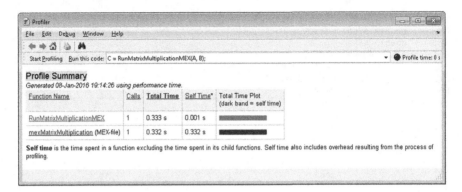

FIG. 10.11

Profile summary for the *RunMatrixMultiplicationMEX* function.

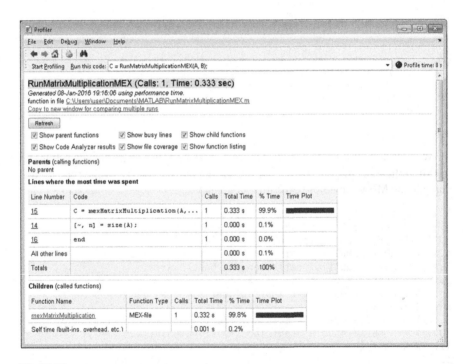

FIG. 10.12

Profile results for the *RunMatrixMultiplicationMEX* function.

We can observe that the most time-consuming part of this code is the execution of the matrix multiplication but we cannot get more information about that. In the next section, we will use CUDA profiling tools to accomplish that.

10.2 **CUDA PROFILING**

As we already found out in the previous section, MATLAB *profiler* cannot display much information for CUDA kernels or MEX files that contain CUDA code. However, we can use NVIDIA Nsight to profile these codes. NVIDIA Nsight is a development platform for heterogeneous computing. There are two different editions of NVIDIA Nsight, the NVIDIA Nsight Visual Studio Edition for Windows and the NVIDIA Nsight Eclipse Edition for Linux and MAC OS. In this section, we will demonstrate profiling using NVIDIA Nsight Visual Studio Edition but similar steps can be followed to profile CUDA application on Linux and MAC OS (for more information, see http://docs.nvidia.com/cuda/nsight-eclipse-edition-getting-started-guide/).

Initially, we profile the execution of the matrix multiplication kernel presented in the previous section. Functions *matrixMultiplicationKernel* and *RunMatrixMultiplicationKernel* will be used for this reason. Initially, open Microsoft Visual Studio and select the "Start Performance Analysis" option from the Nsight menu (Fig. 10.13).

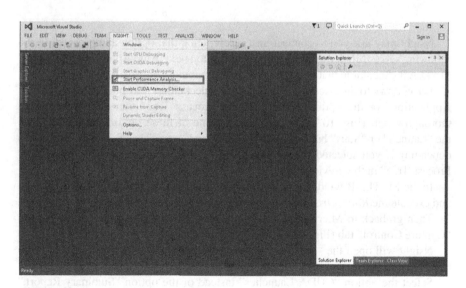

FIG. 10.13

Start performance analysis.

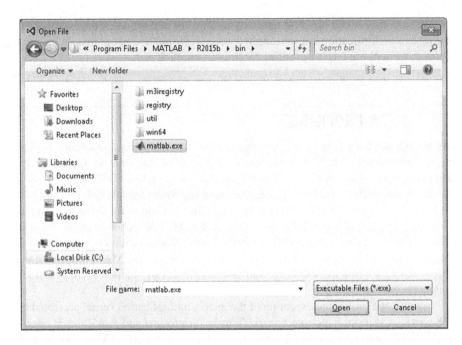

FIG. 10.14

Select MATLAB as the application to profile.

Nsight may ask you to connect unsecurely; click that option and proceed. In the following screen, click on the folder browser button next to the Application and select MATLAB executable that is installed in your computer (Fig. 10.14).

Scroll down to the "Activity Type" tab and select either the option "Profile CUDA Application" or the option "Profile CUDA Process Tree" that generates a more thorough report (Fig. 10.15). After selecting one of these options, Nsight enables the "Launch" or "Start" button in the "Application Control" or "Session Control" tab depending if you selected the "Profile CUDA Application" or the "Profile CUDA Process Tree" in the previous step.

In the MATLAB window that opens, go to the location that your functions exist and execute the *RunMatrixMultiplicationKernel* function (Fig. 10.16).

Then go back to Microsoft Visual Studio and click on the option "Stop" in the "Capture Control" tab (Fig. 10.17).

Nsight will open the "Summary Report" window that includes various information (Fig. 10.18).

Select the option "CUDA Launches" instead of the option "Summary Report." This report contains information for every aspect of the execution (Fig. 10.19). For more information about the profiling results, see the NVIDIA Nsight user's guide [27].

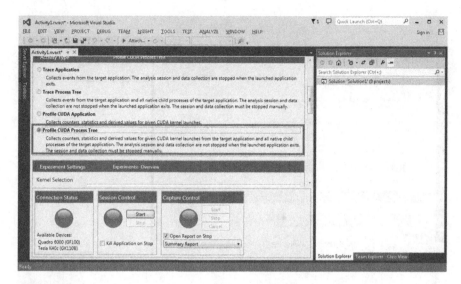

FIG. 10.15

Select activity type to profile.

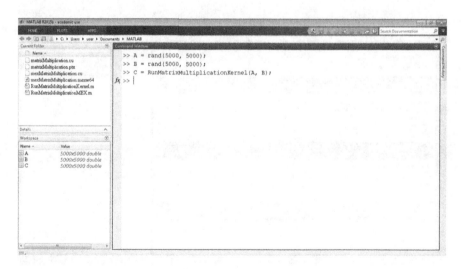

FIG. 10.16

Execute the *RunMatrixMultiplicationKernel* function.

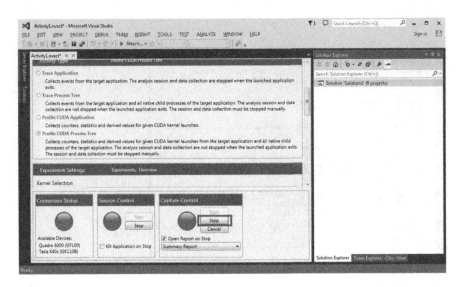

FIG. 10.17

Stop profiling.

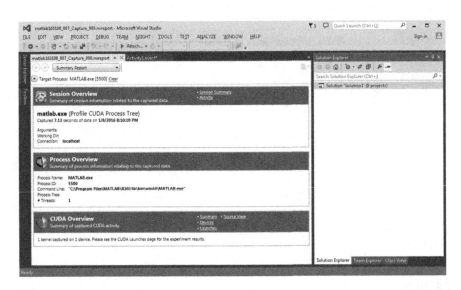

FIG. 10.18

Summary report for matrix multiplication kernel.

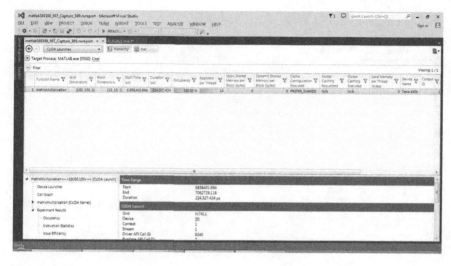

FIG. 10.19

CUDA launches report for matrix multiplication kernel.

Following the same steps, we can profile the matrix multiplication that is implemented through a MEX file containing CUDA code (Fig. 10.20). Functions *matrixMultiplicationMEX* and *RunMatrixMultiplicationMEX* are used as an example for profiling MEX files that contain CUDA code (Fig. 10.21).

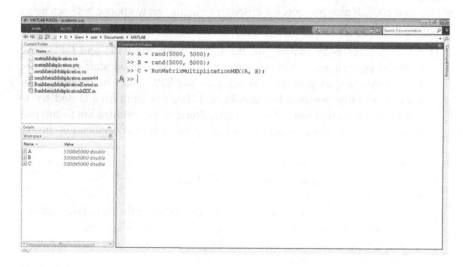

FIG. 10.20

Execute the *RunMatrixMultiplication* function.

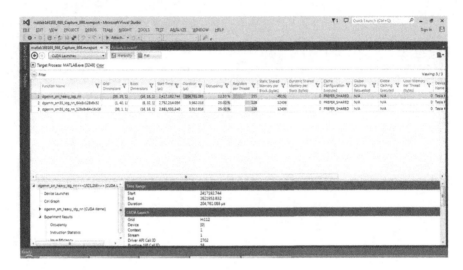

FIG. 10.21

CUDA launches report for matrix multiplication MEX file.

10.3 BEST PRACTICES FOR IMPROVING GPU PERFORMANCE

The purpose of GPU computing in MATLAB is to speed up your applications. This topic discusses concepts and practices that can help you achieve better performance on the GPU, such as the configuration of the GPU hardware and best practices within your code. It also presents the criteria you might use to choose between using *gpuArray* functions, *arrayfun*, MEX-files, or CUDA kernels.

(1) *Optimize your code running on the CPU*: While the CPU and GPU have different performance characteristics, it is always a good start to optimize the performance of your code running on the CPU. Start by profiling your code to identify possible bottlenecks and time-consuming parts and try to reduce the execution time of these parts. Some other optimization techniques that you should take into account when optimizing your application are the following [28]:

- Preallocate your variables.
- Avoid using dynamically growing variables.
- Vectorize your code.
- Operate along the column dimension (see following for more information).
- Use sparse linear algebra when possible if your data is sparse.
- Use built-in functions instead of writing custom algorithms because built-in functions are optimized.
- Avoid using non-numeric types, for example, cells, strings, structs, and class objects.

- Use functions instead of scripts.
- Prefer local functions over nested functions.
- Use modular programming.
- Place independent operations outside loops.
- Create new variables if data type changes.
- Use short-circuiting logical operators, && and || when possible.
- Avoid global variables.
- Avoid overloading built-ins.
- Utilize multiple cores on a computer or multiple processors on a network.
- Reduce the amount of I/O.
- Avoid using "data as code," that is, instead of generating variables with constant values from calling a code, consider constructing the variables and saving them in a MAT-file.
- Avoid clearing more code than necessary.
- Avoid functions that query the state of MATLAB.
- Avoid functions such as *eval, evalc, evalin,* and *feval,* when possible.
- Avoid programmatic use of *cd, addpath,* and *rmpath,* when possible.

(2) *Use GPU-enabled MATLAB built-in functions as a start point*: Start converting your code using GPU-enabled MATLAB built-in functions. MATLAB enhances the list of the MATLAB functions that support *gpuArray* objects in each version, so it is likely that you can implement your code on the GPU with minimal changes. For example, let's assume that you have a function that performs a matrix multiplication:

```
function C = matrixMultiplication(A, B)
C = A * B;
end
```

You can easily implement this function on the GPU without any changes. Just call this function with *gpuArray* objects as inputs (see examples in Chapter 4).

(3) *Write custom CUDA kernels for specific operations in your algorithm that are either not GPU-enabled or that are not fast enough*: Using the *CUDAKernel* object, you can either implement functions that are not GPU-enabled or improve the performance of GPU-enabled functions (see examples in Chapter 7).

(4) *Write MEX files in case there are several parts in your application that are either not GPU-enabled or that are not fast enough*: GPU MEX interface lets you work with low-level features of the GPU, such as shared memory and texture memory, that are not directly available in MATLAB code. It's always preferable to use the GPU MEX interface when your variables in MATLAB are *gpuArray* objects because you do not have to transfer them between the CPU and the GPU. Moreover, you can utilize multiple GPUs in your MEX files (see examples in Chapter 8).

(5) *Use optimized libraries when writing MEX files*: Writing an optimized custom CUDA code is not an easy task. So, if you are a beginner in CUDA, use the highly optimized libraries that are installed with CUDA Toolkit (see examples in Chapter 9).

(6) *Decide wisely which NVIDIA GPU to buy*: Be careful when considering to buy an NVIDIA GPU. First of all, you need to buy an NVIDIA GPU with compute capability 2.0 or higher (as of MATLAB R2015b). Depending on your available budget, you should consider all different aspects of a GPU, like memory size for memory-consuming applications, CUDA cores, base clock, memory clock, memory bandwidth, and so on. Moreover, if you want to implement algorithms using multiple GPUs, you need to purchase several devices. Make sure that you can install multiple GPUs in your computer. Finally, it is always easier to implement algorithms on identical multiple GPUs because you do not have to worry about assigning more tasks or a larger portion of data to the faster device.

(7) *Configure your hardware*: It is usually not practical to use the same GPU device for both computations and graphics because the system is constantly using the GPU device for graphics. In general, you can achieve the best performance when your GPU device is dedicated to computing. So, if possible, obtain a separate device for graphics. Make sure that your operating system uses your less powerful device for graphics and your more powerful device will be used only for computations. Finally, on Windows systems, a GPU device can be in one of two modes: (i) Windows Display Driver Model (WDDM), (ii) or Tesla Compute Cluster (TCC) mode. For best performance, set your device used for GPU computing to TCC mode.

(8) *Limit data transfers*: Although the PCI bus is an efficient, high-bandwidth way to transfer data between the host memory and the GPU memory, it is still much slower than the overall bandwidth to the global memory of the GPU device. Moreover, transfers from the GPU device to the host memory cause MATLAB to wait for all pending operations on the device to complete before executing any other statements. This can significantly reduce the performance of your application. So, try to limit the number of times you transfer data between the host memory and the GPU memory. If possible, transfer data to the GPU once at the start of your application, perform all the calculations and then transfer the results back to the CPU at the end. Finally, when possible create arrays directly on the GPU using either the *gpuArray* option, for example, *A = rand(100, 'gpuArray');*, or the 'like' option, for example, *B = zeros(N, 'like', A);* where *A* is an existing *gpuArray* object. For example, consider the following two functions:

```
function [E, F] = test1(A, B, C, D)
gpuA = gpuArray(A);
gpuA = gpuA + 5;
gpuB = gpuArray(B);
gpuB = gpuB + 3;
gpuE = gpuA * gpuB;
E = gather(gpuE);
```

```
gpuC = gpuArray(C);
gpuC = gpuC + 2;
gpuD = gpuArray(D);
gpuD = gpuD + 4;
gpuF = gpuC * gpuD;
F = gather(gpuF);
end


function [E, F] = test2(A, B, C, D)
gpuA = gpuArray(A);
gpuB = gpuArray(B);
gpuC = gpuArray(C);
gpuD = gpuArray(D);
gpuA = gpuA + 5;
gpuB = gpuB + 3;
gpuE = gpuA - gpuB;
gpuC = gpuC + 2;
gpuD = gpuD + 4;
gpuF = gpuC - gpuD;
E = gather(gpuE);
F = gather(gpuF);
end
```

Both functions perform the same operation. However, the function *test2* transfers data to the GPU once at the start of your application, performs all the calculations and then transfers the results back to the CPU at the end. This technique can reduce the execution time. Calling the preceding functions with four random two-dimensional arrays of size 1,000 × 1,000, function *test2* is ~20% faster than function *test1*.

(9) *Vectorize you code*: Vectorizing the code helps both the CPU and GPU versions to run faster. However, vectorization helps the GPU version much more than the CPU (see the example in Section 4.5). Whenever possible try to vectorize your code and make use of *arrayfun, bsxfun,* and *pagefun*.

(10) *Operate along the column dimension*: MATLAB arrays are stored in column-major order. It is always best to operate along the column dimension. If one dimension of your array is significantly longer than the other, you might achieve better performance if you make that the first dimension. Furthermore, if you frequently operate along a particular dimension, it might also be beneficial to make that the first dimension. For example, consider the following two functions:

```
function sum1 = test1(A)
[~, n] = size(A);
sum1 = rand(n, 1, 'gpuArray');
for i = 1:n
    sum1(i) = sum(A(i, :));
end
end
```

```
function sum1 = test2(A)
[~, n] = size(A);
sum1 = rand(n, 1, 'gpuArray');
for j = 1:n
sum1(j) = sum(A(:, j));
end
end
```

Function *test1* calculates the sum for each row, while function *test2* calculates the sum for each column. Before calling function *test2*, we transpose array *A* to achieve the same operation with function *test1* (function *test2* will calculate the sum for each column but since the array has been transposed, it is like calculating the sum for each row). Calling the preceding functions with a random two-dimensional array of size 10,000 × 10,000, function *test2* is ~25% faster than function *test1*.

(11) *Use single-precision floating-point operations if possible*: By default, all operations in MATLAB are performed in double-precision floating-point arithmetic. However, GPUs have much higher throughput when performing single-precision operations. For example, NVIDIA Tesla K40c has a peak performance of 1.43 Tflops for double-precision arithmetic and 4.29 Tflops for single-precision arithmetic. Moreover, single-precision floating-point data occupies less memory. Hence, if your application's accuracy requirements allow the use of single-precision floating-point, it can greatly improve the performance of your application. However, be careful when to use single-precision floating-point accuracy because many applications will not output the correct results. For example, let's compute a two-dimensional fast Fourier transform of an 10,000 × 10,000 array in single- and double-precision:

```
>> A = rand(10000, 'gpuArray');
>> gd = gpuDevice(); tic; B = fft2(A); wait(gd); toc
Elapsed time is 0.160764 seconds.
>> sA = single(A);
>> gd = gpuDevice(); tic; sB = fft2(sA); wait(gd); toc
Elapsed time is 0.068319 seconds.
```

The two-dimensional fast Fourier transform in single-precision arithmetic is ~2.35× faster than the two-dimensional fast Fourier transform in double-precision arithmetic.

(12) *Utilize multiple GPUs*: When possible utilize multiple GPUs to achieve better performance (see examples in Chapter 6 and Section 5.3).

(13) *Avoid for-loops*: As already mentioned, vectorizing the code helps both the CPU and GPU versions to run faster. However, vectorization helps the GPU version much more than the CPU (see the example in Section 4.5).

(14) *Avoid code branching*: As already mentioned, conditional statements should be avoided. For example, consider the following two functions:

```
function C = test1(A, B)
n = length(A);
C = zeros(n, 1, 'gpuArray');
for i = 1:n
    if A(i) < 0.5 && B(i) < 0.5
        C(i) = A(i) + B(i);
    else
        C(i) = A(i);
    end
end
end
```

```
function C = test2(A, B)
cond = A < 0.5 & B < 0.5;
C = cond .* (A + B) + ~cond .* (A);
end
```

Both functions perform the same operation. However, we eliminated the conditional statement and the *for-loop* in function *test2* by using a logical array. Calling the preceding functions with two random vectors of size $1,000,000 \times 1$, MATLAB evaluates function *test1* in 251.2623 seconds and function *test2* in 0.0026 seconds. Hence, function *test2* is $\sim$96,639$\times$ faster than function *test1*.

(15) *Work on large data sets*: GPUs are only efficient for massively parallel data processing. For example, consider the following two functions:

```
function C = test1(A, B)
C = A * B;
end
```

```
function C = test2(A, B)
gpuA = gpuArray(A);
gpuB = gpuArray(A);
gpuC = gpuA * gpuB;
C = gather(gpuC);
end
```

Both functions perform the same operation. Function *test1* performs a matrix multiplication on the CPU, while function *test2* performs a matrix multiplication on the GPU. If we execute the two functions with two arrays of size 10×10, function *test1* is $\sim$9$\times$ faster than function *test2*. However, if we execute the two functions with two arrays of size $10,000 \times 10,000$, function *test2* is $\sim$11$\times$ faster than function *test1*.

(16) *Use the latest GPU drivers and CUDA Toolkit*: GPU drivers and CUDA Toolkit enhance their performance, so remember to keep them up-to-date with the latest version.

10.4 CHAPTER REVIEW

This chapter presented two advanced topics for better utilization of GPUs on computationally intensive applications: (i) profiling a code running on GPUs, and (ii) improving GPU performance. Didactical examples were given for the reader to understand these topics. Moreover, best practices that you should follow to improve GPU performance were discussed in detail.

References

[1] Flynn MJ. Some computer organizations and their effectiveness. IEEE Trans Comput 1972;100(9):948–60.

[2] NVIDIA. CUDA C programming guide; 2015. Available online at: http://docs.nvidia.com/cuda/cuda-c-programming-guide/ [accessed 15.12.15].

[3] Khronos OpenCL Working Group. The OpenCL specification; 2015. Available online at: https://www.khronos.org/opencl/ [accessed 15.12.15].

[4] MathWorks. Image Processing Toolbox User's Guide; 2015.

[5] MathWorks. Parallel Computing Toolbox User's Guide; 2015.

[6] Altman YM. Accelerating MATLAB Performance: 1001 tips to speed up MATLAB programs. CRC Press; 2014.

[7] Kepner J. Parallel MATLAB for multicore and multinode computers (Vol. 21). SIAM; 2009.

[8] White RE. Computational Mathematics: Models, Methods, and Analysis with MATLAB® and MPI (Vol. 35). CRC Press; 2015.

[9] MathWorks. Platform road map for the MATLAB and Simulink product families; 2015. Available online at: http://www.mathworks.com/support/sysreq/roadmap.html [accessed 15.12.15].

[10] NVIDIA. CUDA GPUs; 2015. Available online at: https://developer.nvidia.com/cuda-gpus [accessed 15.12.15].

[11] MathWorks. Distributed Computing Server User's Guide; 2015.

[12] Mathworks. Parallel computing support in MATLAB and Simulink products; 2015. Available online at: http://www.mathworks.com/products/parallel-computing/parallel-support.html [accessed 15.12.15].

[13] Mathworks. Scheduler support in Parallel Computing Toolbox and MATLAB distributed computing server; 2015. Available online at: http://www.mathworks.com/products/distriben/supported/ [accessed 15.12.15].

[14] MathWorks. Communications System Toolbox User's Guide; 2015.

[15] Malshe M, Raff LM, Rockley MG, Hagan M, Agrawal PM, Komanduri R. Theoretical investigation of the dissociation dynamics of vibrationally excited vinyl bromide on an ab initio potential-energy surface obtained using modified novelty sampling and feedforward neural networks. II. Numerical application of the method. J Chem Phys 2007;127(13):134105.

[16] MathWorks. Phased Array System Toolbox; 2015.

[17] MathWorks. External Interfaces User's Guide; 2015.

[18] NVIDIA. GPU-accelerated libraries; 2015. Available online at: https://developer.nvidia.com/gpu-accelerated-libraries [accessed 15.12.15].

[19] NVIDIA. cuBLAS; 2015. Available online at: https://developer.nvidia.com/cublas [accessed 15.12.15].

[20] NVIDIA. cuFFT; 2015. Available online at: https://developer.nvidia.com/cufft [accessed 15.12.15].

[21] NVIDIA. cuRAND; 2015. Available online at: https://developer.nvidia.com/curand [accessed 15.12.15].

[22] NVIDIA. cuSOLVER; 2015. Available online at: https://developer.nvidia.com/cusolver [accessed 15.12.15].

[23] NVIDIA. cuSPARSE; 2015. Available online at: https://developer.nvidia.com/cusparse [accessed 15.12.15].

[24] NVIDIA. NVIDIA Performance Primitives; 2015. Available online at: https://developer.nvidia.com/npp [accessed 15.12.15].

[25] NVIDIA. Thrust; 2015. Available online at: https://developer.nvidia.com/thrust [accessed 15.12.15].

[26] MathWorks. Profile to improve performance; 2015. Available online at: http://www.mathworks.com/help/matlab/matlab_prog/profiling-for-improving-performance.html [accessed 15.12.15].

[27] NVIDIA. NVIDIA Nsight Visual Studio Edition; 2015. Available online at: http://docs.nvidia.com/gameworks/index.html#developertools/desktop/nsight/nvidia_nsight.htm [accessed 15.12.15].

[28] Mathworks. Techniques to improve performance; 2015. Available online at: http://www.mathworks.com/help/matlab/matlab_prog/techniques-for-improving-performance.html [accessed 15.12.15].

List of Examples

Index

Printed in the United States
By Bookmasters